FIELD LINGUISTICS
A Guide to Linguistic Field Work

WILLIAM J. SAMARIN

Hartford Seminary Foundation

FIELD LINGUISTICS
A Guide to Linguistic
Field Work

HOLT, RINEHART AND WINSTON

NEW YORK   CHICAGO   SAN FRANCISCO   TORONTO   LONDON

PREFACE

This book has few predecessors. The best of them are two small works published over twenty years ago, Bloomfield's *Outline Guide for the Practical Study of Foreign Languages* (1942) and Bloch and Trager's *Outline of Linguistic Analysis* (1942). There were at that time a few books about general linguistics, but not one of them was designed for the investigator taking up for the first time the study of a hitherto "unknown" language. Methodology was an important subject of discussion, but it was treated almost exclusively in technical articles. One learned how to describe languages, as it was then termed, by working with people who had already grappled with problems of analysis. To meet the need for more guidance among the growing number of field workers, Nida produced his *Morphology* (1946, 1st edition) and Pike his *Phonemics* (1947). Although these volumes were acclaimed for the contribution they made to linguistic pedagogy, they were not, strictly speaking, field guides.

Linguistic researchers have been extraordinarily silent—in print—about the field aspects of their investigations. In the preparation of this book I tried to draw from what published material was available, although no pretense is made that my research was exhaustive. Undoubtedly there are significant contributions tucked away in the vast linguistic literature, including those by dialectologists, ethnographers, and even nonprofessional students of language.

The emphasis of this book is on the collection of linguistic data. Chapters 2–7 are in one way or another devoted to this subject. Chapters 8 and 9 deal with the handling of the data. As a treatment of linguistic analysis, Chapter 9 is far too brief, but field work cannot be discussed without reference to analytical methodology; analysis does go on in the field. This chapter will not teach a person how to analyze, but it ought to alert him to certain techniques and problems in this aspect of field work.

This book is meant to serve a practical purpose, to prepare investigators of language for their confrontation with the source of their data—the living speakers of languages. In this category are included linguists, ethnographers, musicologists, folklorists, sociologists, and psychologists. It should be of use also to nonprofessionals who are faced with the task of learning languages for which there are inadequate grammatical descriptions. But since every language learning situation is in some sense a "field situation," parts of *Field Linguistics* can be viewed as a contribution to the literature on learning a foreign language. However, the principal audience is made up of those who propose to collect specimens of language for analysis, either as a goal in itself or for some other purpose (for example dialectology, and ethnography of speech).

We do not restrict our discussion to the study of languages in far-off or exotic places in the world. Indeed, it would be a serious error to restrict field linguistics to the investigation of languages other than one's own. As a matter of fact, there is opening up before us an exciting era in which the various forms of national languages will be studied. In the United States, for example, the language of the "culturally underprivileged" is the growing concern of educators, sociologists, and psychologists as well as linguists. The latter are insisting—with favorable response from the others—that the only firm ground for any program to help these people, whether in the cities or in the rural areas, is to determine the structure of their language. This will be done on the basis of field work very similar to the kind which might be done in some part of Africa or the Caucasus. There are, of course, differences of detail, some of which are not insignificant; for them the reader must be referred to the technical literature.

This book will serve its principal purpose best if the reader has some acquaintance with the field of linguistics. It is quite possible, on the other hand, to use the book when being introduced to linguistics, for the secondary purpose of *Field Linguistics* is to encourage the serious discussion of field problems within the discipline of linguistics. It may be true that linguistics is not identical with discovery procedures, but it is also true that linguistics cannot do without them.

In a book of this type it is easy for an author to be more prescriptive than he means to be. One needs to give advice, but one must not give the impression that there is only a single way of doing something when there may be equally good alternatives. There is no more a best way of studying a language in the field than there is a best way to survive if stranded on a raft in the middle of the Pacific Ocean. But it does help to have had some coaching in survival techniques, and it does help to go prepared with a survival kit. Ultimately, however, the survivor is one who can cope with his situation. This is equally true of the field worker as my last field trip to Africa reminded me. Carefully designed research projects may have to be jettisoned under circumstances beyond one's control.

Here and elsewhere in this volume I may give the impression that field work is more awesome than it really is. A field worker should take his work seriously, but he need not do it lugubriously, for an exciting and life-enriching experience awaits him. Field work is characterized in one word—at least for me; it is *fun*. It is fun to be intimately involved with people of different linguistic (and therefore cultural) backgrounds; it is fun to respond to challenges never confronted at home; it is fun—simple and exhilarating fun—to try to work out the puzzle of some aspect of linguistic structure. There is pleasure indeed in solving an analytical problem in the privacy of one's study, but to me there is more pleasure, because it is more exciting, in working at something step by step with an informant.

Many people have contributed to the making of *Field Linguistics*. It gives me real pleasure to publicly acknowledge their help.

In private conversation or in correspondence the following people furnished me with language data: Harvey Pitkin (Amharic), Sheila Tremaine (Aripaktsá), Virginia Morey Austin (Ata), H. Allan Gleason, Jr. (Badaga, Hindi), John Banker (Bahnar), Norman Abrams (Bilaan), Carolyn P. Miller (Brôu), Bruce R. Moore (Colorado), John Ellenberger (Damal), Geneviève Calame-Griaule (Dogon), David Shinen (Eskimo-Yupik), Charles R. Taber (French), Leslie H. Stennes (Fula), Kenneth Griffes (Gio), Karl Franklin (Kewa), Wayne and Elizabeth Snell (Machiguenga), Sarah Gudschinsky (Mazateco), Eva Radanovsky (More), Arlo Heinrichs (Mura-Pirahã), Dow F. Robinson (Nahuat), Donald Olson (Southern Cheyenne), Stewart Hussey (Tagbanwa), Howard M. Law (Tausug), Albert Buckwalter (Toba), Jack Berry (Twi), Ronald Manus (Uscarira), and David Smith (Zulu). Several of these people are members of the Summer Institute of Linguistics, Inc. Other S.I.L. personnel contributed to the typescript document on "The monolingual approach in linguistics" which was made available to me by George M. Cowan, one of its contributors; the others are: Patsy Adams, Lorrie Anderson, Doris Cox, Esther Matteson, Ruth McLeod, and William

Oates. A lectureship at the Summer Institute of Linguistics of the University of Oklahoma in 1964 provided me with the opportunity of talking with many investigators fresh from the field and of using the air-conditioned library of the University. I am indebted to Kenneth L. Pike, the Director of the Summer Institute, for the invitation.

About other matters the following people either contributed information or helped me to sharpen my thinking: Paul Friedrich (randomness in sampling), T. Gerald Dyar and John Wiedenheft (tape-recording equipment), Martin Joos (reverse playback with tape recorders), Floyd G. Lounsbury (language learning in field work), Harold C. Conklin and William Sturtevant (light-filing system), and Peter Ladefoged (palatography).

Many people kindly gave of their time to read an early version of the manuscript. I am especially grateful to those who read and commented on the whole manuscript: H. Allan Gleason, Jr., Howard M. Law, Clifford Nixon, Donald N. Olson, David L. Olmsted, Herbert Purnell, Earl Stevick, and Charles R. Taber. Others read parts of the manuscript: George Appell, John Banker, Paul Brennan, Robbins Burling, Harold C. Conklin, Kenneth Hale, Carleton T. Hodge, Allen Maxwell, Joe E. Pierce, and Uriel Weinreich.

The name of H. Allan Gleason has already been mentioned twice in these acknowledgments. A third is necessary to allow me full expression of my appreciation for his encouragement and interest in the writing of this book. He may recognize several of his own ideas in these pages; this cannot be helped, for I have learned much from him. But I must accept full responsibility for my use of this knowledge; this responsibility extends to the help given by all the other contributors whose names have been mentioned. To my students in "Linguistic Field Methods" I am also indebted, for it was from them I learned how much was teachable about field work. If their faults have been mentioned in these pages, they will understand that all of us begin by making mistakes. However, *Field Linguistics* was written with the hope that it would prevent others from making similar mistakes.

As with much of field work, the writing of a book separates a person from his family. A geographical separation would not have been as difficult, for it would not have lasted as long. For the patience with which my wife and children endured this burden I am deeply grateful.

W.J.S.

Leiden, the Netherlands
October 1966

CONTENTS

THE PURPOSE
OF FIELD
LINGUISTICS

1

Field linguistics is primarily a way of obtaining linguistic data and studying linguistic phenomena.[1] It involves two participants: the speaker (or speakers) of a language and the linguistic researcher. The means of carrying on investigation is the most direct possible, by personal contact. The speaker of the language, the *informant*, is the source of information and the evaluator of utterances put to him by the investigator. Hence this approach to language study has also been called the *informant method* and might also be called the *contact method* (Hockett 1948:119).

Field linguistics can be carried on anywhere, not just *in the field*, as its

[1] The term *field linguistics* is not to be confused with *anthropological linguistics* which, according to Carl F. Voegelin (1959*b*, 1961) is coordinate with five other aspects of linguistics, namely, *theoretical, psychological, critical, communicational,* and *comparative*. Anthropological linguistics "comprises the analysis . . . of either a wholly unknown language or of some unknown part of a language that is known in other parts" (1959*b*:122). Under this term is stressed the discovery part of linguistic research, whether it be of whole linguistic systems (that is, grammars), of certain aspects of these systems (for example, phonemic systems), of differentiation over an area or through various classes of society (for example, dialectology). Hoijer's definition is even more at variance with our concept of field linguistics: anthropological linguistics is that "area of linguistic research which is devoted in the main to studies, synchronic and diachronic, of the languages of peoples who have no writing" (Hoijer 1961:110).

1

name implies. A "field archeologist" must go out to where he expects to collect his data, but a linguist can bring his source to himself. Thus, some field work is done by bringing jungle dwellers to a city and is conducted in an office instead of a lean-to.

Field linguistics is generally thought of as work done on languages which have either never been studied before or only poorly, but field work can be done on any language for any purpose. Thus, when a person teaches Vietnamese with the aid of a native speaker of that language—because he himself has less than a native control of the language—and seeks to learn something about the language that the available descriptions give no help on, he is engaged in *field work,* brief though it may be. But if one wants to restrict the term "field work" to more prolonged or more intensive investigations, one can still say that the teacher in our illustration was conducting language research under *field conditions.* In this book field linguistics will be applied to the more or less intensive study of linguistic behavior.

Field linguistics has played an important part in man's study of language. If we had to depend only on the written records of language, our knowledge would be severely restricted indeed. Fortunately, for several centuries now inquisitive men, some more talented and careful than others, have personally collected data about little known languages and dialects. Not infrequently the investigations were characterized by theories about the origin and nature of language and the relationships between languages.

As inquires about language became more and more sophisticated, there was an increase in the direct study of living languages. Oftentimes this was of dialects of the cultural languages or of their culturally less important "sister" languages. And although it was a long time before some language scholars could look upon the "primitive languages," as they were known, with any degree of seriousness, there was nonetheless a considerable amount of research in non-Western languages. Some of this was quite good even by our present standards. But since the beginning of this century the amount of field work engaged in has risen dramatically. It is not coincidental, moreover, that this same period saw an equally dramatic development in the science of language. In fact, the history of linguistics cannot be told without proper recognition being given to the contribution made by linguists working on living and for the most part non-Western languages.

The coming of age of linguistics has in no way diminished the importance of linguistic field work. If anything, the need is even greater, because we see its value more clearly. There is today no need to justify linguistic field work in general. There are literally hundreds of individuals currently engaged in some form of field linguistics. The money being expended in this research amounts to several millions of dollars each year. By way of illustration, however, there are four ways in which field linguistics can serve some important purpose.

1. There is still a dearth of basic information about the languages of the world. We are not even certain exactly how many languages there are. The more we learn, the greater the number becomes. About thirty years ago a very rough estimate put the number between 2500 and 3500 (Gray 1939:418), but a more recent guess was that it was between 4000 and 7000 (Ferguson 1964). In West Africa alone, where some people thought there were 300 languages, field work led one investigator to raise the number to "well over 500" for 15 countries south of the Sahara from Senegal to the Cameroun, and there certainly are areas more linguistically diverse than this one (Ladefoged 1964:xiii). There are, of course, languages all over the world which are disappearing with the passing of their monolingual speakers or with the assimilation of their speakers into a dominant society through bilingualism. For example, of the 181 North American Indian languages in use today, 49 have fewer than 10 speakers of whom most are over 50 years old (Gursky 1963; see also Chafe 1962, 1965). We shall be the poorer for not having studied the dying languages.

As for linguistic descriptions of one type or another, most languages are hardly known. Even the 11 languages which together account for over one half of the world's population are inadequately described (Ferguson 1964). The other languages suffer more acutely. It is too much to expect all languages of the world, or even all languages spoken by one million or more people, to be fully described, but descriptions of specific aspects of grammar (for example, sound systems, grammatical categories, clause types) for many languages are realizable. The gathering of all this information is incontestably the business of linguists.

2. Field work is indispensable for the development of linguistics. As put by F. G. Lounsbury (in C. F. Voegelin 1950:299), "The recording and description of every one of these [dying languages] is as important to the science of linguistics as is natural history to the science of biology. When the 'natural history' of language is fairly adequately written, . . . we can look forward to much more of a 'science of general principles' in language than we now possess." The following paragraphs reveal only a few ways in which field work can lead to the development of linguistics.

Linguistic research can contribute data toward the understanding of language universals. There have been recent attempts to delineate some of these universal characteristics of language (Greenberg 1963), and field work since these publications has already challenged some of the assertions (Ladefoged 1964). When languages have been described and the information about them is easily retrieved, there will be less excuse than there is today for statements such as "There are many languages where . . . ," "There may be languages in which . . . ," and "The possibility that some languages do not clearly distinguish . . ." Thus, until K. L. Pike had done field work on Campa, an Arawak language of Peru, it had been held, even by him, that there were no languages in which contiguous syllables could have primary stress, but Campa has series of three and occasionally of even four primary stresses, such as ´ ´ ´ ´ —— (Pike and Kindberg 1956). Even more significant is recent concern with the identification and use of language universals in the stratificational and generative-transformational models of language (Teeter 1966).

There is also a direct relation between field work and language description. The more field work, the more information we will have about the variability of language. This information will reduce the amount of time required for arriving at the distinctive structures of languages being described. The Campa case serves to illustrate this point. It presented special difficulties to the investigators because they "were not psychologically prepared to recognize the nature of the system when the evidence began to appear" (Pike and Kindberg 1956:415). Progress is spiral and cumulative. As put by John Lyons (1962:127):

> . . . the history of science is full of examples to support the opinion that the actual cannot be properly described, perhaps not even recognized, except in the framework of what has previously been envisaged as possible. At the same time, of course, the sphere of what is thought of as possible is being constantly revised under the impact of discoveries made in the description of actual languages.

The field is also the laboratory of the linguist. First, because in his attempt to write a grammar which will be comprehensive, he must test every generalization. This is done by checking statements with informants and with texts. The texts can be studied away from the field, but their validity as a measuring rod is itself a matter to be decided after some field analysis. This means that without proper precautions, a linguistic generalization may be valid only for a specifiable corpus and not for the language as a whole. Secondly, the field serves as a laboratory for all of linguistics insofar as all theories and generalizations are tested by new data. Without these data we will not easily discover the Achilles' heel of whatever theory may be in vogue.

Field work is also an antidote for excessive theorizing. Theorizing becomes excessive when the same problems or the same data are looked at again and again at the expense of ignoring other significant issues.

3. Other disciplines besides linguistics depend on linguistic field work for data, experimentation, and problem formulation. Anthropology is one discipline which early recognized its dependence on it. The two sciences— anthropology and linguistics—in fact developed in the United States each supporting the other. The importance of language to ethnographic field

work is first of all that of a tool. As put by Boas (1911:60): "A command of the language is an indispensable means of obtaining accurate and thorough knowledge." (Other ethnographic field workers, however, have argued among themselves about the skill that they ought to demonstrate in the use of the "tool language," some pushing for fluency and others for a minimum control necessary in interviewing.[2])

For a long time the collection of texts in the native language constituted a considerable part of ethnographic field work. The text publications of Franz Boas, for example, run up into thousands of pages (White 1963). Ethnographic texts are an important source of explicit information about the culture being studied (Radin 1949). They also serve as a stimulus for particular investigations, for in the process of translating the texts the ethnographer sometimes discovers valuable clues. Thus, Suttles discovered a set of kinship forms in his texts which could not have been elicited by the genealogical method, because they cannot be used with possessives (1965: 161; see also Lounsbury 1954:226). Radin (1949) points out another value of text collection. By being able to write down and then read the text with a fairly good approximation to the informant's pronunciation, the ethnographer gives the impression of understanding what he has obtained. Encouraged by this comprehension, the informant, who perhaps has hitherto been psychologically at a great distance from the investigator (or the race or class represented by him), becomes more interested in giving him information.

Anthropologists are concerned today with many problems—historical, structural, and functional—which must be studied linguistically. What, for example, are the correlations between various aspects of cultural behavior and semantic structure; the relation of perception to linguistic structure; the semantic structures typical of specific cultures or universal in all cultures? For each problem there may be necessary a specific set of data obtainable only from native speakers. For such work investigators must be sophisticated in both anthropology and linguistics.

But anthropology is not the only science to profit from the techniques of linguistics. Bloomfield once said (1925:1): "The science of language . . . is most closely related to ethnology, but precedes ethnology and all other human sciences in the order of growing complexity, for linguistics stands at their foot, immediately after psychology, the connecting link between the natural sciences and the human." All that has happened in the intellectual world since then has only confirmed his assertion. Today linguistics cannot be ignored by philosophers, logicians, psychologists, or theolo-

---

[2] For example: Mead 1939; Lowie 1940; Beals 1957; P. Bohannan 1958 *a, b;* McEwen 1959. For a statement as strong as Boas' see Radin 1949.

gians. Some of the questions they pose to linguists can be answered on the basis of what we already know about language and its use. Others must await further research.

4. Finally, field work is necessary if linguistics is going to be applied practically to human affairs. For example, with the eclipse of the colonial era and the rise of new nations, there is an urgent need for language planning and "language engineering." Nations need to determine how many languages are spoken within their boundaries, which ones should be used for education and other purposes, and how they are to be adapted to modern life (Le Page 1964). Some of these languages, like Arabic, have an ancient literature but are fragmented by dialects. Others, like recently resuscitated Hebrew, must be fully equipped for the scientific era. Trade languages, like Malay, Fula, and Sango, must be standardized. There are also vernacular languages which only recently have been raised to official status. For example, the declaration of Pashto as an official language of Afghanistan along with Persian in 1935 (Shafeev 1964) meant the establishment of an Afghan Academy for the purpose of carrying out research on the Pashto language, folklore, and literature. The academy has also sponsored the publication of Pashto classics, folklore collections, grammars, and dictionaries.

In this century we shall undoubtedly see a whole series of linguistic revolutions, some the effects of political developments but others the result of the population explosion. If "minor" languages were so classed because of the number of their speakers, some of them are becoming less "minor" because of the population explosion. They will demand more and more attention from linguists or linguistically trained people.

HUMAN FACTORS
IN FIELD WORK

2

In his preoccupation with data—in the tangible form of notebooks, slips of paper, lists of words and sounds, and so on—the linguist can very easily forget the human factors in his investigation of language. His collection and analysis of language phenomena are dependent on and in some way influenced by the people among whom he works and by his own personality and training. Without some understanding of himself, the language community, and the informant the linguistic investigator goes ill-prepared to the field. So much has to be said about the informant that the whole of Chapter 3 is devoted to this subject.

The Investigator

Not everyone who is attracted by the study of language is qualified to carry on linguistic research in the field. Veteran field workers can tell of investigators who have increased the difficulties of their endeavors by their insensitivity to the subtle elements of harmonious interpersonal relations. Anticipating problems, many have fulfilled their linguistic ambitions in studies where human factors were less crucial. This is not to say, of course,

7

that outgoing persons cannot be found among those whose studies are less dependent on the first-hand collection of data from speakers of a language. It is simply a fact that one who is embarrassed by too much exposure to the challenges of interpersonal and cross-cultural relations can nonetheless find satisfying pursuits in other fields of linguistics.

To the field situation the investigator brings not only his personal psychological makeup but also his training and skills.[1] There must be training in articulatory phonetics and methods in linguistic analysis—phonological, grammatical, and to some extent lexicographical (or semantic). Occasionally one finds statements by linguists who in describing their field techniques seem to undercut the need for intensive training in phonetic transcription. The following is one example. It is said (Voegelin 1949:81) that whether the investigator starts with a phonetically over-differentiated [that is, with narrow transcription] or under-differentiated [even to the point of leaving out contrastive sounds] text, he must "check again and again with native speakers before arriving at a text identified entirely in terms of phonemes." If this is a procedure to follow in field work, it is (a) extremely wasteful of the time of both the investigator and informant, (b) unnecessary, and (c) perhaps even detrimental to the research, since it would tend to undermine the informant's confidence in the investigator. Checking will always be necessary, but it should never be done on a text in such an unsystematic way.

The more that one knows of the diversity of language structures and of the different ways they have been handled by grammarians, the more successful he will be in dealing with the language at hand. Reading of various types of linguistic descriptions should therefore be an integral part of linguistic training. Unfortunately, finding good grammars is not accomplished by an examination of the reviews. Rarely do grammars receive accolades like the one Hockett gave Bloomfield's Algonquian work: "one of the finest indoctrinations into the best of linguistic method" (1948: 117).

Linguistic "internship" is practice in the analysis of a language. Knowing the principles of linguistic analysis—as demonstrated by a lecturer, revealed in the reading of descriptions, or worked out in problem-solving —has proven to be inadequate for all but the rare individual.

---

[1] There will, of course, always be gifted people who can collect data and write a description which is accurate and comprehensive without the benefit of formal training in linguistics. One such person was Lt. Col. D. L. R. Lorimer. This "amateur linguist," whose major responsibilities were those of an administrator in the British civil service, wrote a grammar of Burushaski of which it is said: it is "one of the best 'amateur' efforts that has ever appeared in linguistics, and is marked by acuteness both of recording and of analysis." Lorimer, it is claimed, "had little to learn . . . [in field methods] from the professionals, apart from the field of phonetics and some of the very latest developments in phonemic and morphophonemic analysis" (Emeneau 1940:354.

If intensive training in field procedures is assumed for the anthropologist, it can figure no less in the training of a linguistic researcher. Yet in some quarters there seems to be a minimizing of its importance. In a paper read to a conference of anthropologists, linguistic analysis was made to seem an easy task for them:

> In order to do his linguistic work, accordingly, the anthropologist does not need to be trained in a whole separate science. He has only to comprehend the phonemic method of discovering what sounds are functional in a given language [that is, what are the phonemic contrasts], and the combinatorial technique of stating which combinations of linguistic elements occur in speech" (Voegelin 1952:325).[2]

What this statement says is that a skilled ethnographic interviewer who is acquainted with the principles of linguistic analysis should have no difficulty in producing a satisfactory grammatical description. The implication is that ethnographic and linguistic techniques are fundamentally the same; one must only add some supplementary skills to those he already has. It is doubtful, however, that the results will always be the desired ones. For the anthropologist as well as the nonanthropologist there must be training, and it will be incomplete without practice in linguistic analysis, using an informant.

The field worker's preparation must also include becoming acquainted with the culture of the people whose language he is going to study and with previous work on this language or others either related or found in the same area. This is the testimony of one linguist in this regard: "I once attempted a grammar . . . of a single idiolect of Kalmyk Mongolian at a time when I knew little of present-day dialects. The result of the analysis seemed linguistically adequate; it was only after studying related idiolects and dialects that a full awareness dawned on me of the vital importance in linguistic field work of some background in—and feeling for—the family of languages involved. (It is appalling how many hours one can waste working on problems already solved by others.)" (Street 1963:336).

The reason that ethnographic reading is important is that in language analysis one must make inquiries that will be judged culturally relevant or irrelevant by the informant. Irrelevant inquiries will have the effect of slowing down the elicitation and perhaps of undermining the informant's confidence in the researcher. When eliciting words from the pastoral Tamachek of northern Mali, for example, one does not simply ask for the generic terms for domesticated animals: camel, horse, cow, and others. The investigator should expect that the Tamachek would have a profusion

---

[2] This statement appears to contradict an earlier one: "Everyone acknowledges this [that is, that language is part of culture] theoretically and then tends to treat the two separately in actual work because the techniques of gathering data and making analyses are not the same for both" (Voegelin and Harris 1945:456–457).

of terms in this lexical domain distinguishing male from female animals, young from mature, those in good condition from those in poor health, and so on. The more relevant to the culture that a linguist can make his inquiries, the more interested his informant becomes.

The Community

Linguistic field work does not have to be done in the native habitat of the speakers. Many Americans have worked with single informants who were away from home. Thus Morris Swadesh (1951*b*:66) was able to elicit about 500 words, a few paradigms, and a short text from a Unaaliq Eskimo at a Sportsmen's Show in New Haven, Connecticut, in 1936.

Idiolectal grammars have been the target of repeated criticism, but there is no denying their contribution to our knowledge of the languages of the world. Nevertheless, if linguistics is going to concern itself with more than structural descriptions, as indeed it should, the linguistic researcher must expose himself to the normal use of the language.

There are two principal reasons why field work should be done *in situ,* not necessarily with several different informants (whose number is taken up in Chapter 3), but where one can see people realistically interacting in the language being studied. The first reason is that field research will make it much easier for both the informant and the investigator to collect a corpus which is culturally relevant and linguistically accurate. A careful study of examples in grammars often reveals utterances which quite clearly show the bias of the investigator. Examples of poor analysis are more difficult to detect unless the reader happens to know the language as well as or better than the analyst.

The second reason is that by restricting himself to working away from the community, the investigator precludes the observation of important linguistic phenomena. It is not just that the "meaning" of utterances can be ascertained with greater accuracy—and meaning discrimination *is* an important tool in linguistic analysis—but also that there is much data of sociological or psychological significance that can be obtained in no other way. It is becoming increasingly important for the linguist to be able to relate his findings to other fields of linguistics and to other disciplines.

An example of the limitations of the informant technique is my own linguistic investigation of Gbeya dog names (1965). My purpose in collecting them, along with personal names, proverbs, and riddles, was primarily to increase my vocabulary and to investigate the possibility of there being different styles of language. Except for a few syntactic features, my investigation turned up nothing linguistically significant, but many new insights into Gbeya culture were obtained. When these names were being described for publication, however, I discovered that I had very little information about their most interesting aspect from a theoretical point of view. What turned out to be extremely interesting was not their lexical content or syntactic structure but their use in bringing attention to the behavior of others or to one's own attitude to life.

Entrance into a community can be extremely difficult. In a few instances investigators have lost their lives even after great effort was made to establish rapport with the people.

More common than danger to life or limb is the problem of being accepted by a community. Communities vary considerably in their attitudes toward outsiders. Some are extremely hospitable and others treat strangers with great suspicion and lack of cooperation. Some, like the Auca Indians of Peru, consider the approach of any person outside the immediate homestead a threat to life. More typical is the treatment afforded strangers by the people of Sirkanda, a peasant village of North India. The following is a statement by an Indian school teacher from fifty miles away who was assigned to Sirkanda:

> I have taught in several schools in the valley and people have always been friendly to me. They have invited me to their homes for meals, have sent gifts of grain and vegetables with their children, and have tried to make me feel at home. I have been here four months now with almost no social contact aside from my students. No one has asked me to eat with him; no one has sent me so much as a grain of millet; no one has asked me to sit and talk with him; no one has even asked me who I am or whether I have a family. They ignore me (Berreman 1962:5).

Another fairly well described case of cautiousness, suspicion, reticence, and sensitiveness is that of the Gullah Negroes who live along the coast of South Carolina and Georgia. Their language had never been adequately studied until Lorenzo Dow Turner, himself an American Negro, established rapport with them in the forties. His work *Africanisms in the Gullah Dialect* has been acclaimed for its demonstration of what good field techniques can accomplish.

Another reason for a community's reticence in accepting a stranger is its inability to understand the nature and purpose of a linguistic project. People whose days are taken up with caring for their own needs do not understand the presence of a foreigner who comes to simply ask questions. Even in our own society where interviewing as a basic technique in research is known superficially by a large proportion of our society, one's avowed research goals are invariably questioned. When, for example, I was using the sentence-completion device to get information in the United States about English syntax and had quite frankly explained what I was doing, I was still asked: "Is this some kind of a trick?"

One might expect people to be flattered by having their language studied, but this is not always true. Lack of interest is in fact to be expected where one is studying a nonstandard dialect or a language which does not have the prestige of the national or official language. People may fear revealing a bumpkin mentality or ungrammatical speech. Since it is with language that people transmit information about their culture, they may also resist its study for fear of revealing secrets about themselves. Unsophisticated users of language do not see the difference between structure and content, so questions about their language are taken to be questions about their lives.

It is not always obvious to a linguist how he gets into the back region of the community as he investigates its language. His work is certainly not comparable to that of the ethnographer who must get bits of information that have cultural relevance by direct means. But the linguistic investigator also handles bits of information which can take on special significance when he is working in the community. He might innocently ask his informant to translate a sentence he overheard. Embarrassment or even anger would indicate that the informant considered this repetition equivalent to tattling or slandering. The linguist must therefore expect to arouse his informant's emotions by calling his attention to the content of utterances. This is also true as one works with traditional utterances such as proverbs and tales. One of the times my own Gbeya informant was most severely criticized for helping me to learn Gbeya was after I had publicly used the proverb *hérɛ́ŋ á dɛà b'árá wí-ré nɛ rékɛ́t á dɛà wí-zú* "Escaping makes a righteous person but getting caught makes a thief." The community's resentment must have been based on being "defeated" in an argument with one of its own weapons, a proverb.

Illustrative of a community's language shame is the case of the Coatlán Zapotec of Oaxaca, Mexico. Field work among these people is described in the following words:

> From the initial language contact with the Coatlán Zapotecs it was evident that the language, as far as the people were concerned, branded them as "indios," as ignorant peasants. Progress up and out of this social level was to come through the acquisition of Spanish. A village school, "primaria," had been in operation for some twenty years. Hence for a foreigner to enter the village and express interest in their native language, to learn to speak . . . , to write it with an alphabet that looks like Spanish—all this for the people was incomprehensible. In fact, the attitude towards our linguistic efforts became that of sustained aloofness and, for a few, hostility. To recognize the Zapotec language as a language and worthy of being studied was interpreted as an effort to regress to a previous generation—the time, in the memory of not a few adults, when the presence of the "mestizo" in the village would find every door shut, with the women and children inside, and only a few of the bravest men outside to exercise their meager vocabulary of Spanish (Robinson 1963:iii).

The Mazatecs of Mexico also hold their own language in contempt.

Eunice V. Pike reports (1956:73) that the word for "Indian language," meaning their own, is a compound consisting of the word for "word" plus an adjective which is also used in describing a cripple, an idiot, and a person lacking in money or goods.

Finally, entry into a community will be affected by its power structure. One must expect some kinds of "political" forces whether the community be formally structured or not. They may be kinship or occupational groups, political parties, religious castes or leaders, and others. In a less overtly structured society, such as one finds in many parts of Africa, one does not necessarily find less opposition. Cliques and old rivalries may stand in the way of any productive work whatsoever. In the novelized description of ethnographic work among the Tiv, Laura Bohannan (writing under the pseudonym of Elenore Smith Bowen, 1964) very effectively portrays the frustrations experienced by investigators as they become involved, sometimes unwittingly, in communal problems.

Acceptance by a community even under the best of circumstances is not achieved without some effort on the part of the investigator. He must reveal himself as a harmless individual who in no way threatens the existing state of affairs. This means fitting into the scheme of things as a neutral person or as one who can actually contribute something to the community's well-being. To accomplish this the investigator must assume a role which is acceptable to the community. Since acceptability is determined by the community's expectations, it may take several weeks or even months of rather intensive and systematic investigation to ascertain what these are. Of his work at Sirkanda, Berreman says (1962:9): "Three months were spent almost exclusively in building rapport, in establishing ourselves as trustworthy, harmless, sympathetic, and interested observers of village life." But the field worker, whose time is always severely restricted, will want to use every opportunity to the greatest advantage. When this determination affects a person's behavior, making out of him an efficient, and perhaps impatient, machine, he will violate the ideal behavior demanded by the community. The people of Larteh, Ghana, for example, required one investigator "to be . . . pliant, passive, easy-going, docile, a follower rather than a leader" (Brokensha 1963:533).

The variety of experiences people have had in finding their place in a community is truly astounding. Wayne Snell and his family had to be adopted by one of the Machiguenga families since the only other alternative among these Peruvian jungle dwellers was to be considered and treated as an outsider. Benjamin Paul and his wife were given a role by the Guatemalan Indians on the day of their arrival, for the people thought that because of the amount of goods they had arrived with they surely must be merchants! (Paul 1953:433).

The case of the Snells in being adopted into a family is an extreme form of an otherwise effective way of finding an entrance into a community, that is, sponsorship. This simply involves being endorsed by someone in the community. The sponsor does not necessarily have to be a prominent or influential person; such a person sometimes creates more problems than he is worth. On the other hand, one must not be sponsored by a person against whom there is resentment.

Acceptance by a community can also be achieved by various avenues of participation: (a) The first has already been mentioned—membership or relationship of one type or another—in a family, club, society, work gang, ritual team. Some of these are more or less permanent, but others may be temporary. One recent investigator of the Yupik (Eskimo) language on St. Lawrence Island, Alaska, became a regular member of a boat hunting crew at the invitation of its captain. Through two hunting seasons, four or five days a month, he had the full responsibilities of a crew member. ". . . I was expected to be ready to go out with the crew on a moment's notice and take part in all the work involved on a hunt. This included getting the equipment down to the beach, preparing the boat for launching, implicitly following the orders of the boat captain, doing my share of the butchering, and finally helping land the boat and securing it. All this entitled me to have an equal share in the game that was taken on the hunt." In this natural setting the field worker escaped the stilted conversations which had characterized all his previous contact with the Eskimos, and he was able to note linguistic material which had been difficult to elicit or which had not even occurred to him, such as various types of humor. (He also discovered that the Eskimos continued the practice of casting certain parts of animals back into the sea as an offering to the goddess who releases animals for the hunters to capture.) (b) The avenue available to everyone is the solidarity he has because of his age or sex with certain members of the community. A man, simply because he is a man, has the right to sit in the men's house among the Damal of New Guinea. There are very often certain obligations, of course. Among some people it may mean bringing tobacco. Among the Damal it means being properly and modestly dressed. To the Damal men, indecent exposure, comparable to the exposure of the genitals among us, is an uncovered head of hair. (c) One can also participate in some communal activity appropriate to one's sex like drawing water, planting rice, setting traps, and the like. (d) Finally, one can render services which the people would otherwise be without, such as pulling teeth, writing letters, and acting as intermediary with government representatives.

Participation exacts a great price from the field worker. There will be physical discomforts as one lives at a level and under circumstances to which he is unaccustomed. More trying will be the obligation to behave in an unaccustomed way. Everyone wants to indulge his own idiosyncracies from time to time. In our own societies we know which ones we can favor, where and when. In a foreign community it may be difficult or impossible to "do what we want." The toll that participation exacts of one's time is another factor that one must face. Getting alone to do one's work, as many Europeans are accustomed to, may be difficult indeed. Privacy in many communal societies is unknown as we think of it. Sending people away would be taken as an affront. My own solution to this problem did not come until I had been in Africa for several years. If my visitors wanted only to chat at a time when I was otherwise preoccupied, I told them that I—speaking about myself in the third person—had gone to weed the garden. By using a common phrase, I conveyed the message that although I did not have a real garden to weed, I did have work which kept me equally busy. The good will with which this explanation was always received testified to its cultural relevance and effectiveness.[3]

The greatest danger in participation is that it undermines the psychological distance that is necessary in scientific investigation. What is studied must be "out there" where one can look at it objectively and holistically. The linguistic field worker must never become so involved with people that he loses sight of the object of his study. Even as he talks with people in the target language, he consciously filters out, in addition to the message, all kinds of information about sounds, use of certain affixes, phrase structure, and gestures.

At some point or another the investigator will have to explain what he is doing and why. In other words, he must identify his role in the community. Inevitably, this role has a direct bearing on (1) to whom he has access or (2) from whom he is excluded and (3) on what he is or is not told about persons and activities. If he has the backing of some local governmental body, his project will not be difficult to explain, but where government officials and government interference are looked upon with distaste and distrust the investigator might be advised to omit references to the government support. Another danger of sponsorship by an external body is that the investigator's work may be misrepresented. For example, when Hollingshead did his study of "Elmtown" youth, he had been preceded by the Chicago Committee on Human Development which had informed the leading people of the town that the study to be undertaken was primarily interested in the development of character in boys and girls. By "character" the people understood "goodness." For this reason they were very much in favor of the projected study, but Hollingshead was primarily interested in the sociological correlations of the behavior of youth,

---

[3] This paragraph has mentioned a few of the many cultural differences that make it difficult to establish and maintain rapport with members of another society. Shelton (1964) discusses one that is easily overlooked, that is, inability to make physical contact with village folk.

not in prescribing good behavior. The result of this misinterpretation was a limitation of what he could do (Hollingshead 1949:8). If the investigator declares that he is alone in his project, his words may be taken with incredulity. What the investigator must look for is some independence mixed with endorsement from a well-received prestigious institution, be it political, educational, or commercial.

Language study for its own sake will hardly ever be comprehended. More acceptable are explanations in terms of what the study could contribute to education, mass information media, and the learning of the standard language. When I was conducting a sociolinguistic study on the use of Sango in the Central African Republic, I explained that although French was the national language, not everybody knew French. Therefore it would be a very good thing for the government and others to ascertain how many people knew Sango. This was one thing I was trying to do.

The role of the "learner" is a very effective one. Among the Japanese, for example, a researcher who presents himself as a student of human behavior will probably find, as one sociologist did, that he is equated with a "scholar," a very respected person in their society (Wax 1960). The role of learner has the advantage also of increasing the intimacy between the investigator and his informants. However, in preliterate societies, where there is no scholarly tradition of any type, the image of a learner is impossible except in a personal, practical sense. In such societies the investigator is obliged to give the appearance of being actively engaged in worthwhile projects, especially if the community has a low opinion of "dawdlers." This might mean engaging in red-herring studies, that is, doing valid work which is approved by the community but which is not central to the project.

There are obviously questions of ethics when one assumes a role and states a purpose in a community. The first one concerns the ethics of role-playing itself. Is it deceitful to assume a role which is in conformity to the local role expectations even when these are far removed from the explicit purpose of the research? The answer to this question will be decided in part by the amount of disparity there is between the role and the purpose. It will be decided also by the expectations of the community. It is not unethical to act in harmony with these expectations.

A more specific question is this: how can a linguistic investigator take from the people of a community a vast amount of data—much of it given free, all of it given in good will, with the hope, perhaps, that it will do them or their children some good—and use it exclusively in scientific publications which in themselves can serve no practical purpose? To some degree the linguist is obliged to his helpers to meet their expectations. Looking upon linguistics as an "objective" science does not make us less dependent on human beings for its pursuit, nor does it make us less obligated to use our findings for the satisfaction of their desires. How all of this is done is, of course, a matter of personal decision. One linguist, a rare one indeed, begins his notes to the user of his dictionary with the following words: "Many times during the course of fieldwork the author's Klamath friends and informants expressed the hope that the Grammar and Dictionary might be of use to them as a guide for writing Klamath and also as an instruction book for younger Klamaths wishing to learn the language." Then follows an apologetic statement concerning the purpose and use of the dictionary which is fully in good taste (Barker 1963: 10).

With the greater availability of education and literature in the newer nations scientific field workers, especially ethnographic ones, are coming into greater and greater disfavor. One African spoke sarcastically about how he had been invited to tea whereas the real purpose was to get information from him. It did not seem that he criticized the elicitation of information nor how it was used; he seemed rather to look upon his conversation as a commodity over which he should have had some control. "When people make a study," he added, "they should leave behind a copy of all that they write down." Another African discouraged a missionary from studying anthropology after he had himself taken such courses. Similar attitudes are held concerning linguistic work. Two non-Africans saw the wisdom in criticizing, by implication at least, the work that many had done on African languages. At a conference in Africa at which Africans were present John Spencer declared that African languages have been looked upon by academics as "rich linguistic raw material awaiting export for processing" (1963:37). At this same conference Pierre Alexandre said (in my translation from the French): "Some [Africans] . . . experience suspicion towards non-Africans who are interested in African cultures and languages, seeing in this interest a disguised means of keeping Africa at the level of the folkloristic and picturesque so as to exploit it" (Spencer 1963:57).

In a politically sensitive Africa there are frequent reminders to the field worker to be circumspect about the role that he assumes and the use to which he puts his study, but in other areas there are far fewer demands for alertness. Thus, investigators among the recently pacified groups of Brazil or New Guinea will find it difficult to think of their work in a historical perspective. Yet resentment against academic exploitation or "cultural imperialism," as it is being called today in some areas, can be retroactive, which is all too evident in the newer nations. The fact that two well-known Africans were at one time linguistic informants, namely Kwame Nkrumah and Jomo Kenyatta, should prevent field linguists from being too casual about their obligations.

Gross deviations from our society's ethical code, of course, we do not expect. It is therefore surprising when we read in an anthropology textbook: "He [the house-servant acting also as informant] was not always scrupulous, but he got me what I wanted and needed. His methods and motives perhaps would not stand up under close inspection, nor mine either. But moralizing seems inconsistent with the hard facts we had to deal with in the bush." One would hope that no amount of casuistry will ever be adequate to justify the devious activities implied in that confession. Away from the field, that is, in publication, a certain standard of uprightness is assured by a large and critical audience. In the field there are no such sanctions to control the behavior of the investigator. Each man is his own king, but he must also be his own judge.[4]

The reader has by now come to the conclusion that field research can be a difficult experience. It can indeed. The reason is that the researcher must cope with innumerable problems, some of which he has never before had to face and others he is very much unaware of. It will be an entirely new and trying experience, for example, to be completely responsible for one's own water supply, lighting, and sewage disposal. Even more difficult perhaps will be the problems which arise in his involvement with people of a different culture. The point is tellingly made in the anthropological novel *Return to Laughter* by depicting the field worker's trials during a smallpox epidemic:

> It is an error to assume that to know is to understand and that to understand is to like. The greater the extent to which one has lived and participated in a genuinely foreign culture and understood it, the greater the extent to which one realizes that one could not, without violence to one's personal integrity, be of it. . . . I had discovered that there were moral values which I could not willfully abandon, no matter what the dictates and interests of science and no matter how impossible it had been for me to live up to those standards (Bowen 1964:291, 289).

The problem which the field worker least expects, therefore, is a psychological one. For many a neophyte researcher field work will resemble a birth experience his student life has poorly prepared him for. Ejected from the university's womb into a foreign culture where the most important values are in personal relations, where technical or scholarly competence is either not understood or not appreciated, the field worker will indeed feel out of place. He will find himself asking questions he had never heard raised: What is the relation of my project to humanity's crucial needs? By pursuing this project am I most adequately fulfilling my own personality and destiny? Am I truly qualified to interpret these people

---

[4] For recent discussions of ethics in field work see Barnes 1963, Hanna 1965, Shelton 1965. Published discussions by linguists have not come to my attention.

with my inexperience? Why do the people see me more and less than I truly am?

For one sociological field worker the most difficult aspect of field research was the discovery of a role which was satisfying, in being authentic, both to herself and the people she was studying. In assessing her own difficulties twelve years after the experience she writes: ". . . the fundamental process involved in the initiation into full-scale field experience does not differ significantly from the process of learning any new role. The neophyte passes through an initial period of anxiety and distress, during which he and the persons with whom he interacts contribute to the definition of both his and their roles. If both parties are able to agree on these definitions and are able to communicate the fact that they agree, much of the anxiety disappears and is replaced by the complex phenomena which we call 'self-confidence'" (Wax 1960:177). Her problems were due to the initial failure to identify this role: ". . . during this period of initiation she [writing of herself] found herself trying to defend what to her was an ideal rather than a real self-image against the community's already well-defined derogatory appraisals. Desperately she tried to see herself as a 'person to whom one gave information,' while everyone about her regarded her as 'a person to whom one gave no information'" (175). Her frustrations became grave. Very frankly she describes them with these words: "She [the author herself] spent days alternately crying or writing letters to relatives and academic friends. Then she refused to associate with the Caucasian staff members, hoping that this irrational rudeness would make her more acceptable to the Japanese. She repulsed the overtures of a few kindly and insightful staff members who tried to draw her out of her self-imposed solitary confinement, interpreting their offers of friendship as 'attempts to steal her data.' . . . Finally, she succumbed to an urge to eat enormously and in three months gained thirty pounds" (175).

The first way to avoid some problems and to cope with others is to be fully aware of them. One must understand the nature of the psychological crises one will have to face. The second tactic is simply to avoid the ordeal of having to work alone for a protracted period of time, especially in a hostile and uncooperative community. The field worker should arrange to have visits made to him by an experienced and understanding person who can, among other things, reinforce the approved image of the worker's developing self. Trips away from the field are also salutary and need to be recommended whenever circumstances permit. So important is this move to a more congenial society that the field workers of the Summer Institute of Linguistics stay no longer than six months even when working in teams.

THE LANGUAGE
INFORMANT

3

The linguistic investigator is an outsider to the language he studies. As long as he remains an outsider, the language will be nothing but noise. It is only as he enters into the experience of the community that he begins to "understand," that the noise begins to take shape and "make sense." Little by little he learns the rules of the language and relates them to the rules of his own language. This would be a very long process—as long as it is for children—if the investigator did not have the help of an "insider," someone who interprets for him and helps him to bridge the gap until the equation is established. This person is the *informant*.

More specifically, the informant is one who furnishes the researcher with samples of the language, either as repetitions of what has already been said or as creations of what somebody might say. He also explains how the utterances were used or what they meant, using for this explanation either his own language or some other. The informant can be a chance speaker of the language from whom the researcher has obtained data, but he is more normally one who more or less regularly meets with the researcher for language study.

The term informant is therefore a technical one and should be used judiciously outside of linguistic circles. Educated people have been known to become embarrassed when referred to by the phrase "my informant." To some people the term seems to have the same connotation as "informer." To avoid causing this embarrassment and misunderstanding one can use less loaded terms, such as assistant, helper, aid, or colleague.

Need for Informants

From what has just been said it should be apparent that informants are indispensable for linguistic research of the kind being treated in this book. Yet nowhere in linguistic literature has there appeared an adequate treatment of the part that informants play in linguistic analysis. It would almost seem as if informants were not the indispensable collaborators they really are. In grammars almost always and in journal articles sometimes authors will express their appreciation for the patience, faithfulness, help, and encouragement of the informant, but it is not often that the appreciation is expressed at such length and with such apparent sincerity as it is in the following acknowledgment by Bronislaw Malinowski. That he was speaking as an anthropologist makes no difference, for the linguist depends no less on his informant than does his colleague:

> The Anthropologist takes full credit for some of his discoveries, but for the real toil, as well as for the degree of intelligence in the approach, he can only take part credit. To a large extent my informants are responsible for the correct interpretation and perspective, for the sincerity and relevance of what is contained in these volumes, as also in my other ethnographic writings (1935, I:x).

But why precisely do we need informants?

First, we need informants in order to get the body of data (the *corpus*) which is necessary for making generalizations about the structure of a language.[1] This is a particular kind of corpus, because the linguist is working under special conditions with special goals in mind. The characteristics of this corpus are not described here, for they are treated in Chapter 4. All that needs to be said now is that a very convenient method for obtaining the crucial data is by working with an informant. One does not have to wait for further occurrences of something already heard; he can

[1] The linguist also collects information which, although not strictly linguistic in nature, may nevertheless be part of the whole speech act, such as gestures. Here are several different categories of gestures one should pay attention to: (1) gestures of negation and affirmation; (2) gestures indicating measurement of height, length, depth, width, weight, volume, size, direction, position; (3) gestures used to warn, hush, frighten, beckon; (4) gestures and patterned expressions showing emotion (pain, fear, sorrow, surprise, disgust, derision, admiration, smell, and so on); (5) suggestive gestures such as snapping of fingers, winking, staring, whistling; (6) gestures used in counting; (7) symbolic gestures and dance postures; (8) gestures and postures used in conversation, whispering, oratory, singing; (9) greetings, handshaking (Conklin 1950).

obtain them by asking for them. (One cannot say that he uses an informant to get "exactly" what he needs. Linguistic research is exploration; one may know in general what to expect, but he has no assurance that he will get to precisely where he wants to go. There will be many opportunities for getting lost along the way.)

One cannot obtain the corpus from everybody in the community. Without knowing what diversity there is in the speech under investigation, the researcher may acquire an extremely diversified corpus: women's speech may be different from men's as among the Koasati of Louisiana; different dialects may be represented by the population; the speech of the oldest generation may be different from that of young people, as among the Badaga. All of these variations within the speech community must in time be incorporated in the linguist's complete description, but he only complicates his task unnecessarily by starting with them. He will not, of course, ignore any utterances from any speaker which he can possibly write down with a reasonable degree of accuracy. They too become a part of the corpus, carefully labelled.

Checking the data for accuracy is also an important function of the informant. There is probably no linguistic researcher alive, nor will there ever be, who can write down at the first hearing everything which is linguistically significant. The more different the language is from our own the more chance there is for error in transcription. The errors can be of several types: not hearing enough phonetic differences, hearing differences in the wrong places, wrongly segmenting the stream of sound into phonological units, and so on. Improvement in transcription is spiral and cumulative: as the researcher makes progress in one area of phonology or grammatical analysis he will see the need for going back to earlier utterances. All of this work requires a patient, trained, and reliable informant.

Further reasons for the informant's importance are seen in comparing analyses based on written texts and those based on informant texts. A grammar based entirely on written texts is dependent on the orthography for its statements about the phonology. In spite of the success that linguists have demonstrated in historical reconstructions, they can only guess at the subphonemic characteristics of a language. On the level of the morphemes, identification is made on the basis of the translation. When one has been confronted with extremely knotty problems in living languages, one can appreciate the difficulty of analyzing only from translations. An analysis of Early Archaic Chinese serves to illustrate this problem. In addition to nouns and verbs there seems to be a class of words which show formal characteristics of both nouns and verbs but are translatable into English adjectives, adverbs, or intransitive verbs. Whenever these words turn up in verb position they can be translated either "bring [the noun] into being" or "treat others or behave oneself as [the noun]" (Stimson 1963). Without an informant to provide more data, we have no way of knowing how to better classify these words.

Another difficulty with working exclusively with written texts is that one can never be sure that the relations established between grammatical elements are not simply *ad hoc* descriptions instead of true patterns. The analyst is at the mercy of his corpus. What this means is that without an informant one cannot test hypotheses (that is, one's tentative analyses) and cannot make statements concerning the productivity of morphemic relations—one cannot predict.[2]

Selection of Informants

Not every speaker of a language can qualify as a language informant. There are good informants and bad informants, but criteria for considering one good and another bad are difficult to enumerate. One linguist who got on famously with an informant might not understand why a colleague found it impossible to accomplish anything with the same person. How the informant is classified does not depend entirely on the informant himself but also on the personality of the investigator and on other factors.[3] The nature of the study, the circumstances under which it is done, the informant's health, and innumerable other factors will influence one's judgment about a candidate. Difficulties in agreeing on the qualities of a good informant do not, however, justify ignoring the consideration of who best serves the investigator.

Proper deliberation in the selection of an informant is required by the fact that it is so often difficult to dismiss one. Where the informant in some way represents the community to the field worker or where he is in some special relationship to an important personage in the community, the dismissal of an informant will engender ill will. So great might be the animosity be that the linguist, not being able to find a replacement, might have to give up his project.

For this reason and others one should make a thorough reconnaissance before selecting the informant. This involves soliciting, if possible, the help of the language community in determining the availability and aptitudes

---

[2] This statement is not meant to be categorical. One can, for example, always divide his texts: one part for the analysis and the remaining part for testing the analysis. If the nonanalyzed part is describable in terms of the analysis, then one has succeeded. Obviously, the problem of judging adequacy is a statistical one.

[3] Kurath (1939:41) documents how field workers for the *Linguistic Atlas of New England* tended to show preferences for certain types of informants (one for "the interesting old-fashioned local type," another for "the quicker middle-aged type") in spite of the precise instructions they had received concerning the three types of informants they were to seek out.

of several candidates. The informant must first of all have enough time to more or less regularly meet with the field worker. He must also be a good speaker of the language. People show a surprising ability the world over in evaluating the verbal gifts of their fellow men. Comments people make about individuals in the community will often contain information which is useful in identifying potential candidates. One ethnographer was alerted to the existence of a truly remarkable informant by the statement that he was always eager to talk at great length about the work that he was doing (Osgood 1940:51). One can also use questions such as the following in assessing the usefulness of a particular candidate: Does he speak your language well? Does he use words from other areas? Is there anything wrong with his pronunciation? Is he a good conversationalist, storyteller, orator, quoter of proverbs? Can he explain things well? Answers must never be taken at face value, for a particular question may have been interpreted in a way different from the intended one. For example, an affirmative answer to the question "Does he know your language well?" might only mean that the man was a good storyteller and would not indicate that having lived away from the community for several years, he used forms which no one else did.

Recommendations for an informant should always be carefully scrutinized. Inquiry might reveal that a recommendation issued from a desire to sponsor a nephew or cousin. If the sponsor had learned the qualities that the investigator was looking for, he could make a very convincing case for his candidate. Bad recommendations can also issue from a misunderstanding of the nature of the project. If the people somehow should imagine that the investigator was interested in flora (perhaps because he simply had asked for the names of ten or fifteen trees and plants in the neighborhood), they might suggest a person whose special craft made him well acquainted with this part of the environment.

The foregoing discussion may have given the impression that potential informants were in such abundance that the linguist had only to take his choice of the most suited individual for his work, but getting informants can be a most frustrating experience. Where the communities are small and few in number, one will first have to locate the people. This is not always an easy task. Finding Bushmen, for example, can require weeks of exhausting and patient search over the desolate plains of South Africa. The Indians of the Amazon will disappear with hardly any warning whatsoever to be gone for days in search of monkeys, pigs, or bees. Such is the case among the Brazilian Aripaktsá who frequently depart on three-day hunting or fishing expeditions, leaving in the village the few children under six and the lame adults. Very often one must take what informants he can get. In Brazil this may mean working with captured Indians. When Kenneth L. Pike was trying to analyze the tonal system of Mixtec (a language of Mexico), he went several months without a regular and dependable informant with whom he could do the tedious checking. The informant who did finally agree to work with him was available for only two hours before sunrise, after which the informant would go to his cornfield (E. V. Pike 1956:43).

Often the only people who are more or less willing to spend time at the apparently meaningless activity of saying things for the investigator are irresponsible and derelict members of the society. One may have trouble with such people because of their undependability, but one may also have trouble with the rest of the community. Such people, being marginal to the society, are often under suspicion because of the danger they pose to the established order by exposing the full workings of a society (Berreman 1962).

Overcoming all these difficulties will hardly ever be easy. One may leave the field without ever having had an informant of whom he could be proud. Tact, patience, ingenuity—and some luck—will all figure in one's complete or partial success.

It might be thought that remuneration in the form of money, goods, or services would be a compelling reason for a person to make himself available as informant. Sometimes pay is the only means of getting informants, and when work is regular and intensive, the informant will usually expect it; but often the winning of an informant is achieved by ingenious ways of gaining his confidence or interest. Because Lowie had had the foresight to learn to make a number of cat's cradle designs as part of his preparation for field work (in 1907), he was able to enlist the help of a Blackfoot interpreter. It happened in this way: "[I strolled] through the camp, developing different figures with a piece of string while apparently looking neither right nor left. The Blackfoot came out of their tipis, staring at me in rapt attention, and finally themselves summoned Rex [the only Blackfoot bilingual in the camp] to discover the meaning of my strange antics" (1959:17). The accomplishment is all the more remarkable since the Indians were at that time in a state of passive rebellion against the white authorities.

In some places the promise of pay is enough to entice almost anyone to work as informant, but in others hardly any amount of remuneration would strengthen an individual to go against the will of the community. If the researcher has established friendly relations with the community, a person might even be embarrassed in receiving pay publicly. He might want to consider the service an act of friendship.

The rate of pay depends most of all on the local conditions—and not on the resources of the investigator. Where a money economy is well established one will probably have to rate his informant as some kind of semi-skilled employee: a schoolteacher, clerk, professional letter-writer.

He certainly would not be paid less than a house-servant or grass-cutter. Wherever possible it would be advisable to begin with a lower rate than what one intended on finally giving. There are two reasons for this procedure. First, it is easier to dismiss a poorly paid employee than a highly paid one. Second, the increase in salary can serve as an encouragement for good service. Different pay scales can also be attached to different kinds of work. In fact, the field worker should not lead people to think that everything done for him is of equal importance. Survey work would be well-nigh impossible if interviewees demanded the same pay that a regular informant received.

More important than the actual salary is the kind of relationship it establishes. The informant might think of his part as an act of friendship or as a disagreeable task which is justified only by the financial return. For his part, the investigator may feel that the arrangement is strictly business and that the pay must be returned in equal value of work. It would therefore be wise for the investigator to give his views on this matter careful scrutiny. One of the undesirable aspects of our money economy in field work is that it allows us to think that the informant is obligated to us for the salary he receives. This puts us in the position of power from which we can make all kinds of demands. The rightness of our position may appear to us incontestable since the work-pay pattern is so easily taken for granted in our Western society. The informant would see little sense in our view if it were explained to him, and when he does not understand the reasons for the investigator's demanding attitudes and words, he will be hurt, embarrassed, or angered. A good example of the kind of understanding which the field worker must exhibit is found in the following words by Robert Lowie about his Crow Indian informant:

> Our relations were on a plane of *noblesse oblige*. Theoretically, I was paying him four dollars a day [in 1910] for interpreting and transportation, but to insist on the eight hours' daily stint would have proven fatal. If Jim had been on a spree the night before, there was no use expecting him at nine in the morning; he might turn up at noon or he might not turn up at all. I gained stature in his eyes by never reproving him for such irregularities and actually lost nothing at all. For when [Jim] Carpenter had once overcome his initial suspicions, he worked for me whether I was about or not [that is, in getting information for Lowie] (Casagrande 1960:430).

Financial remuneration may actually be impossible in some situations, not because the informants do not want the money or cannot use it, but because they prefer another way to seal the bargain. In some societies the giving of gifts is the only acceptable behavior, sometimes because a loosely structured relationship permits more freedom in making demands upon the donor: the chicken may not have been big enough, the last gift was given three weeks ago, the service that was rendered was especially difficult, because the informant should have been working in the garden, and so on. Again, the refusal to take pay may be motivated by the desire to put the investigator under the obligation to "act like one of us." Thus, when a sociologist was making a study of attitudes among the Japanese interned in American concentration camps, her informants—and even her teacher of Japanese—refused any pay. The resultant relationship is described in the following way:

> Informants had indicated that they were willing to accept me as a friend or friendly acquaintance but not as an employer. The value of the role hinged upon the fact that it put me under an unverbalized obligation. My informants and I knew that I was getting information on the strength of a personal relationship. I had no means of recompensing them except by returning their friendship and accepting the obligations it implied, the most important of which was observing the complicated taboos of the in-group (Wax 1960:169).

The principle here is one that field workers in sociology and anthropology have long recognized, that the relationship established in field work can be conceived of as involving a reciprocal exchange between the participating parties: the investigator wants data, but the interviewee has his own set of motives. He is not cooperating "for nothing." If for no other reason, there is some psychological satisfaction such as ego-building or curiosity (Gusfield 1955). By bringing the informant into the project, we satisfy his curiosity and repay him in some small measure. My own Gbeya informant was repaid in part by the prestige that he acquired by constant association with me which led eventually to his being able in spite of his blindness to marry a respectable widow with children.

The investigator should not overestimate the "rewards" that apparently accrue to the informant. His cooperation must be seen from the viewpoint of his peers. They may consider him a shirker of culturally-approved work (such as going to the corn gardens as every man must do to support his family), a betrayer of village secrets and traditions, a gossip, a toady of the stranger. The suspicion and criticism he must endure must be overbalanced by the rewards he finds in cooperating with the investigator.

Tricking informants into rendering free service is an extremely dangerous undertaking; an investigator who practices duplicity usually deceives nobody but himself. An investigator who is suspected of committing this evil may find himself tricked and obstructed by an irate community. A better motive for reciprocity in field work is the respect the investigator maintains for himself and his endeavors, a commodity whose value greatly exceeds the price which must be paid for it.

Number of Informants

In a critical appraisal of American field linguistics the statement was made that "the linguist must not restrict himself to only one informant" (Uhlenbeck 1960:433), because a grammar which ostensibly comprehends the whole language must necessarily be based on a fully representative corpus. But the question of how many informants one should use cannot be answered with a single categorical statement.

There is indeed a relation between the kind of linguistic investigation being undertaken and the number of informants who are used. The most obvious kinds of study which require many informants are dialectological and sociolinguistic ones. Where language features are to be correlated with age, class, occupation, or any other sociological factor, a scientific study demands careful sampling.[4] But where one is concerned with determining the structural outline of a language in its broadest form, there is usually no need for more than one good informant. (The word "good" is crucial in that statement. What this term implies is explained in the next section.) A representative speaker has had built into him all the linguistic rules needed for interacting efficiently with the other members of the speech community. We can say that he has within him a microcosm of the linguistic structure.

The more one expects diversity in the language at some point or another, the more he needs to have a plurality of informants. It would have been foolish for me, for example, to have based my description of Sango on one or even half a dozen speakers of this Central African language. Since it is a lingua franca used by about a million speakers, mostly as a second language (although many children learn it along with the language of their parents), it was necessary to determine to what extent there were variations correlated with geography, language background, amount of acculturation to European culture, age, sex, and religion. The final corpus of about 37,000 words represents the speech of 56 informants (see table).

There are dangers surely in working with just one informant; one is wisely cautioned against doing it. But the reason is not that an informant can so adulterate elicited data as to conceal the structure of the language. Native speakers of languages have, of course, reported instances of such sabotaging. One well-educated Mexican Indian reported that he knew of one informant who had been encouraged by his fellow villagers to distort the language for a period of seven years. After a change of heart, he confessed his action and advised the linguist to destroy everything he had written down. There is evidence that something like this did in fact happen, but we demonstrate extreme naiveté in believing with the informant that he alone could be responsible for a poor analysis of the language. What he had in mind was very likely certain words which had great

[4] The relevance of sampling to linguistic field work has generally been ignored in linguistic literature, but the naiveté of linguists is probably not as bad as Pickford (1956) would make it out to be. For a sophisticated use of data obtained in a sociological survey see the work of Labov on the social stratification of English in New York City (1964*a, b*).

SANGO INFORMANTS

Sex	Age	Degree of sophistication	Religion
		(1)–14	p–10, c–0, o– 4
	Adult—32	(2)– 5	p– 2, c–0, o– 3
		(3)–13	p– 0, c–2, o–11
Male—37			
		(1)– 3	p– 2, c–1, o– 0
	Youth—5	(2)– 1	p– 0, c–0, o– 1
		(3)– 1	p– 1, c–0, o– 0
		(1)– 7	p– 7, c–0, o– 0
	Adult—15	(2)– 5	p– 2, c–0, o– 3
		(3)– 3	p– 0, c–0, o– 3
Female—19			
		(1)– 2	p– 0, c–0, o– 2
	Youth—4	(2)– 0	p– 0, c–0, o– 0
		(3)– 2	p– 2, c–0, o– 0

Degree of sophistication: (1) refers to the lowest degree, (2) to people who have had a minimum of education and/or travel and broadening employment, and (3) to those with a fairly high degree of education and/or travel and employment. *Religion:* p = Protestant, c = Catholic, o = Other or unknown religion.

cultural value to him and his fellow villagers. If a person did try to deliberately corrupt the data, we should, in any case, find it out soon enough because of the inconsistencies.

Even in the best of circumstances one will find the use of several informants profitable. It will turn out, for example, that one person is a very good storyteller, another very keen on the use of words, another adept in paraphrasing, and so on. A plurality of informants is especially important in the collection of texts, for one needs to avoid making the error of attributing to the whole language characteristics of one informant's style. Even a dullard can be of real assistance, as Sarah Gudschinsky has pointed out. One of her Mazateco informants was ideal for tonal study, because she never tired of repeating words in frames as the complex tone changes were being carried out. The imaginative and gifted person very soon grows weary of such routine, monotonous work.

One does not necessarily want several of one's informants at the work session together. The relations between the informants may be such that some will be reluctant to speak in the presence of the others. When William Labov was conducting his study of English on the island of Martha's Vineyard, Massachusetts, he had no difficulty in interviewing individuals. However, when he tried to observe what happened in natural speech among acquaintances, he was less successful; the people did not want to talk casually in a group. Sometimes informants disagree so much among themselves and over inconsequential matters, that the field worker finds it difficult to make progress. On the other hand, the presence of another person at the work session might serve to check the desire of the informant to please the investigator by not correcting wrong or unnatural constructions.

If the investigator is adept, he can also use groups of people in less structured work sessions. By acting as their host but letting them carry on their own conversations and activities, he can stimulate linguistic discussions among them. In a description of a "typical" day among the Parina of the Philippines the anthropologist Harold C. Conklin describes this technique in the following way (the time is 7:30 in the morning):

> Pinungu, the old man of Arasa'as and the best archer on Mt. Yagaw, arrives with a gift of 5 fresh eggs and a handful of medicinal jungle plants which he thought we might have missed (we had). Ayakan and two other Parina elders come into my house to join Pinungu in a chew of betel and a round of gossip. It seems "Nungu" has just come from a nearby settlement where he officiated, as eldest relative, in the trial of his grand-nephew for polygynous marriage sans *pangagduway* (compensatory payment to first wife). Sitting in a circle on the floor, the others [at least 11 people] listen intently as the old boy relates the whole affair blow by blow. I appear to be attending to some other business at my bamboo desk, but actually I am recording on 4" x 6" slips as much of the sociological information uncovered in their conversation as possible (1960*b*:119–120).

Qualifications of Informants

AGE.   Since the investigator needs to select informants who are truly representative of the speech community, he must find people who are thoroughly experienced in it. A young age generally disqualifies a person from this point of view; a six-year-old obviously has not had as much experience in his language as his senior by 30 years. There are exceptions to this generalization; a very good one is Conklin's remarkable seven-year-old Hanunóo informant.

> . . . Maling had demonstrated an astonishing maturity of interests and experience, richly illustrating the way in which a Hanunóo child, without formal instruction, acquires an increasingly detailed acquaintance—direct or vicarious—with all sectors of the local adult world. Geographically, this is a small universe, limited often to an area within ten kilometers of one's birthplace. . . . But this small orbit comprehends a comparatively vast realm of knowledge in all provinces of which any member of the society is expected to be at home. In this setting, Maling's parents never thought it particularly precocious that on some occasions she should be as interested in contraceptives as in learning to spin cotton or take care of her younger sister. Nevertheless, I was constantly impressed with her independent thinking and utter frankness which seemed

to recognize no boundaries, except of degree, between child and adult knowledge (Conklin 1960a:107–108).

In a strongly bilingual community, where one language is more prestigious than the language being studied, there will also be the danger of incomplete knowledge on the part of the children. Such is the case among the Coatlán Zapotec where only about 10 percent of the children have any control of Zapotec (Robinson 1963). In this community the men, though knowing Zapotec, carry on their marketing and political and religious activities in Spanish. As for the women, only about one-third of those of child-bearing age can speak the language. Obviously one would have to find his informants here among the adult men. A similar situation obtains among the Chontal (Waterhouse 1949).

Children make poor informants also because they very often do not seem to understand what is wanted in elicitation. Their intellectual powers not having fully matured, they have more difficulty in making sense of particular lines of inquiry. They also have a shorter interest span. One other difficulty in working with children is the possibility of insulting their seniors who might consider their own relation to the investigator a prestigious one. (If a child is a better informant than some elder, one can get around this problem by using the child to elicit—or pretending to elicit—from the elder, writing down instead what the child repeats.) There are, on the other hand, some advantages in working with children: they very often are patient about repeating things and in giving utterances slowly; in some societies too, children of a certain age do not have many responsibilities, so they are available for questioning when the adults are otherwise occupied.

Old people present different problems and opportunities. In their favor, obviously, is their experience in the culture. Again, their age often makes them more available as informants than younger people, and they appreciate the attention which comes to them in an investigation. On the other hand, advanced age can be responsible for things which make informant work quite difficult: deafness, poor health, tendency to fall asleep, inability to concentrate on one problem for a long period of time, lenis articulation, and so on. It is probably also true that elderly informants would not be good for elicitation which did not have immediate cultural relevance.

SEX.   There is no reason why female informants would not be as good as male informants,[5] but it is probably wise for an investigator to

---

[5] The claim has sometimes been made (Pop 1950, I:725) that women preserve a more archaic usage than men, but this has been disproved. In Atwood's study of Texas speech the women represent a slightly older group, but their use of archaic forms is almost equal to that of men (1962:118).

work primarily with informants of his (or her) own sex. In some instances the investigator might be disturbed by the physically determined speech differences. Women, for example, have greater difficulty in adjusting to the pitch levels of men's speech than of women's speech, an important fact when working on tone languages. In those languages which require women to speak to men and women differently, a man might find it disconcerting, at least in the initial stages of his investigation, to have to make the proper adjustments throughout the work session. There might also be rules of etiquette which would make it difficult to work with a person of the opposite sex. For example, among the Gbeya of the Central African Republic it is improper for a woman to look directly into the face of a man who is not closely related to her. A women investigator working with a Gbeya man would stand the risk of being considered "loose." A man working with a Gbeya woman would have two difficulties: he would be annoyed by not being able to watch her face closely for greater accuracy in transcription; she for her part would be embarrassed by the stare.

One must also reckon with difficulties accompanying the investigation of a cultural domain which is proper for only one of the sexes. In most preliterate societies there are large portions of the culture which only the men are supposed to know anything about. That the women are not entirely ignorant of the lore might very well be conceded by the men, yet their *right* to the knowledge would never be. Of course, what constitutes the men's and the women's worlds can hardly be predicted without preliminary investigation.

CULTURAL AND PSYCHOLOGICAL QUALITIES.   There are several different attributes of good informants which are not easily discussed under separate headings; they overlap at one point or another. The first group concern the informant's relation to his own culture.

A good informant is one who can talk freely and naturally on a wide range of subjects relevant to his own culture. This does not mean that he must be a specialist in every art and skill—in a highly specialized society this in any case would be impossible—but that he should be as informed as one can possibly be in his own society. Ignorance of the basic activities and values of the society will be evidence either of an inferior intelligence or of incomplete enculturation. It is evident that when a person has been away for many of the formative years of his childhood, he will have less knowledge of his culture than his peers who stayed at home. Imperfect knowledge will affect the relations between the investigator and the informant by the fact that embarrassment at his own ignorance will progressively undermine the informant's self-confidence; but any discomfiture on the part of the language assistant is something which the investigator must consciously avoid. Secondly, an imperfect cultural knowledge will lead to an uninteresting content in the corpus. Although information about the people's lives is not the primary goal of a linguistic investigation, no field worker can be excused for ignoring a wealth of ethnographic data which no one might ever again have the opportunity of getting. Besides, grammatical exemplification can just as well be based on interesting texts as it is on uninteresting and uninformative sentences as, "He bought two yellow bananas."

One must be careful not to reject people too quickly as candidates for the job of informant. A "bad reputation" might be the clue to a truly independent spirit and creative mind, qualities which eminently qualify a person for being an informant. Such a person Casagrande's Ojibwa informant seemed to have been:

> Everyone at Court Oreilles seemed to know John Mink. His name was one of the first mentioned to us when we arrived on the reservation in June of 1941. And the more we heard about him the more redoubtable he appeared and the more curious we became. Some called him medicine-man, priest, friend; others called him sorcerer, pagan, scoundrel. But all, Indian and white alike, agreed that his knowledge of the old ways was unsurpassed by any of the 1700 Ojibwa on the reservation (Casagrande 1960:468).

A few more words need to be said about the independence of an informant. Unless he is free from the pressures of his kin or other members of the community, he will work reluctantly and sporadically. This is a corollary of the statement that the informant most useful to an investigator is one who, like Lowie's Crow interpreter, identifies himself with the investigator and the project.

There is again a whole array of qualities which we recognize as distinguishing the superior person. Only a few are mentioned here. *Intelligence* is the hardest to define. It is enough to say that an intelligent informant, by whatever standard we measure this quality, is going to be more helpful than one who is not. Bernard Bloch gives an amusing description of a nearly illiterate butcher in a Massachusetts industrial town whose mental sluggishness impeded the dialect study he was engaged in: "[the informant] persisted through a dozen hours of interviewing in the belief that it was only my pitiful ignorance that led me to ask him such questions as, for instance, 'What do you call the thing you fry eggs in?' Instead of giving me the word he used (*frying pan, skillet, spider*), he would stare at me in astonishment, then say, as if he could hardly believe his ears: 'Don't you *really* know the name of that?'" (1935:4fn). In this same place Bloch explicates the need for "sympathetic intelligence" on the part of the informant: "A man with quickness enough to understand our purpose, with alertness enough to co-operate in our work, and with a memory good enough to call up old words and idioms from his childhood, is naturally preferable to one who hardly knows the words he uses himself and has to be coaxed or dragged along over every step of the way without a notion of the object" (3–4).

Locating an intelligent informant may not be an easy undertaking. It is unlikely that all societies will understand intelligence as we do. Any attempt to talk about an "intelligent person" in the Gbeya language would be a failure; I know no way of circumventing the difficulties linguistically. There are practical means, however, of evaluating the intelligence of informant candidates. If they are literate, one can ask them to submit lists of names of plants, animals, kinship terms, and others, a procedure which was used by Conklin in his work in the Philippines.

The importance of a good *memory* is seen in the work session when the investigator asks the informant to repeat something he has already given, perhaps the day before or just a few minutes ago. If an informant cannot recall exactly what he said, there will be moments of malaise between him and the investigator as the latter, puzzled, says, "No, that wasn't what you gave before," or "Didn't you say it another way before?" Unable to recall having said anything different, the informant may interpret the linguist's statement as a criticism of his lack of competence.

Alertness is related to memory. What is needed is a person who pays attention and is not easily distracted either by his environment or his own fleeting thoughts. Nothing can be more exasperating in a work session than repeatedly having to bring the informant back to the task at hand. The alert informant will also be aware of mistakes or contradictions he has made in response to the questions of the investigator.

No less important are some social qualities: *patience, honesty, dependability, cheerfulness.* Patience is a virtue which the informant demonstrates in his relations to the investigator when the latter fails to pronounce words correctly, forgets words which have already been obtained, and so on. Impatience on the part of the informant can lead an embarrassed investigator to respond in several ways detrimental to the project: by pretending to know something he had really forgotten, thus giving evidence to the informant of his own dishonesty; by going on with the point under investigation in a careless and superficial way; or by becoming angry. Honesty on the part of the informant prevents him from accepting anything from the linguist which is not completely natural in his own language. Dependability characterizes the informant who fulfills all the obligations agreed upon with the field worker, for example, to work for so many hours a day on such-and-such days, and so on. My own Gbeya informant Gounnté was truly remarkable in this respect. When I was first working on the language, I met with him five days a week after lunch for about one hour or so. In spite of the fact that he was totally blind and had to make his way from his village a couple of miles away, he failed to show up without advance notice on only a few occasions, all of which were fully justified. He never arrived at my house late, and if he arrived early (which he often did because no one in the village had a clock), he would patiently wait until my siesta was over. His dependability was not only a credit to him, but it was also a challenge to me, for there were many times when I had other work to do or when I simply did not feel like doing language work.

Quite different was the experience of the person trying to analyze the language of the Amuesha Indians of Peru:

> After hiring someone as an informant with good pay, we have found that he comes one day and misses a week. He may have good intentions when he promises to come each day, but outside circumstances change his mind. He must get his food supply almost daily. If he sees the river rising, he knows that the catfish will bite. When it drops and the water becomes clear, he takes advantage of spearing fish. If it looks like a fine day, he goes hunting. . . . If there are several sunny days in succession, he remembers that his new clearing needs to be burned if he is to plant for the next season. If it rains, he stays at home. Some day he runs out of kerosene or matches and comes to buy some from us. Then we take the opportunity and get some language data from him while he sits down to visit a while. . . . Again we repeat our offer and give him a special gift, hoping this may induce him to come more often" (Fast 1952:80).

LANGUAGE.   Of all the qualifications for an informant none are so important as the linguistic ones. Anyone who serves in this capacity must be chosen for his ability to provide a corpus which is abundant, accurate, and thoroughly representative.

The requirement is that the informant be a native speaker of the language and dialect being studied. In some circumstances one may need to add that he be monolingual or "monodialectal," for where there is contact between speakers of several languages or dialects, one runs the danger of selecting a person whose speech shows the result of much interference. (This topic is more fully discussed in Chapter 4.)

The speech of the informant should also be characterized by good diction. Some speech defects will be identified by the field worker, but unless he has some familiarity with the phonological norm of the language, he may be unable to spot others. For example, he may mistakenly accept a particular kind of postdental voiceless fricative as the normal realization of an /s/ phoneme instead of identifying it as the aberrant phone that it is. There is one published grammar based on data obtained from an informant with a speech defect. If there are not more, this is not to say that other field workers have not had to redo much of their work after belatedly making the discovery of their informants' idiosyncracies.

There must also be precise articulation and voice resonance that is both sharp and pleasing.[6] Mumbling, slobbering, and strident talk can make informant work disagreeable and difficult. In a contact situation some of these defects can be overcome by careful attention to the inform- ant's face as he speaks. For tape recording, however, it is extremely im- portant that the informant have the closest approximation to a "radio voice." This should be ascertained by test recording before he is fully committed.

Contrary to what one might imagine, certain practices of personal orna- mentation do not seem to affect speech seriously. Thus, in New Guinea men wear elaborate discs and rods in their noses, usually on special occa- sions; in some African tribes—like the Yakoma and Kaba of the Central African Republic—there is the filing of teeth or the removal of two upper incisors; among the Gbeya, large plugs are worn by women in each nos- tril; some people also insert circular objects, reeds, or sticks at the center of the upper or lower lip—or both. However, such deformations as the enlarging of the upper and lower lips (as among the "Ubangis"—really Sara-Madjingay of the Chad) affect speech to a greater extent.

An informant should also be talkative (see Chapter 5). Work sessions can be extremely tedious when a taciturn informant gives only what is asked of him. If he cooperates only to the extent that a food-vending ma- chine cooperates—milk or coffee or cocoa, depending on what button is pushed—the analysis will be doomed to a snail's pace. But when the lin- guist's questions stimulate a whole array of associated responses, his corpus will be richer and more varied. My first Gbeya informant was brighter and more sophisticated than Gounnté, but he braked my study by being both dour and linguistically unresponsive. Although I could oftentimes improve his humor by small talk at the beginning of our ses- sions, I cannot recall having taught him to make unsolicited contributions to my study. The opposite kind of informant poses different problems. When my Tamachek informant at Timbuctoo responded very congenially to my requests for names of objects and short sentences with a torrent of words, I was unable to capture the part that I had asked for. A good informant must therefore be able to control his talk, providing first of all what is requested and, if necessary, at a speed that will permit easy tran- scription.

Some informants have been so naive about language use that any speed slower than the one they were used to seemed unnatural and ridiculous. Such people are almost impossible to use when the linguist is still un-

---

[6] McIntosh (1952:90) is right, however, in insisting that certain speech defects, like tooth- lessness and adenoidal trouble, not be overemphasized. Some people with these handicaps may be better informants than those without them. Besides, if the characteristic is a common one in a speech community, the investigator would err in expecting a different standard of articula- tion than that which exists.

familiar with the language. One investigator amusingly describes his first elicitation of verbal forms from a Waunana informant in the following words:

> I was so eager to get ahead in the work that I skipped my siesta and began furiously writing out verb forms in the paradigms: I run, you run, she runs, it runs, we run, you run, they run. Then followed all the other tense forms, as far as the English grammar permitted. The idea was that in the afternoon we would only have to fill in the equivalent Waunana forms beside the English pattern already worked out.
>
> Finally the informant arrived and we started our work. "How do you say 'I run' in your language?" The Indian was quiet for a while. First he looked down; then he looked out. Suddenly his face lit up as if struck by a sudden flash of inspiration. He spoke very rapidly. If I had been able to transcribe what he said, it would have spread across the page several times. I gulped and bravely started to write; but after a few syllables, I was already hopelessly bogged down.
>
> "How did you say that?" With his repetition I added two more syllables, then bogged down again. When I asked for the third repetition, the informant began to waver and finally to change his story, and so I had to give up entirely. To my half self-justifying and half self-accusing, "But that surely doesn't all mean just 'I run,'" he said, "Why of course not. It means I was sitting here with you; then I looked out of the door and saw a deer, so I quickly grabbed my spear and now I am running after it." Then, almost philosophically, he added to himself, "Only a fool would run for nothing" (Loewen 1964:189).

When an informant can add to all his other virtues the ability to be analytical, he will be able to serve as the field worker's colleague. A poor informant is not able to see the components of long words in an inflected language such as Nyanja (spoken in Malawi and Zambia). He can pick out from a stream of speech the nouns and perhaps the verb phrases, hardly more. He finds it difficult to relate parts of words to linguistic environment or meaning. A good informant is one who can make fine discriminations quickly and realistically. This ability is of considerable importance to the linguist for whom meaningful differences are the keys to analysis. A Gbeya who tells me that *gó* and *sókó* are the "same" is telling the truth to the extent that they both are connectives in identical sentences, but he would have rendered a much greater service if he could have pointed out that the second one implies that the action of the first clause was completed before the second was performed. (Informant help almost never comes in statements as sophisticated as that one, however!)

Akin to the informant's ability in distinguishing fine shades of meaning and use in his own language is his intolerance of unrealistic and muddled sentences. To a good informant the language is a model which must be accurately copied by the field worker. He remains frank and critical in his appraisal of the linguist's every attempt to approximate the model.

These analytical qualities are not generally found among "naive" speakers of a language. Linguistic sophistication implies the ability to reflect on how one uses language. It takes language out of the realm of the unconscious and automatic and puts it in the realm of the conscious and deliberate. Neither control of a set of verbal arts (for example, poetry, storytelling, proverbs, orations, and eulogies) nor bilingualism are in themselves sufficient to release one from naiveté, although a person so gifted is in some respects more qualified as an informant than one who is unskilled. The use of these arts, however, can be applied to linguistic analysis only with the guidance and training of the field worker.

Empirical studies have not yet been made of the analytical skills of language informants. It is therefore impossible to suggest how the best candidates might be found in a society. One opinion is that a more exactly verbalized and deeper knowledge of the structure of one's language is one of the fruits of being fluently literate in one's own or another language. This correlation might hold only when the literates have had formal education of the Western type. My own experience with informants literate in the Sango language leads me to this view. In the Central African Republic people learned to read Sango either from some religious literature or from a set of primers but always in informal classes, usually led by an African. The acquisition of the skill of reading is rarely accompanied by any process of intellectualization which would better qualify a person for objective discussion of his language. This is not to say, of course, that literacy is a skill to be ignored (see below).

Hitherto the terms "naive" and "unsophisticated" have been used in talking of an informant's lack of skill in dealing objectively with his language. It should be understood that these terms, and their opposite, "sophisticated," are useful only at the extreme ends of a continuum of characteristics. One informant might be more sophisticated in some respects than another informant, and the same informant may be less sophisticated at one point in time than he will be a year later. In fact, by virtue of being involved in an investigation of his language the informant becomes progressively sophisticated. This kind of sophistication is what the linguist seeks to develop; more is said on this topic in the next section.

"Sophistication" can also be used in connection with a person's acquaintance with the world beyond the boundaries of his own speech community and culture. Thus, it can be said that because a person lived for a year or two in his nation's capital, he is more sophisticated than when he was still in the village 200 miles up-country. It should be obvious, however, that cross-cultural awareness and linguistic objectivity are two very different kinds of sophistication, neither one of which implies the other.

A culturally sophisticated informant is not necessarily a better informant, not for purely linguistic research at any rate. In fact, an awareness of values different from his own might lead to some skewing of the lexical

information he provides. For example, when a Philippine Tausug informant was asked for the word for "house" in a field methods session at an
American university, he furnished a word which did not refer to the mud
houses of his own community but to the more prestigious city houses. At
that moment he had rejected his own crude mud house as something inappropriate in a highly sophisticated university context.

An informant's attitude toward his language is determined by personal
and cultural factors. The cultural factors are implicit in the role that language plays in the speaker's culture. McIntosh states (1952:91) that the
Scots "will not react in a linguistically unsophisticated way, no matter
how they are questioned," for they are used to thinking about the relationship between Scots and English and between their own and other
forms of Scots. In some societies language is little more than a useful but
unconscious tool for communication. In other preliterate societies language has a very important role. In these correct or elegant speech may
be highly prized. Those learning it, whether children or outsiders, will be
expected to strive for the culturally-determined norm. Two such societies
are the Dogon of Mali (in West Africa) and the Tewa of First Mesa, Hopi,
Arizona (Dozier 1951). The Dogon cosmology is an extremely complex
one approaching the sophistication of a well-articulated philosophy. In
the creation myths language is described as partaking of the original sub-
stance from which the universe was made; the use of language is viewed as
a continuation of the creative process. With such respect for language the
Dogon naturally place great emphasis on proper speech and take great
pains to teach their children about words and their use.

This section on the qualifications of an informant cannot close without
the reminder that there are great differences between verbal skills among
all human beings. In our own society we know people whose intellectual
brilliance is not matched by oral articulateness. One would expect of the
more intelligent person a better control of his native language, but the
facts clearly contradict this assumption. Speaking is an oral skill different
in many respects from writing. It is a myth which is tenaciously held that
there is one model language to which all forms of speech must conform.
Where language style is a ticket to upward social mobility, the existence
of this myth is not difficult to explain, but it is nonetheless false. In short,
since the investigator wants samples of the best possible use to which a
language can be put, he will do his best to seek native speakers who can
produce this speech. This simply means that he wants texts which demonstrate the highest level of verbal planning.

Equally false is the myth which states that because preliterates live in
face-to-face, communal societies where pluralism and diversity are at a
minimum, there will be little diversity in the skill of speakers of the native
language. It might be summarized in the statement, "One informant is as

good as another." No person did more to debunk this myth than Leonard Bloomfield. By carefully describing his Menomini informants he not only sets a standard of linguistic and cultural perceptiveness which field workers should strive to achieve but also outlines the variety of verbal skills which they must expect:

> Red-Cloud-Woman, a woman in the sixties, speaks a beautiful and highly idiomatic Menomini. She knows only a few words of English, but speaks Ojibwa and Potawatomi fluently, and, I believe, a little Winnebago. Linguistically, she would correspond to a highly educated American woman who spoke, say, French and Italian in addition to the very best type of cultivated, idiomatic English.
>
> Her husband, Storms-At-It, a shaman, is half Potawatomi, and speaks both languages. Of English he knows not even the cuss-words. In Menomini he often uses unapproved—let us say, ungrammatical—forms which are current among bad speakers; on the other hand, slight provocation sets him off into elevated speech, in which he uses what I shall describe as spelling-pronunciations, together with long ritualistic compound words and occasional archaisms. He corresponds, perhaps, to a minister who does not put on much "dog," speaks very colloquially in ordinary life, but is at the same time very intelligent and able to preach or exhort in the most approved semi-biblical language.
>
> Stands-Close, a man in the fifties, speaks only Menomini. His speech, though less supple and perfect than Red-Cloud-Woman's, is well up to standard. It is interlarded with words and constructions that are felt to be archaic, and are doubtless in part really so, for his father was known as an oracle of old traditions.
>
> Bird-Hawk, a very old man, who has since died, spoke only Menomini, possibly also a little Ojibwa. As soon as he departed from ordinary conversation, he spoke with bad syntax and meagre, often inept vocabulary, yet with occasional archaisms.
>
> White-Thunder, a man round [*sic*] forty, speaks less English than Menomini, and that is a strong indictment, for his Menomini is atrocious. His vocabulary is small; his inflections are often barbarous; he constructs sentences on a few threadbare models. He may be said to speak no language tolerably. His case is not uncommon among younger men, even when they speak but little English. Perhaps it is due, in some indirect way, to the impact of the conquering language.
>
> Little-Doctor, a half-breed, who died recently in his sixties, spoke English with some Menomini faults, but with a huge vocabulary and a passion for piling up synonyms. In Menomini, too, his vocabulary was vast; often he would explain rare words to his fellow-speakers. In both languages his love of words sometimes upset his syntax, and in both languages he was given to overemphatic diction, of the type of spelling pronunciation.
>
> Little-Jerome, a half-breed, now in the fifties, is a true bilingual. He speaks both English (the dialectal type of the region) and Menomini with racy idiom, which he does not lose even when translating in either direction. He contrasts strikingly with the men (usually somewhat younger) who speak little English and yet bad Menomini (Bloomfield 1927:437).

It would be valuable to know if in preliterate societies there were any sociological correlates of language proficiency such as one finds in our own society. It has been demonstrated, for example, that at the economically lower strata of American and English societies language structure is not as "rich" as it is in the higher strata, even at an early age. This is so not only in the use of more unusual adjectives and adverbs but also in the use of sentences with dependent clauses (Lawton 1963, 1964).[7]

The Training of the Informant

For everyone but the person who has already served as a linguistic informant, the first weeks or months will be a time of training. Even the best of candidates will have failings which must be corrected. The extent to which an informant is trained depends on the informant himself and on the skill of the investigator in teaching him.

The general goal of training is to make of the informant an enlightened, interested, and cooperative coworker. The training involves getting him to understand the routine and mechanics of the work sessions: the time and place, the way he should respond when asked a question, how often he should say an utterance before and after it is written down, when additional information is to be given and what kinds are most desired, not accepting ungrammatical or meaningless utterances from the investigator, and looking toward the investigator (if not directly in his face) when giving an utterance. Comprehension of these details does not follow the first explanation of the nature of the linguistic project and the informant's part in it. Even college students who have acted as linguistic informants have required several explanations from different points of view before they began to understand.

The ultimate goal is to get the informant to think about language as the investigator does, that is, in terms of broad generalizations based on what is actually said or could be said. Success in this type of training can be achieved only by deliberately and carefully explaining the purpose and techniques of linguistic analysis, not in a few informal "lectures" but over a prolonged period of time in connection with specific problems that the investigator is working on.

The investigator should not assume that the informant will appreciate being told about the problems and nature of linguistic analysis. Either because he has little capacity for abstract reasoning or because he does not see the relevance of analysis to the speech that everybody, even children, has obviously grasped, the informant will waste the investigator's

[7] However, R. Robinson (1965) concludes after experimentation that the contrast between restricted and elaborated codes may exist only in formal writing and that there may be other reasons, motivational and attitudinal, for explaining why working-class children use the restricted code informally.

time with his disinterest; he may even resist the investigator's excursions into seemingly irrelevant discussions.

If the informant should become only partially sophisticated, he may take more liberty in talking about his language than he is qualified to. It is for this reason that people who have been used as "language teachers" have often made such bad informants; they take their experience as a certificate of competence in all linguistic matters. Whether or not the observations by a partially trained informant are accurate, he may monopolize too much of the work sessions with discourses about matters of interest to himself. The investigator's task in training the informant therefore involves restraining both his imagination and his discussion.

The full responsibility for analysis lies on the shoulders of the investigator, not those of the informant. Yet there have been grammars produced by well-trained investigators which contained inaccurate descriptions based on the opinions of the informants. One recent grammar of an African language errs in this respect. For example, the word *mòkònzī* ("chief") is described as being "most often considered as a compound," that is, *mò* ("mouth") + *kò* ("death") + *nzī* (a segment whose meaning is not identified here although in other places it is "memory"). How "mouth + death + X" results in "chief" is not explained (Thomas 1963:46). Only linguistically naive people who had learned the trick but not the science of morphemic segmentation could have produced such an unrealistic compound. They could not possibly know that *mòkònzī* is a borrowing from Sango which in turn borrowed it from a Bantu language.

It should be obvious from the foregoing discussion that there can be great variation in the degree to which an informant can be trained. Although no informant can remain "naive" after three or more months of working with a linguist, it is wrong to say that all informants become "sophisticated." Much depends on the intelligence of the informant, the nature of the linguistic project, the length of exposure to the habits of the field worker, the amount of training the field worker attempts to give.[8]

Up to this point we have been talking about the linguistic training of the informant. There also are skills that he can be taught with great profit to the linguistic project. The most important of these is writing. A literate informant becomes extremely valuable, because he is set free as an independent collector. He may be asked to collect names of objects (plants, insects, animals), further examples of the use of certain words or mor-

---

[8] It is surprising, therefore, that it should be held that American undergraduate students in beginning rhetoric were less sophisticated than field informants who "become something more than naive native speakers of the language being described" (Maclay and Sleator 1960:276). Although some field informants may be more sophisticated linguistically than some university students, the converse must also be true. For other reasons too the statement just quoted is not useful as a generalization about the two groups of people. Gudschinsky (1958) clearly docu-

phemes, and connected texts. This ancillary collecting adds to the efficiency of the work sessions, since corpus collecting is always extremely time consuming.

The immediate problem is training the informant to write legibly and according to the conventions established by the investigator. Unless the field linguist wants to prepare his own writing lessons, he should try to obtain writing manuals in his own language or in the standard language of the country being visited. Even where the Roman alphabet is used, there may be local styles of writing which the informant, as a member of that society, should be taught to master.

With a truly illiterate person, one who neither reads nor writes in any language, the field worker must recognize that he is obliged to teach the concept of the visual representation of speech. This is not a highly complex task, but it demands some sophistication nonetheless, that is, an awareness of what letters are most easily confused with each other, what letters have the greatest usefulness because of either frequency or occurrence in productive morphemes, and so on. In short, one needs some familiarization with the art of primer writing (Gudschinsky 1957). Because the introduction of letters in a primer will follow a sequence determined by criteria different from those which determine the sequence in learning to write, the would-be teacher must carefully distinguish between the two operations and the difficulties involved.

The investigator must expect inconsistencies and inaccuracies even though the informant is recording his own language. Consider the case of an Osage Indian who was serving as informant for a field methods course:

> A reading of Bighorse's word lists reveals nothing, unless the reader happens to know both English and Osage. The Bighorse orthography is no more than an interesting failure because it is not systematic—at least not recognizably systematic. Not only was the recording of every form a problem in itself, but, as the many variant spellings in the corpus show, every recurrence of a form presented an entirely new problem which had to be solved without reference to the fact that the form had already been recorded at least once. This is all the more surprising in view of the fact that the informant apparently had a "good ear" . . . and was striving for phonetic accuracy (Wolff 1958:35; see also Hockett 1948:121).

As for other skills—such as typing, manipulating a tape recorder or duplicating machine—nothing needs to be said except that the time involved in teaching must always be weighed against its return. Nothing must be taken for granted. Even a recording session has many aspects

ments the way in which a native speaker's training affects awareness of linguistic contrasts in his own language. Her conclusion is that the responses of a linguistically naive speaker are different from those of a linguistically sophisticated one.

which demand a certain amount of skill or knowledge on the part of the informant. The more that the linguist makes explicit and prepares his informant for, the better will be the returns in quality of work accomplished.

By now the reader will have seen the justification for spending all these pages discussing the language informant; he is an important member of a linguistic field project. Unfortunately, circumstances may require a field linguist to work with far less than the optimum. The first informant of K. L. Pike's long and productive linguistic career was a Mixtec Indian who was old, blind, toothless, and bedridden with illness!

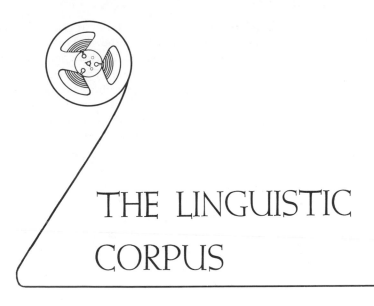

THE LINGUISTIC
CORPUS

4

For linguistics, as for any other science, there must be a body of data from which patterns, systems, or generalizations can be discovered by induction. In this chapter we are to examine the nature of this corpus and consider the ways in which it can best be obtained. Since, however, it is impossible to discuss the corpus without raising questions about its analysis, there is some overlapping between this chapter and Chapter 6 which deals with elicitation, a particular way of obtaining a corpus, and with Chapter 9 which deals with analysis.

Factors Which Determine the Kind of Data Obtained

What kind of corpus a field worker obtains is determined by the purpose and the techniques of the data collection. Poorly conceived notions of the data's influence on collection can result in incomplete or unsuitable linguistic material. Hence the first step for any field project is a specification of its goals and a justification of the techniques to be used.

1. Among the several uses to which linguistic data can be put, the one

with which we are primarily concerned is language description. Either because the object of study has been poorly analyzed or because it is completely unknown, the field linguist seeks to obtain whatever is necessary for discovering the language's basic structure. This means that the outcome of the project will be a grammar describing its phonological and morphological-syntactic structure with enough texts to permit a verification of the analysis. Like the traditional ethnographic monograph, it paints in bold outline the characteristic features of the linguistic patterns and their constituents. For this purpose great demands are put on the field linguist for a "good" and abundant corpus, the nature of which will be discussed in subsequent sections. Here we might simply note that American field linguistics has a poor reputation in some circles, because some of its friends and foes have inaccurately represented it. Some time ago, for example, Margaret Mead summarized the description of languages in the following words: "[the assumption of the American method of teaching linguistics is] that the task of analysis is to achieve a final understanding of the form of the language from a mass of phonetically accurate and absolutely unintelligible material, plus a literal translation furnished by an interpreter" (1939:201). This characterization of the linguist's corpus reduces the discovery of grammatical structure to a mechanical process. It also obscures the fact that at many points in his project the field linguist knows what he needs and how to go about getting it. He is no more satisfied with "a mass of . . . unintelligible material" than an ethnographer is with a miscellaneous collection of statements and observations about human behavior and artifacts. When a linguist is working at his best, he, like his ethnographic colleague, has specific problems which can only be solved on the basis of particular kinds of data.

2. The compilation of a dictionary is a goal very much different from that of a language description, especially when the dictionary has a strong ethnographic bias. What constitutes a good dictionary is not the question here—that will be taken up later; we are interested in how one's field work is affected if one wants the dictionary more than the grammar. An investigator might be able to arrive at a fairly accurate phonemicization and "part-of-speech" identification quite quickly, and then go on to collecting, analyzing, and annotating the vocabulary. The collection of a mountain of texts, whether he can translate them or not, is an insufficient corpus for such a project, for it has been adequately demonstrated that long texts do not necessarily show up new words (Lawton 1963:139). For dictionary projects one needs a fairly good prior acquaintance with the culture so as to elicit the vocabulary which reflects it. One especially needs word lists and other such elicitation instruments.

The following is a useful guide to a few kinds of lexical material that one can obtain (1951 appendix to Conklin 1950). One should also consult research guides such as *Outline of Cultural Materials* (Murdock *et al.*) and *Notes and Queries on Anthropology* (Royal Anthropological Institute).

Parts of human and animal anatomy
Clothing and personal adornment
Artifacts, tools, utensils, weapons, machines, conveyances, furniture
Occupational and professional terminology
Geographical and astronomical items: directions, winds, types of weather,
    phases of the moon, seasons of the year, constellations
Flora and fauna
Foods and methods of food preparation
Measurements of time, space, volume, weight, quantity
Diseases, medicines
Games, amusements
Religious objects, beings
Etiquette and tabooed words, insults, curses
Colors, textures, shapes
Systems of enumeration: counting money, telling time, and so on
Classifiers: "bunch," "flock," "handful," "piece of," and so on

3. Archiving is another kind of project which requires its own kind of corpus.[1] Since the ostensible purpose of any archive is to store up linguistic information for future analysis and comparison, there must be more stress put on the comparability of the corpora than on their usefulness for monographlike descriptions. An archive is therefore set up with a plan which is strictly adhered to. This is the ideal which no archive has yet achieved because the financial, administrative, and practical problems involved in an archiving project are monumental. Of a more modest nature are projects such as the Franz Boas Collection of Materials for American Linguistics, Library of the American Philosophical Society, Philadelphia, and the Indiana University Archive of Languages of the World, Bloomington. There are undoubtedly other national archives throughout the world such as that maintained by the Brazilian National Museum. Apparently more common are the archives of dialectal data such as the American Library of Recorded Dialect Studies, Ohio State University (established around 1957), Archives de la Parole, University of Paris, and others. Magnetic recording makes archiving in many ways much easier than it was 30 years ago, but it does not reduce the need for good informants and a considerable amount of data processing. The time required by the simplest of archiving projects will always far exceed the expectations of the inexperienced field linguist, published programmatic statements to the contrary notwithstanding (for example, Voegelin and Robinett 1954). The problem is that there is more information on what

---

[1] For a general discussion of archiving as well as practical suggestions see the papers in the archiving issue (No. 2) of the *International Journal of American Linguistics,* Vol. 20 (1954).

linguists think should be done than on what procedures were actually followed.

4. Field linguistics can be undertaken with the purpose of investigating the linguistic aspects of cultural behavior. Hitherto such studies of the "ethnography of speech" have been ancillary to specifically ethnographic or linguistic (descriptive) ones. Many interesting observations have been made in this area as the result of accidental discoveries in the field or post-field considerations of the linguistic and ethnographic data.[2] But if the ethnolinguistic concerns of anthropologists, linguists, sociologists, and psychologists continue to develop at the present rate, we can expect increasingly more precise goals and techniques. We do not have to wait for that day, however, to say that a specifically ethnolinguistic field project starts with a problem. One does not just arrive among the Dani of New Guinea, say, with a nebulous intention of discovering what correlation there is between speech behavior and cultural patterns! Rather, one begins with the assumption that there are pronunciation, lexical, or stylistic differences in the speech of the community and that these are somehow related to social structures or cultural values. One then proceeds to get more information within the framework of a hypothesis. An illustration of this kind of study is that of the apparently strange use of formal speech with dogs, cats, and Indians in the Spanish-speaking village of Tzintzuntzan in Mexico. As usual, the investigator gives no indication of the steps he took in the study, but we can safely assume that it was the use of *usted* where one would expect *tú* (among other things) that first caught his attention and raised intelligent questions. The result of the study in any case is the hypothesis that there are several speech uses that give evidence to the way that the people of Tzintzuntzan perceive social distance and try to increase or decrease it (Foster 1964).

The principal requirement of any ethnolinguistic project, regardless of its proportions, must be the careful documentation of the nonlinguistic correlates of speech behavior. Since it is primarily speech *differences* that are being studied in such a project we must know who said what and under what circumstances. One can sometimes discover clues in the careful analysis of texts, especially those which reflect contemporary life, but for most of his data the field worker must seek in the verbal exchange between people in face-to-face situations. So rapid is normal speech and so subtle are the functions of speech variations that the investigator is required to have a near-native control of the language if he hopes to make a contribution to ethnolinguistic studies.

---

[2] Two useful readers in this area are Hymes (Ed.), 1964, and Gumperz and Hymes (Eds.), 1964.

What has been said in connection with ethnolinguistic field work concerns the descriptive linguist only insofar as he must understand the linguistic data he obtains. This is the point of the statement that "the linguistic scholar working in the field has perforce to be or become something of an anthropologist. . . ." (Emeneau 1958:314; *cf.* Bloomfield 1925:2). For the "cracking" of a linguistic code, which is what grammatical analysis is mostly concerned with, we do not need a profound knowledge of the culture of which it is a part.[3] It is as if we were studying behavior on one dimension only; the other dimensions need also to be studied, but at another time and perhaps in another way. In this manner do we explicitly exclude the position taken by Malinowski forty years ago "that linguistic analysis inevitably leads us into the study of all the subjects covered by Ethnographic fieldwork" (1923:305).

5. Language learning can be either the goal or technique of data collection. Both of these matters shall now be discussed, but a further consideration of various other techniques for collecting data and their relation to the corpus will be discussed below.

When language learning is the goal of data collection, we can expect three factors to affect the resultant corpus. In the first place, data will be obtained for personal and immediate practical needs. This means that the learner will attempt to translate messages coded internally in his own language according to the situations he finds himself in rather than to get a systematic view of the language; in a sense he is solving translation problems rather than storing up information systematically. The result of such an approach is generally, but not necessarily, an incomplete grasp of the language. The person for whom language is a tool and not the object of study too often, and too soon, stops learning when his practical needs are met. It is only a linguistically trained person who can combat this pragmatic approach to language learning with a definite program for ultimately describing the whole language structure.

The second aspect of language learning in the field is that it is so often spasmodic. There are periods of considerable progress followed by periods of inaction. Finally, language learning tends to result in a very limited corpus. For no part of a total description is there as much data as is necessary: a lexical file may contain entries with the barest of definitions, grammatical notes may show many paradigms uncompleted; in short, whatever a person collects for the primary purpose of learning a language will be far from adequate for a description of it. In the long run the structure which a skillful language learner can mirror in his own speech may

---

[3] But it is necessary in a linguistic project for other reasons. See, for example, "Morphology and Syntax" in Chapter 9.

be the same as that which the linguist arrives at by more explicit procedures, but there is always the difference in time. A linguist can reveal basic
linguistic structure with far less data and in less time.

Language learning can also be looked upon, not as a goal in itself, but
as technique for collecting linguistic data, making structural inferences,
and testing hypotheses. The questions we ask ourselves here are, for example: How useful or necessary is language learning to field work? What
are the problems involved in learning to use the target language? What is
the difference between language learning and language analysis? In what
ways is language analysis different when it is accompanied by language
learning from when it is not so accompanied?

There have been many who have deplored the "hit-and-run" tactics
of American field linguistics, much of which is admittedly in the context
of fulfilling requirements for doctorates in linguistics or anthropology.
Their declaration that "the linguist should converse with the informant
without using an intermediary language" (Uhlenbeck 1960:433) is uncom-
promising. But one has the feeling that their attitude is based less on being
able to demonstrate the superiority of their approach than on an incredulity that an accurate grammar can result from a five-month exposure to
a language with no speaking knowledge of it. Their attitude may also be
in part due to their *déjà vécu*: having had the opportunity for learning the
languages they have studied, they look upon the less fortunate as practicing an inferior kind of field linguistics. The whole question deserves an
objective appraisal. Here are a few of perhaps a long list of reasons why
a field worker will find value in learning the language under investigation:

(a) The learning of a language serves to feed the field linguist's drive.
It can be one of his many accomplishments, like paddling a dugout canoe
or playing an African "hand-piano," which will entertain and satisfy him
during difficult months of isolation from his own society. It is simply fun
to be able to talk and joke with people with whom one is working. And
if the investigator is somewhat successful in learning the language, he can
have the real satisfaction in being told: "You don't even talk like a white
man."

(b) Being able to speak the target language (the language being studied)
serves also to identify the investigator with the host community. Generally, people find it easier to accept an outsider with whom they can
communicate in their own language. Some people see it as the chief characteristic of ethnicity. As one Kewa told a linguist in New Guinea, "Your
skin is white and mine is brown, but now we talk the same language, so
we're the same inside."

(c) Speaking the language vastly increases the possibility of getting a
greater and more diversified corpus. Knowledge of the language will put
the investigator in contact with more people in more different situations

and cause him to talk about a greater variety of things than would be otherwise possible. In this way randomness is increased, an extremely important feature of a good corpus which is not easily achieved in elicitation or restricted text collection. As informal teachers, the members of the community bring new things to the investigator and test his knowledge of things he has already been told. Such was the experience of one linguist among the Mazatecs of Mexico: "When they realized that we were trying [to learn their language], most of them had an irresistible desire to check up on us. That desire was realized by some of the women almost every time we went for water. . . . It was while we were waiting our turn that they quizzed us. They didn't believe that it was possible for us to learn their language, but they thought it a big joke that we were trying" (E. V. Pike 1956:17).

(d) Speaking a language forces one to make constructions which one otherwise would not think of; or some constructions will be uttered which will be rejected by the native speakers. In any case, the investigator is forced to make a more explicit analysis of the problems he has encountered. A speaking knowledge of the language can also affect a final description. Unless all of the exemplification is derived from actual utterances, for example, from a body of texts, one must rely on his own ability to construct utterances as the need arises.

(e) A knowledge of the language also has the value of building up the internalized corpus which the linguist can draw upon in his analysis. This is saying that he makes of himself another informant whom he can use for introspective eliciting. Not many use language learning in this way, but one redoubtable polyglot of my acquaintance claims that this is the only way that he conducts linguistic analysis: first learn the language and then discover structure on the basis of what is known. There is no gainsaying his ability to learn languages, for he has a near native-control of, among others, French, Haitian Creole, Portuguese, Pidgin English, and Spanish. Unfortunately, his truly remarkable abilities are bestowed on too few of us! Hence the danger of making wrong inferences from what we *think* we have learned. This was the mistake that a European speaker of Sango made when he insisted that the connective *sí* could never be used to join a subject to a predicate: *babá sí avɔ* "It was Father who bought (it)." In spite of the fact that he had learned the language from native speakers and had used it for much of his childhood, he accepted the "doctrine" prevalent among Europeans that this word meant "then" or "so that," probably in violation of his own unconscious use. Another danger of introspective elicitation is that we can easily produce an empiric-looking but highly speculative description. "Flying planes can be dangerous," a veritable pet of linguists studying English syntax, is an authentic but ambiguous English sentence; it is all too easy, however, to conjure up others that have the same or similar structure but lack the note of authenticity.[4] My own procedure is a much more cautious one than that of my linguistic colleagues': learn as much of the language as possible but rely ultimately only on well controlled utterances obtained from native speakers.

(f) Another value of having learned the language is that it permits the investigator the liberty of working on the texts independently and perhaps even away from the field. My own experience with translating texts makes me cautious, however, about recommending the processing of texts away from the field, even if one speaks the language. The problem lies not only in being unable sometimes to make out the sense of a passage, but also in not being able to distinguish between grammatical and ungrammatical utterances. Indeed, the intractability of a passage may be due to its being ungrammatical. It is possible that dictated texts will have far less of these kinds of problems than tape-recorded texts which are the only ones I am experienced with. Of course, if the investigator has a literate informant, the two of them can carry on a correspondence which will permit the investigator to extricate himself from all but the most difficult passages which, in any case, can be identified as such in publication.

The nature of language learning is always determined in part by the structural complexities of the target language. Some languages have extremely difficult phonological systems, whether they be in the consonantal system (like Xhosa with its full set of clicks or some Athapaskan languages with their glottalized stops and affricates) or in the tonal system. Other languages have extremely complex verb or noun morphologies sometimes made more opaque by morphophonemic changes whose patterns do not emerge until a very large amount of the data is in. Such is the case in Fula, illustrated by the following words from the Adamawa dialect:

		SIMPLE	AUGMENTATIVE	DIMINUTIVE
dog	sg.	*rawaandu*	*ndawaaŋga*	*dawaaŋgel*
	pl.	*dawaaɗi*	*ndawaako*	*ndawaakoy*
male	sg.	*worduru*	*ngorga*	*gorgel*
	pl.	*gorɗi*	*ngorko*	*ngorkoy*

The adjectives for "male" occur in these forms with "dog" or any other noun in this, that is, the *ndu,* class (since Fula is a class language). Add

---

[4] Excepted here are people like Samuel P. Kleinschmidt, 1814–1886, who made such an astounding contribution to Greenlandic studies. In addition to his knowledge of German and Danish, the languages of his father and mother respectively, he learned Greenlandic from his playmates for whom it was a native language. He did not leave for Europe until he was 14 years old and came back 12 years later, apparently retaining his original command of the language (Rosing 1951).

to these problems the one of having to learn the vocabulary and there is reason to wonder if the great effort expended is truly justified by the returns. I maintain that it is, in part for the reasons already given and in part because language learning can be selective.

Knowledge of any language is always partial. Even the native speaker of a language does not have a knowledge of his language which is fully congruent with that of all the other speakers. If this is true, then it is all the more true of one for whom this is a second language. Moreover, there are many paths to a near-native control of a language. One person may have an excellent control of pronunciation, but another person may know the verb system better. Since this is true under ideal circumstances—when the full grammatical system of a language is known—it must be true under field conditions. The field linguist therefore must not be frustrated by his failure to control all that he should like to. Unattainability of native control is no excuse for not acquiring *some* control. What he must do is select those parts of the language which will accomplish the following objectives: acquire and maintain the confidence of the informant in his abilities, build up in himself the satisfaction of being a partial master of the language, and know whatever is most important for the analytical part of his work.

Unfortunately, the field linguist cannot always know what part of yesterday's or today's data will be important for work a week or a month from now. Still, he can learn and use whatever bit of corpus he happens to be working on with specific problems in mind. If, for example, he is trying to determine the explanation for the lengthening of the vowel of the Kikuyu copula *ne* in some environments, he memorizes what data he has and tries to use similar constructions with his informant or other speakers at every opportunity. For a day or so the field linguist is on a *ne* "binge," but no one knows it except himself, and he will end up knowing more or having a better picture of the problem than when he first began.

The next best thing that the field linguist can do in learning the language is to memorize connected discourse. This may be something he has had his informant help him to translate or, better, something which the informant has given more or less spontaneously. It could, for example, be a short narrative about someone's trip or an illness in the village. Long before I had a good picture of the general structure of Gbeya I was getting my informant to tell me about my own activities. I would take these short texts, change the pronouns to the first person singular, and then use them whenever possible. Each new telling was enriched by my having found new things to say and new ways to say the old things. Where I faltered, questions were put to me, making dialogue out of a narrative. Where I used one tense, my interlocutors used another and thereby introduced other necessary changes.

We have very little information about the techniques and uses of language learning of field linguists.[5] Hoijer claims that "the anthropological linguist rarely achieves more than a casual practical facility in the language he is studying" (1961:110). Although it would be interesting to know what "casual practical facility" is, it would be more important to know to what extent and in what way it helped the linguist in his field work.

Because individual language learning ability, language complexity, field conditions, and other factors vary so much, it is hardly worth venturing any guess as to how much time a field linguist would need before he could understand most of what people said to him. (It is always much more difficult to follow a conversation when several people are involved.) Yet it seems reasonable to expect a field worker to arrive in six months at the point where he is able to satisfy routine social demands and limited work requirements. People with less training and less time to devote to specifically linguistic study would naturally require more time. Of anthropological field workers Lowie says, ". . . I cannot bring myself to believe on the basis of my experience that even an unusually gifted person could achieve thoroughness in less than approximately a year" (1940:89).

The learning of the target language is not the only technique for data collection which affects the nature of the corpus. Every technique moulds the "shape" of the final body of data that the field linguist must work with. If he uses word lists or questionnaires or a grammar of a related language to the exclusion of others, his data will in some way be circumscribed. There is no need at this point to specify the characteristics of such corpora nor to enumerate their limitations. All of this can be inferred from subsequent treatments of the nature of a good corpus and the various techniques one can use in obtaining it.

The final factor which influences the nature of a corpus is the investigation itself. An interest expressed in how a person speaks very often makes him self-conscious and perhaps even ill at ease. The result may be speech which is unnatural in some way. The most common errors produced in this way are in pronunciation; an informant's articulation of a certain sound will be different or he will segment a stream of speech in an abnormal fashion. Again, where speakers are insecure vis-à-vis another prestige language, they very frequently modify their speech if the investigator speaks this language or if he is a representative of the culture with which it is identified. Thus, Turner observes that when white men have studied the Gullah Negro speech, the informants used far fewer African-based words than ordinarily (1949:12). The white man's presence therefore

---

[5] The collection of unpublished papers by Summer Institute of Linguistics people is an exception. Statements have been published about Bloomfield's technique (Voegelin 1959*b*:114), but demurrers expressed outside of publication indicate that confirmation is needed.

temporarily increases the rate of borrowing from English. The Hopi and Taos, on the other hand, tend to purify their speech of loan-words under some circumstances (Dockstader 1955:157).

Another form of distortion which results from the contact between a community and the investigator is simplification. More than one field worker has discovered that the material he first obtained contained far too few noun or verb affixes, if the language was complex in these areas, or a rather monotonous series of too similar sentence types (Aitken 1955; Henry 1940). Even the most "simple" folk have a remarkable talent for diagnosing the linguistic skills of a foreigner and will adapt their speech according to his limitations. Yet out of fairness to some field workers, we ought to say that the native speakers' prior experience with others might account for this simplification.

The Characteristics of a Good Corpus

No body of generalizations, however broad or restricted it may be, is any better than the data on which it is based. In linguistics, a poor analyst can misuse a good corpus and a good analyst can sometimes outguess a bad corpus; the human factor is never to be ruled out in an investigation.[6] But since the ease with which the project is accomplished and the value of the final product are determined in large measure by the quality of the data used, the maximum of care should be exerted in its collection. What is it that the field linguist must try to obtain? This question will be answered by discussing six of the outstanding features of a good body of data. They are presented here as if they were all coordinate in a single list. Some apply only to the requirements of the phonological analysis, others to grammatical analysis. Some are crucial to the description of the language, others are important from the point of view of the reader of the description; but in one way or another all of them contribute to the making of a good body of data. Their absence, in part or in whole, will conversely characterize a bad corpus.

1. *Dialectally uniform.* All of the data in the linguist's corpus must represent a single idiom. Thus, if a description includes the statement that the phoneme /v/ is articulated as a voiced labio-dental fricative, but a speaker of this same language is found who uses a voiced bilabial fricative, it has failed in some way: either there are different dialects or idiolects or the investigator erred in the identification of the sound. This is not to

[6] Witness the excellent description of Tunica based on material collected with the assistance of an elderly informant who had not spoken the language for 25 years and whose parents had each spoken a language different from Tunica (Haas 1941).

say that the linguist is uninterested in speech variation. He is very much interested indeed, but he seeks to sort out the various kinds of recurrent differences so that his final description will accommodate all of them, in some cases by explicitly ruling out some of them, with a limited set of generalizations.

At the beginning of the project, when one does not yet know what variations are going to turn up, it is possible to assure considerable uniformity in the corpus, because we know in what ways languages tend to be internally divergent: over geographic areas, through social classes, from polylingualism, because of age or sex, and so on. The most obvious way to avoid the problem of getting a nonuniform corpus is to select a single informant. But this is like jumping from a burning building before you know that there is a fireman's net below. Native speakers of a language do not necessarily speak "pure" Banda or Turkish or anything else. The following is the kind of informant in whose speech one might expect a considerable amount of interference from the languages he has been exposed to: He speaks Dakota, but his parents speak Yankton, and his schoolmates Teton. He has for many years lived in English-speaking environments, paying occasional visits to Yankton-speaking communities (Matthews 1955). A phonemic analysis of data from this speaker which purported to represent a Dakota dialect is understandably tentative.

It should be well understood that when we speak of "purity" of speech we mean neither a form of speech which is "standard" (by contrast with an inferior "substandard") nor one which supposedly has not changed as much as others since a given period in the past. In the first instance, we ought certainly to know if there are different linguistic systems (they may be called dialects) recognized by the native speakers and rated in some more or less consistent way. All classifications, of course, must be subjected to independent scrutiny. The reasons for choosing one particular idiom for description are outside the tastes and dictates of the language community as long as the investigation is a purely scientific one. In the second instance, it is doubtful that any so-called archaic speech is "pure" in any proper sense of the term. Yet this is its implication in some statements. In any case, it is not archaic bits of language that we are at all interested in when we set out to describe a language.

2. *Natural.* Strictly speaking there is no objective "natural speech," either from the speaker's point of view or from the analyst's. A discourse is deemed appropriate or inappropriate according to its purpose, speaker, and conditions which surround its use. What is "natural" in one circumstance is not natural in another; what is acceptable for one speaker is not acceptable for another. As native speakers of a language, all of us can unconsciously account for the way a person is talking, and speech is rejected only if the speaker is considered to be demented. The ultimate

judges of naturalness are therefore always the speakers of a language. Internal evidence cannot be used by the investigator for making an independent evaluation. He must depend on his informants.

It might be argued that grammaticality is one of the aspects of natural speech about which native speakers would not dispute. Among transformational grammarians, in fact, the assumption is made that one of the characteristics of a good grammar is that it produce only those utterances which are judged grammatical by the native speakers. As one might expect, much of the evaluation of the claims made for this approach to language description has consisted of exploring the nature of grammaticality. It has been found, however, that native speakers arrive at a point in a test where they have difficulty in distinguishing between semantic nonsense and structural incorrectness. There is certainly no question about some constructions that one presents to a native speaker: they neither make sense nor are structurally typical of the language; but between these and those sentences which everyone would accept as entirely normal, there are sentences about which there would be hesitation, doubt, and disagreement (Maclay and Sleator 1960). For the field linguist this is an important thing to remember. He must avoid influencing his informant to accept as grammatical those utterances which a majority of his fellow-speakers would possibly reject.

Having identified naturalness as whatever is appropriate under a given set of circumstances, we add that it is this natural speech which a linguist works with. He does not create an artificial language which will be more amenable to linguistic analysis than the one that exists independent of his investigation. Yet it must be admitted that some descriptions are indeed based on a corpus which consists of hardly anything more than words in citation forms, paradigms, and sentences which are translations of utterances put in the contact language. Such constrained corpora are often supplemented by brief texts, such as descriptions of pictures, narrations, folk tales, or conversations. The greatest limitation of this type of corpus is obvious: it sheds very little light on the great diversity which every natural language displays; it prevents the investigator from observing the extreme ranges of tolerance permitted by a community of speakers.

The only possible defense for these artificial corpora is that they are convenient and that they reveal the structural core of the language. There is no denying their convenience. The newcomer to a language rarely—if ever—has the competence to transcribe complete utterances in an accurate way. He must start with the smallest possible fractions of meaningful utterances—words and short sentences. Although there is some danger in obtaining utterances which are phonologically aberrant, one can generally expect these utterances to be compatible with the normal patterns of the language, for "clarity norms" are, as Hockett has suggested, probably universal (Hockett 1955:220). Where the linguist errs is in leading others to believe that his phonological description is natural to the whole language rather than to just a part of it. Unless a "clarity norm" description is diligently compared to one based on other forms of discourse, it must be judged incomplete.

Artificiality is certainly one Scylla which the conscientious field linguist seeks to avoid, but opposite it stands the Charybdis of informal, casual speech. Casual speech can nowadays be collected with very little difficulty by using tape recorders. This ease can tempt the neophyte to dispense with other types of corpora. He should be warned, however, that as raw data for phonological analysis, tape-recorded casual speech can be almost intractable. The difficulty of using this material is due not so much to the mechanical distortion which is inevitable with even the best of portable recorders as to what happens in casual speech generally. As long as a speaker feels that he is being understood, he unconsciously reduces the contrastive features (used in the most general sense) of his language. It is not uncommon for phonemic contrasts to be levelled out, articulation to become less precise, and so on. This phenomenon was particularly in evidence when I was studying the distribution of lexical tones in connected Sango texts. Over several syllables and words there was very often a lowering of high tones and a raising of low tones, that is, a neutralization of these tonemes without the appearance of any pattern. This leveling might be accounted for by the fact that Sango is a lingua franca were it not for the fact that it has also been observed in other languages. Because of this phenomenon, the field linguist should not expect to use tape-recorded casual speech for large-scale spectrographic study: that is, he will not find enough comparable examples of each type of utterance to make valid comparisons (Lehiste 1963).

An artificial corpus is convenient, but does it reveal the hard core of the language structure? We do not know in what specific ways—other than incompleteness—descriptions based on more artificial or more natural corpora would differ. There have certainly been no experiments dealing with this problem. One can only compare two or more grammars whose corpora are fully described. Yet even here one must be able to factor out elements of analytical skill, methodological techniques, and statement. We may nevertheless expect to find the following characteristics of an artificially induced corpus:

(a) A tendency to similarity with the language of the investigator. This would be due not to his having imposed a structure on the target language, although we know that this is always the danger with nonlinguists, but to his having looked for certain structural features. Thus, if one's language has a subjunctive, it is hardly possible that a subjunctive will be overlooked in the language being studied. The error will be in omission rather than commission. The investigator will not see other features, some of which may be equally important to the complete description. It is very often what a grammar does *not* contain that is frustrating to the general linguist or comparativist. A good example of such lacunae is the scarcity of information grammars give on the peculiarities of a particular class of nouns in Benue-Congo (Bantu) languages. These nouns, known as *1a* in the singular and *2a* in the plural, are characterized by certain morphological and syntactic features which are shared by no other nouns except perhaps personal names. Information about these nouns, so important to a reconstruction of the history of the Benue-Congo—if not all Niger-Congo languages—is very easily omitted from a grammar because of their difference from the prevailing system (Gleason 1959).

(b) The absence of low-frequency elements both in phonology and grammar. In phonology those features which carry the heaviest functional load will naturally be more prominent than those with the lowest functional load. Thus, in Gbeya the voiced labiodental flap occurs in only five words (in my corpus), none of them at all common. Low-frequency grammatical elements, by their very scarcity, often defy neat analysis and are confined to a section in our files which our consciences require to be labelled "for future study." For example, in Gbeya I cannot be certain what some occurrences of *gá* are: either assimilated forms of the connective *gó* "then," abbreviated forms of *gende gá ye ge* "in other words, that is to say," or a third connective not yet identified.

(c) Constructions which are most interesting or most tractable to the investigator. The unit that the field linguist generally restricts himself to is the sentence. This is the tool that he can most conveniently handle as he elicits grammatical information. It might in fact be said that many grammars arc "sentence grammars" since this is the top limit of their largest constructions.

Naturalness in content is as important as naturalness in structure, although for different reasons. It has previously been noted (in Chapter 3) that the informant must approve the utterances he is made to produce in his own language. The authenticity of the utterances is linked to his maintaining a personal integrity. The more unrealistic the demands on his language, the more ill at ease he becomes. Much of this realism can be anticipated by the alert and sympathetic field worker, but since linguistic elicitation is artificial even under the best of circumstances, we should be prepared for unprovoked negative reactions from an informant. What accounts for these reactions is his failure to imagine a situation in which the desired utterance would be said. Thus, when a Marathi informant was first asked by a student to give the imperative form "Die!" he became troubled, giving the impression that he could think of no occasion when one would give this command. He gave the form reluctantly, and not until several minutes later did he volunteer the statement that a tired mother might say to her child "Die! Leave me alone!"

3. *Varied.* The importance of a varied corpus can be illustrated by a comparison with archeological field work. When an archeologist must choose to excavate at only one or two of several possible sites, he is led by many considerations, one of the most important of which is this: At which site will the greatest amount of information be unearthed? To this researcher information does not mean large quantities of artifacts or remains; tons of pottery is not what he is looking for. Since he is attempting to reconstruct the history of a particular area, he is most interested in reconstructable diversity. He would like to find several easily distinguished strata, each differentiated by richly variegated remains of human existence. The field linguist likewise explores his terrain for those data that will most readily disclose to him the inner workings of the language. He does not want vast quantities of information; just a little will do if it is the right kind. Therefore all linguistic corpora must be evaluated by the following dictum: the quality of a corpus is in direct proportion to the diversity of the structures it reveals. Conversely, the more uniform a corpus, the less valuable it is.[7]

Two means are available to the field linguist for diversifying his corpus: careful sampling procedures and the inducing of higher frequencies.

Careful sampling is necessary to make certain that every possible structurally relevant linguistic feature has been obtained. One cannot dragnet the whole language, so one does it selectively. What one seeks to acquire is a random sample of the language. This is not accomplished by collecting at random because no such procedure produces a truly random sample: if one is collecting texts, he may be more interested in one kind than in others; if he is building up a corpus by elicitation, the material is determined by the questions he asks; if he is depending on what he hears "on the run" in everyday verbal intercourse with the community, what he files away depends as much on his memory, previous knowledge of the language (which constitutes a kind of interpretive grid), and momentary interest as on what is said. What is meant by collecting "at random" is that any number of external factors may influence the material which is collected; the pulling out of the plum is always determined by a particular kind of putting in of the thumb (Friedrich 1964).

The alternative to this kind of haphazard sampling of a language is a methodical sampling; one makes a conscious effort to increase the scope of the coverage. The technique is simple enough: the field worker sets out to get speech of every possible variety on every conceivable subject indigenous to the community. We shall assume that this text-collection is

---

[7] The nature of this uniformity must be understood from the context of the present discussion. It is not to be confused with dialectal uniformity mentioned above.

to be done with a tape recorder, although this is not necessary. Translation elicitation is definitely excluded; hardly any modification of this technique can be imagined which would increase its yield for sampling purposes.

The sampling project will be limited by field conditions and by how much a single worker can accomplish himself. Since it is all too easy to collect endless hours of texts with a tape recorder, the field linguist must severely curtail the amount of texts he obtains of any particular type. To get short texts one does not always limit his speakers to an arbitrary five minutes or so. The reason is that whenever informants are "put to work" at talking they will be ill at ease for a minute or so. This discomfiture could certainly affect the naturalness of speech. Much more needs to be said about corpus-collecting with tape recorders, but a discussion of all the mechanical aspects of this activity is given in Chapter 5; here we are primarily concerned with the great variety of speech which must be recorded in the texts.

There are at least eight factors which are correlated with speech diversity, each of which should in some way be represented in a good linguistic corpus: age, sex, and social class or occupation of the speaker; speaker's emotion; speed of utterance; topic, type, and style of discourse.

(a) *Age of speaker*. Where a society is structured according to age, one can often find linguistic usage reflecting the differences, a common form of which is in different sets of personal pronouns. In our own society certain forms of slang characterize adolescents. Where a society is undergoing severe culture change or is characterized by a considerable amount of contact with other speech communities, one can also find significant language change which is correlated with the age of the speaker. One such interesting case is that of Badaga in India. In this Dravidian language a rather drastic change has occurred in the vowel phonemes during the lifetime of people still living, with the period 1930–1935 being the dividing line. Before that time there were 20 vowel phonemes; after the change there were only 13. In other words, older folk have 20 vowel phonemes, but the younger ones have only 13. The rearrangement is the following:

Before 1930	*After 1935*
5 vowel qualities:/i, e, a, u, ɔ/	5 short vowels:/i, e, a, u, o/
2 lengths: short, long	7 long vowels:/iˑ, eˑ, ɛˑ,
2 degrees of retroflexion	uˑ, oˑ, ɔˑ/
	1 nasalized vowel:/ã/

The restructuring is illustrated by the following pairs of words.

Before 1930	*After 1935*	
/beˑ/	/beˑ/	mouth
/bȩˑ/(retroflexed)	/bɛˑ/	bangle
/huˑ/	/huˑ/	{ flower
/hṳˑ/(retroflexed) }		worm

(b) *Sex of speaker.* In a few places minor but consistent differences have been found between the speech of men and women. In Koasati, a Musko-gean language now spoken in southwestern Louisiana, there are differences which are limited to certain indicative and imperative forms of verbal paradigms (Haas 1944; see also Sapir 1929). In the following examples ˆ stands for falling pitch-stress and ´ for high pitch-stress:

WOMEN'S	MEN'S	
kã·	ká·s	he is saying
molhîl	molhís	we are peeling it
lakawčîn	lakawčî·s	don't lift it!
lakáw	lakáws	he is lifting it

Sometimes, however, men report speech differences which cannot be corroborated by linguistic evidence. Such is the case for Sango. Men claim not only that the women living in the towns speak the language better than they do but also that the Sango of the women sounds good: *anzere míngi* "it is very sweet." It would appear that they detect some paralinguistic features in women's speech, but no informant I have ever interviewed was able to verbalize his feelings well enough for me to identify these qualities. It is quite possible that "sweet talk" is not so much a particular way of talking as it is the impression given by the behavior of these women, which is much less inhibited than that of the "up-country" women.

(c) *Social class or occupation.* There are sometimes extensive language differences where a society is formally stratified. In the Far East, for example, one finds "honorific" language contrasted with humble or neutral language in Balinese, Chinese, Sundanese, Burmese, Tongan, Marathi, Hindi, and Bengali.[8] Japanese can serve to illustrate this point. In this language there is a distinction between exalted, neutral, and humble (or self-denigrating) forms of nouns and verbs. Thus, the neutral form of "father" is *chichí* whereas the exalted form is *otósan;* the neutral form of "house" is *uchí* and the exalted form *otaku.* A few verbs have humble, neutral, and exalted forms: for example, for "says" there are *mōshiageru mōsu, iu,* and *ossháru,* respectively. Similar distinctions are made by adding certain prefixes or affixes to nouns or verbs. It is not essential to give a description of the use of these status words, but in general it is this: one uses the simple neutral forms in reference to oneself and one's actions and the exalted forms with a superior or even a peer; but if one's actions are understood to involve the other person or his family, then the humble forms must be used by the speaker (Martin 1956:328ff).

[8] *The Bible Translator,* Vol. 14, No. 4 (1963) is devoted to a discussion of the problems of translating into languages such as these.

A very different type of class-correlated speech difference is found among the Barundi in Africa. There is extensive and elaborate formalization and stylization of speech situations leading to norms which govern the use of speech which is differentiated according to sex, age, and caste. The hierarchy in Burundi starts with the king and descends to the low-born pariahs through the princes, the nobles, the herders, and the farmer-peasants. The appropriate speech behavior, for example, of the peasants during relations with the superior castes, is described in these words: ". . . their words are haltingly delivered or run on uncontrolled, their voices are loud, their gestures wild, their figures of speech ungainly, their emotions freely displayed, their words and sentences clumsy. . . . It would be an unforgivable blunder for a peasant-farmer, no matter how wealthy or able, to produce a truly elegant, eloquent, rapid-fire defense before a herder or other superior" (Albert 1964:38, 41–42). In such a society it is obviously necessary to distinguish between the linguistic performances within certain levels (say, among the nobles) and between various levels (say, between nobles and peasants).

Even in less clearly stratified societies one often finds speech forms whose differences reveal information about class consciousness. We can cite our own society where certain forms are approved and others are substandard. There are sometimes subtle differences of pronunciation which are not part of the overt signs of class-identified dialects but which native speakers nonetheless easily identify in tests. One of the advantages of tape recording over elicitation is that the speaker, taken up with his subject, is less likely to correct his speech to conform to the standard model, but in elicitation the informant has time to make what corrections he wants (McDavid 1954).

(d) *Emotion at time of speaking.* A corpus collected entirely from speakers who were calm or bored at the recording sessions cannot be said to fully represent the language in phonology, lexicon, or grammar. We should like to know what regular linguistic features are correlated with various emotions. In general we have very little information on this subject, but in the Kaiwá (Guaraní) language of Brazil it was found that the occurrence of certain intonational features (for example, stress placement and syllable timing) seemed to depend on whether the speaker "seemed to be angry, excited, intensely moved, or interested in confirming facts" or whether he "was expressing fear or discussing religious subjects" (Bridgeman 1961:329). Lexical variation is illustrated by the reported higher incidence of ideophones in well-told African folk tales than in more prosaic narratives. Sentence structure will also vary with the emotion of the speaker: we can reasonably expect, for example, that the discourse of an "excited" person will contain more short and "incomplete" sentences than in deliberate and unemotional speech (Moore 1964).

(e) *Speed of utterance.* It is phonology which is most affected by speech tempo. In some languages the differences between "slow" or "deliberate" and "fast" or "allegro" speech can be correlated with morphophonemic changes; for example, changes in the shapes of words at open juncture, as in Kikuyu or Bambara. One of the most remarkable cases is that of Bini, a language of Nigeria, where there are said to be seven tempos of speech (Westcott 1962). The relations between these various tempos are too complex to describe here, but the following "allologs" illustrate the kinds of variations which exist for the word "now":

Ceremonious	*rlìrlán*
Deliberate	*rlìán*
Slow	*rlìán* or *nìán*
Ordinary	*rìán* or *nìán*
Rapid	*ryàán* or *nìaán*
Hurried	*nyàán*
Slurred	*yàán*

In other languages the differences are subphonemic: thus, in Maidu, a language of northern California, voiceless stops, which in deliberate speech have aspirated and unaspirated allophones in complementary distribution, tend to have only unaspirated allophones in allegro speech; likewise, the six vowel phonemes have centralized allophones in unstressed syllables only in allegro speech (Shipley 1956).

(f) *Topic of discourse.* A comprehensive corpus should cover some of the principal cultural activities and culturally relevant topics of the society. The topics chosen for inclusion in the corpus need not all be covered in the same way, of course. One aspect of the culture may be fairly well covered in the folk tales and another in the conversations or narratives. Since for the Baruguyu of Tanzania, for example, cattle are the focal point, a truly representative corpus would reveal this fact in words which describe the different colors, sizes, shapes, breeds, and behavior of this beast as well as in proverbs, palavers over ownership rights (see Beidelman 1965).

(g) *Type of discourse.* Language can be put to several different uses in every human society. The following is only a partial list:

Narrations: eyewitness accounts, reminiscences, instructions on how to perform certain tasks, or how to get to certain destinations
Conversations: arguments, dialogues over "where have you been?"
Songs: lullabies, dirges, dance songs
Folk tales: legends, how things came to be, amusing stories
Proverbs and riddles
Names: personal, topographic, village
Pseudo-onomatopoeic calls of animals or birds

The value of such a broad spectrum of types of discourse is the information that they are likely to produce on special vocabularies, archaic forms of speech, and others. For example, what may be an anomalous construction in "everyday" narration may prove to be a common feature of proverbs or riddles, as in the Gbeya proverb *dawa-nɛ ŋgɔ́n baà ʔmũkɔ́ te,* "the monkey which travels above seizes (literally, seized) a rotten branch," (meaning "He who lives dangerously will be killed by his deeds"). The characteristic feature here is the use of the perfective form of the verb in stating a general truth. In Jacalteca (Guatemala) narratives the commonest pattern in the verbs is CCCVC, but in the conversations the patterns are simpler (Church 1962). A different kind of speech difference is found in Nahuat: verb forms used by *compadres* in speaking to each other are more highly inflected than they are in other situations. Even personal names may reveal significant features of a language. Among the Bahnar of South Vietnam, personal names are characterized by so many unusual phonological features that one must wonder about the changes that are taking place in the language, either naturally or from contact with other languages. Personal names have one more vowel phoneme than the nonname corpus; in names there is a filling-out of patterns of phoneme distribution (for example /ʔw/ syllable finally as well as initially); and whereas only two-thirds of the nonname vocabulary is monosyllabic, all of the personal names have this form.

(h) *Style of discourse.* Where a particular kind of discourse has features which distinguish it from other kinds, we can speak of a characteristic style. There may be a "conversational style" as opposed to a "narrative style," but narratives may defy a single characterization if they occur in cant, baby-talk, or pseudo-animal speech in addition to the everyday form. For some purposes it is useful to distinguish between "casual" (covering ordinary interactive speech) and "noncasual" (covering almost everything else), but specifically such things as myths, prayers, chants, certain kinds of "deliberate monologues," and others. It is less important for the moment to categorize speech styles than it is to indicate the importance of getting information about them. In obtaining only "noncasual" texts one may fail to see the amount of borrowing going on in the language, for traditional texts may be less hospitable to borrowing than casual language is. By failing to see the stylistic correlations of speech differences, one can also produce an unrealistic description of a language. In Southern Cheyenne, for example, one finds rare occurrences of the vowel [u] where the usual allophones of the phoneme /o/ are expected. What eliminates [u] from the regular phonemic system is the fact that it is the stylistic means of representing a person with a cold. (See also French 1958; Hymes 1958; Wolff 1951.)

It should be realized that a type of discourse which has its advantages may also have its limitations. Descriptive texts (those which tell how to perform certain activities), for example, probably tend to be simpler syntactically and more repetitious. These characteristics may make the linguist's work easier (see below), but such texts do not demonstrate the full potentiality of the language. (Descriptive texts may also be characterized by more hesitation, caused by the speaker's trying to get things in the right order.) Traditional material can be expected to differ from everyday speech in several different ways. One of them, delivery, can make text collection quite difficult. This would be true of Mohave. Devereux writes:

> The Mohave have a traditional staccato, strongly accented and rather rapid manner of delivering traditional memorized texts which are usually couched in brief sentences. . . . This characteristic method of delivery is so completely a part of the recited text, that it is very difficult, even for the most willing informant, to slow down to the point where the text can be conveniently recorded (1949:269).

Careful sampling must be supplemented by other techniques to get more data on linguistic elements which normally are of low frequency. All languages have such elements at different levels of structure. To illustrate, it has been widely observed (and recently called to the attention of linguists by Martin Joos) that of all the members of an open class (such as nouns and verbs) occurring in a body of text, slightly less than 50 percent of them will be *hapax legomena* (elements occurring just once). In contrast to this phenomenon, some frequencies appear to be determined by the type of discourse. It is reported, for example, that when a group of native speakers of French retold the story of a film they had just seen, their narration was entirely in the present tense. However, when they related a personal experience, they used only the *passé composé* (compound past tense): *il a décidé* "he decided." (The one exception was a seven-year old child who used one *passé simple: il décida* "he decided.") A study of the essays of English grade-school children of upper and lower classes also revealed that adjective clauses occurred only in the shorter texts (Lawton 1963).

To induce more occurrences of specific categories of elements, the field linguist must first identify them. Unless he has some prior knowledge of the language or the family of which it is a member, he can acquire this knowledge by performing a pilot analysis of a few short, representative texts. Once the elements are identified, the linguist can either collect more of the kinds of texts which seem to determine the frequencies or elicit utterances which presumably will contain them. Thus, when I found that I had very few examples of the Gbeya connective *só kó* in my texts, I obtained more proverbs because of the frequency of this connective in them. I also took the sentences with *gó* and transformed them, with the informant's assistance, into *só kó* sentences. For example:

bɛrɛ go wa há ŋginza	they give money (habitually) in the dry season
bɛrɛ só kó wá há ŋginza	they gave money in the dry season

4. *Complete.* A corpus is said to have completeness when all the closed classes of linguistic elements are fully accounted for. In general, one would not expect nouns and verbs to represent closed classes, but there may be closed subclasses within these or other open classes. For example, Gbeya adverbs include a small list of one kind of words and an apparently un-limited number of descriptive adverbs, the so-called "ideophones."

Completeness is achieved by being aware of patterns which gradually emerge from the data; one must always know where one is in the analysis and how much more needs to be learned. An illustration from phono-logical analysis makes this clear. Unless one has made an inventory of the phones which occur in the transcription, he may be unaware of the fact that he has only the following consonants:

p	t	k
b	d	g
m	n	

But awareness of the lacuna in the velar position forces him to give greater attention to all occurrences of nasalization, resulting in the discovery that what was perceived as vowel nasalization is in reality lax velar articulation.

5. *Repetitious.* Repetitiousness in a corpus is extremely useful in the early stages of analysis, for each identified element, whether it be restricted or free in distribution, acts as a pivot for the identification of the surround-ing elements. Certain kinds of texts are always more repetitious than others: for example, instructions on how to make beer, butcher a pig, and make a house. In the following Sango recipe for the preparation of kidneys notice the recurrent key words:[9]

¹nzoní tongana mɔ yí tí tɔ́ ní na *vin* só, mɔ goe mɔ vɔ *rognon* ní na lá kúí. ²mɔ gá na *rognon* ní mɔ *fáa* yá tí *rognon* ní kóé, mɔ sukúla ní nzoní, mɔ zía na yá tí sɛmbé. ³mɔ mú l'ail kété, mɔ fáa l'ail da. ⁴mɔ mú *vin* ní verrɛ ɔ́kɔ, mɔ túku ní da.

¹*You* should, if *you* want to cook it with *wine,* go buy the *kidneys* in the evening. ²Take the *kidneys* and *cut* them all up, *you* wash them well, and *you* put them into a dish. ³*You* take a little garlic, and *cut* up the garlic in it. ⁴Take *wine,* one glassfull, and pour it in.

The word *ní* is not so easily identified from the English translation, but one can infer its function from the fact that it occurs after some easily identified nouns. This information and the knowledge of what form signifies "you" help to identify the verbs.

6. *Interesting.* An interesting corpus is one whose content can profit-ably be studied long after it has served in the analysis of the linguistic

---

[9] The nature of the text is due to its being given over Radio Centrafrique. The French words *vin, rognon,* and *l'ail* do not have Sango equivalents.

structure. The scientific discipline which has the most to gain from linguistic texts is anthropology, but psychologists and philosophers—among others—will find increasing profit in the study of good texts. In general, anecdotal texts are to be avoided. Rather than hearing about how the informant had cut himself, we should prefer to learn about its treatment; rather than hearing about the informant's trip to the city, we could learn more about culture change if he should describe how different city life was from village life. Knowing what would be interesting or valuable to other scholars requires a certain amount of sophistication on the part of the field worker. The more intellectually curious he is, the more likely he is to get a valuable documentation of another people's life.

These texts must in some way be confirmed as culturally authentic. On one occasion it was classroom declamatory style that made me suspect that a text was inauthentic. I had gone to an elementary school to get samples of children's Sango. Since I was trying to get "interesting" texts, I suggested the topic of fishing, because it was a major activity of the community; but instead of telling about his own experiences at catching fish, my informant attempted to translate what he could remember of a lesson that had appeared in the class' French reader. By paying attention to *how* the lad was speaking as well as to *what* he was saying, I was thus able to detect and eliminate an inferior narrative.

What this discussion of a good corpus should have demonstrated is that it never comes into existence automatically or accidentally. It results from the application of definite techniques in a skillful manner by an alert investigator. As much as a good analysis, a good corpus always distinguishes the truly competent linguist.

Size of the Corpus

The only factors which should restrict the size of the corpus are the practical ones of collecting and processing; size must have no priority over quality and adequacy. So the only question which a field worker must face is: Is it possible to get a good but restricted corpus? A lot depends, as we have observed in the preceding pages, on the care which is devoted to its collection. Much depends also on the language itself. There are some patterns which very soon emerge from one's data, but there are others which are adequately attested (without elicitation, of course) only in increasingly greater amounts of data. This is why a surprising amount can be learned about a language with a relatively limited corpus, a fact which has been amply demonstrated by philologists working on dead languages and descriptive linguists working on living languages (Bowman 1959).

The size of a corpus is generally controlled by the rule of thumb which states that "When the investigator finds that all additional material [in a collection] yields nothing not already contained in his analysis he may consider his corpus adequate" (Harris 1951:13). But the problem is that the investigator does not know how much more material he would need before finding something new; is it five more minutes or five more hours of tape-recorded texts? The problem is obviously a statistical one.

The problem can be illustrated by the study of a list of Sango words which I ultimately designated "Adjunctives." In trying to determine their classification, I was confronted by a considerable freedom of occurrence (with respect to nouns and adverbs) which was only partially overlapping for some of them. Thus:

finí kɔ́tɔ́rɔ́	new village
kété kɔ́tɔ́rɔ́	small village
mbi hínga français kété	I know French a little
ála tɛ kété kété kété	they ate a very little bit
angbá kété, ála fáa mbi	a little more (literally, it remains little) and they would have killed me
na pɛkɔ́ ní kété, wále tí babá tí lo akúi	a little later (literally, at back little) and his father's wife died
mɔ mú na ála kóbe kété sí	give them a little food
mú na ála kété ní	give them the small one

The 37,000-word corpus with which I was working presented a rather complex picture, but because I spoke the language, I knew that the corpus had not illustrated all of the uses: for example, that some of these words could function as subjects when followed by the determinant *ní*:

kété ní aɛkɛ nzoní apɛ	the little one is not good
kótá ní aɛkɛ nzoní míngi	the big one is very good

In its present form the *Grammar of Sango* indicates those adjunctives which occurred substantively in the corpus and observes that adjunctives, *as a class,* can serve as subjects of verbal predicates.

Statistics are rarely available for anything besides phoneme frequencies. It would be extremely useful for field linguists to know what uniformity or variety there is in the frequency of different types of linguistic elements and constructions in different languages. Information such as the following gives a researcher some idea of the quantity of material he must collect for certain kinds of studies: Eight hours of extemporaneous tape-recorded conversational English consisted of about 4000 utterances of which about 75 percent were subject-predicate clauses; of the remaining clauses only 210 were subjectless, simple-verb sentences, only 129 again which implied a kind of command. In other words out of 4000 sentencelike constructions there were just 81 which required explanation (Bowman 1963). To produce that many more, one would presumably need another eight hours of conversational material. For phonemic analysis field workers have generally

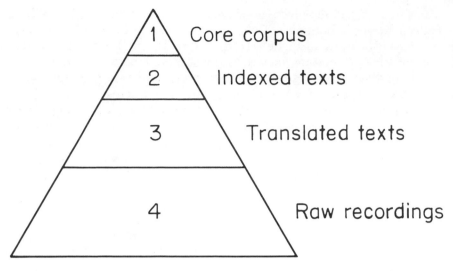

Tapered corpus.

produced creditable results with several hundred words and some connected discourse; some linguists would require about twenty to thirty hours
of connected speech for this purpose (Hoijer 1958:576). The great discrepancy between the recommended size of corpus for phonemicization is undoubtedly due to two factors: what the investigators considered a reasonable goal of phonemicization and what complexities the language
presented for analysis.

We must expect any field worker's corpus to be deficient in some respect.
When one is faced with having to decide between getting more corpus
than one needs or missing something by getting too little the choice must
be in favor of the first alternative: maximizing this error, if such it is, will
minimize the other error about which there is no doubt. In other words,
the greater the corpus, the less the chance of missing something structurally relevant.

Since the size of one's complete corpus is determined in part by how
one intends to use it, there can be different sizes of "subcorpora" according to the various needs, resulting in a "tapered corpus" (Twaddell 1954).
This tapered corpus will actually consist of several corpora processed to
different degrees (see figure above). The first would be the "core corpus"
which is completely analyzed for descriptive purposes. The second would
be a body of texts which are transcribed, translated, and provided with a
lexicon. The third would consist of texts which are not transcribed but are
translated by sentences or groups of sentences. The final corpus would
consist of raw recordings, preferably with either a retelling or a synopsis

in the contact language. If purposes other than linguistic analysis are envisaged for the total corpus, the ratios must be changed. A dictionary project obviously requires a much larger body of translated texts (3) than an archiving project. For the látter Twaddell has recommended the ratios: $(2) = 5 \times (1); (3) = 125 \times (1); (4) = 625 \times (1)$.

Time Required for Field Work

Measuring contact time with the informant, field projects have ranged from a few days to several months, the difference being determined by circumstances; every field linguist would naturally like to spend as long as he could collecting data and analyzing while still in the field. No one argues with the categorical statement that "prolonged contact with the informant is indispensable" (Uhlenbeck 1960:433). Criticizing linguists because they have not had enough time with informants is like condemning shipwrecked sailors for not having provided themselves with food and water. What we can more wisely do is evaluate how much was accomplished in the time a linguist had at his disposal.

We need to discount, first of all, the claims made by linguistically naive people for their own or the accomplishments of others: "It took me only six weeks after my arrival in Africa to learn enough of [Bakuba] to begin teaching classes in the day school." Equally ridiculous is the following advice: "It will take perhaps two months altogether before the grammar is worked out fairly well. These figures are based on working with an informant 4 hours a day and putting in whatever additional study is necessary to keep material organized and up-to-date" (Pittman 1948:154). The error that this writer makes is confounding field work with final analysis: in two months one can learn a great deal about a language, but it will surely take more than two months to extract from the corpus all of the linguistic structure and to write it up in a rigorous fashion.[10] A more realistic statement is the following which is concerned, however, only with the phonemicization of a hitherto unknown language, say, "Martian":

> In a day or so, a well-trained Earth linguist, working with a completely new language, can get the cultural wax out of his ears and begin to hear something that sounds like it might really be a language. Before that, everything is a mumbling buzz. In another ten or so days of hard work, the linguist can get perhaps ninety per cent of what counts in the sound-making and sound-recognizing habits of the language, though his own hearing may not yet be

[10] For example, Mrs. E. O. Lorimer writes that her husband's grammar of Burushaski, based on data collected "in the leisure of one short year" while he was also at work on Shina and Khowar, took four and a half years "of steady desk work to prepare for the press" (E. O. Lorimer 1939:26).

too well trained for the new system. In another hundred days he can get perhaps ninety per cent *of the remainder*. Sometimes it is years before he gets it all (Hockett 1957:48).

No better guide and challenge to the prospective field worker is there than the knowledge of what has been accomplished in given amounts of time. The following information is selected at random from the linguistic literature; some of the workers may have had prior knowledge of cognate languages:

  10 days with an informant: Theodore Stern, A provisional sketch of Sizang (Siyin) Chin, *Asia Major* 10(2):222–278 (1963).
  80 hours (or about 10 days) with an informant in the United States: Samuel E. Martin, *Dagur Mongolian Grammar, Texts, and Lexicon.* 336 pp. 1961.
  One month (four weeks?) in Petrolia, California: Fang-Kuei Li, *Mattole, an Athabaskan Language.* 152 pp. 1930.
  6 weeks in India: Murray B. Emeneau, *Kolami, A Dravidian Language.* 302 pp. 1955.
  11 weeks: Hans Vogt, *The Kalispel Language. An Outline of the Grammar with Texts, Translations, and Dictionary.* 178 pp. 1940.
  12 weeks of ethnographic field work during which time linguistic work was done as a side line: Mary L. and George M. Foster, *Sierra Populuca Speech.* 45 pp. 1948.
  16 weeks (approximately): Norman Balfour Levin, *The Assiniboine Language.* 166 pp. 1964.

Linguistic field work is not easily evaluated even when one has a language description in one's hands. There are two reasons. In the first place, the linguist does not always specify what his field work consisted of: does he simply count the time he was on the field? does he count only the time he worked with the informant? how does he measure a day's, week's, or month's work—does a work-day consist of 8 hours? a work-week of 40 hours? From statements such as the following it is almost impossible to get a good idea of the field linguist's exposure to the language: "My own field work was done in January–February, June–September 1959, a few weeks in April and November of 1960." In the second place, it is difficult to determine to what extent the investigator was equipped with fore-knowledge of the language or its family. Bibliographies are commonly given in the published grammars, but only infrequently are we told how much they contributed to the study. The following account, because it is unusual and rather complete, is cited as an example of the kind of documentation which is needed. The field work covered the period between November to August of the following year:

  The present study was based on taped interviews with informants from 105 villages throughout the Fiji group. The corpus consisted of the Swadesh 200-word list, approximately 200 words used by Capell and Biggs in previous studies, sentences and phrases chosen to illustrate Bauan markers, the pronoun set, 10 sentences used by Milner in his dialect survey, and free discourse, usually an explanation of how either copra or kava is produced and marketed. Some of the items were transcribed with the informant; most were done from the tapes with the help of a Bauan speaker (Schütz 1963:63).

How much one accomplishes in a given amount of time depends on several factors, many of which can be inferred from the subjects which have hitherto been treated, for example, establishing rapport with the community and recruiting an informant. Much depends also on the language itself. Some languages present special problems so recalcitrant that they can be solved only by intensive work with the informant. These are problems of tonal analysis, extreme morphophonemic changes such as one finds in Cherokee, and so on. Other languages can be studied with less dependence on an informant after the collection of a good corpus. In general, advice to the first-timer is this: plan to spend more time in the field than your best plans and judgment lead you to think is adequate.[11]

It might appear that the ideal project would permit one to spend from six months to a year or more in the field after which one would return home to write up one's analyses, but an investigator would do much better work if there were intervals between periods of field work. The value of such interrupted field work has been pointed out by anthropologists (Malinowski, for one [Kaberry 1957:77]) and linguists (Trager 1948).

Organization of Field Work

No plan for a field project was ever devised that did not have to be changed, but without planning, a project will accomplish far less than it ought to. The first thing which must be determined is its primary goal: what can be achieved in the time and with the resources available for the project? This may be a description of the phonology of the language or a sketch of the grammar as compared with another related language or a thorough analysis of the noun derivation and inflection. The primary goal defines and justifies the project, not only to a sponsoring organization (if there is one) but also to the investigator himself. The goal is both a guide and a rule: through the complexity and confusion of living in a foreign society under rustic or rugged circumstances, the field worker can measure his daily or weekly progress.

There also ought to be several secondary goals. For this there are at least two reasons. First, when work toward the primary goal is impossible, one should have other projects which can be pursued in its place. Second,

[11] Even such a highly organized and repetitive project as a vocabulary survey for comparative work requires much time. Morris Swadesh spent from 6 to 12 hours manually transcribing and then machine recording 1000 expressions, that is, words and short phrases (Swadesh 1954).

the tension of single-minded involvement in the primary goal needs to be relieved by other goals which may be less important but have more immediate rewards. Some of these should have nothing to do with one's scholarly or scientific interests: bird watching, geology, photography, collection of children's games. Others can very well be linguistic in nature: spending days observing the language behavior of three-year old children, interviewing people for their opinions about language function or language change, making observations about the mechanisms of language borrowing (where there is a shop in the village one can keep records of how many people come to the shop, where they come from, how long they stay, what they talk about, what languages they use, what they buy).

OBTAINING AND CARING FOR THE CORPUS

5

Knowing what constitutes a good linguistic corpus is certainly a first step to successful field work, but one must also know how to obtain it. The techniques a person uses will determine the nature and quality of what he acquires. It is the purpose of this chapter to discuss these techniques and the way, short of processing the material for analysis, that the corpus must be cared for.

Techniques for Collecting a Corpus

A linguistic corpus is never obtained by a single technique, and no two field workers ever use the same ones. Several techniques are here discussed, with the order of presentation following the order of increasing involvement on the part of the investigator.

1. The corpus-collecting techniques which are least affected by the field linguist's involvement are *eavesdropping* and *selective listening*; the second is just a special form of the first. In them the object is to record whatever

people say to each other or to the field worker without any guidance on the part of the latter, that is, as part of normal social intercourse.

Providing games for children or illustrated magazines for older people is an effective way for getting timid villagers to talk. It may even be necessary to have some food or drink to draw a group together under relaxed conditions. Keeping two pots of coffee on the fire at all times is one of the most effective means of getting the recently pacified monolingual Mura-Pirahá of Brazil to stay long enough for utterances to be recorded. One can also attend social gatherings of a more or less formal nature where speakers engage in long discourses, for example, African "palavers" or legal cases which may last for weeks as people give their testimony, histories and parables are related, and so on. What one does under these circumstances is to record as much as one can for later translation or analysis. The result is not necessarily a great deal of material but a considerable amount of variety in what one collects.[1]

The problem with eavesdropping is twofold. First the material that one records is disconnected and contains little information about the context. Consider these utterances from the notebook of the investigator among the Mura-Pirahá, five months after his arrival in their midst. Below are the English equivalents of his Portuguese glosses:

1. What is your name?
2. Do you want money?
3. Do you eat this?
4. We are going to clean (that is, the land or grass).
5. ants
6. Do you want bread?
7. Yes, I do want some.
8. The otter knows.
9. The coffee is cold immediately.
10. He liked the (chocolate).
11. They ate the bread fast.
12. Are you tired?
13. No, I'm not.
14. Are you sick?
15. No, I'm not.

An informant may find it difficult, if not impossible, to identify such snatches of speech, especially if they are inaccurately transcribed or are incomplete utterances. Secondly, the recording of speech without the knowledge or consent of the speaker may cause resentment. Unless people understand what is being done, they generally are suspicious of having their words recorded.

Selective listening is a very effective technique for collecting many ex-

[1] For an analysis which is based entirely on utterances recorded as heard in conversation see Borgman and Cue 1963.

amples of any particular linguistic element (Nida 1952–1953). All that is involved is deciding first what elements are to be the targets and then listening deliberately for them. A study by this means is best conducted in listening to prolonged discourses: political speeches, folk tales, testimonies at trials (in a folk society). In an experiment conducted with students listening to different sermons in Hartford the following data were collected:

1. The suffix *-ity:* 4 times/in 30 minutes.
   "swept clean of its vulgarity"
   "reveal a reality"
   "until calamity came"
   "in order for independence to have a reality"
2. Verbs in *-ing* form used as attributive of nouns: 6/22.
3. Hortatory expression *let us* . . . : 2/45. But *let me* occurred once and *we've got to* occurred 8 times.

Effective though it may be, selective listening has certain difficulties: (a) It is more difficult to get examples by classes than by items—identifying specific nouns or verbs is more difficult than collecting nouns or verbs in general. (b) The less frequently an item occurs, the more difficult it is to concentrate over a long period of time. (c) Focussing on any item seems to increase the general scope of interest. (d) Becoming interested in content of message leads away from items. (e) Utterances are transformed, leading to uncertainty as to exactly what was said: *while he was cleaning the carburetor* might be heard (interpreted) as *when he was cleaning the carburetor.* (f) Perception of an element may come too late for one to reconstruct enough of the utterance to make a notation worthwhile. The student who was listening for *if* clauses (17/40) obtained utterances like the following:

> *if* . . . *was* . . .
> *if* . . . *were* . . .
> *if* . . . *should* . . .
> *if we are to (infinitive)* . . .

He failed completely to reconstruct the apodosis of any of the sentences. (g) In working on an unknown language, one will also have the problem of wrong identification. For example, having identified the function of the suffix *-ness* (/nɨs/) in English, one might include *keenest* and *alumnus* along with *unwillingness, wickedness,* and *thoroughness.*

2. *Language learning* is another device for collecting a corpus which was discussed in Chapter 4. Its chief value is that it combines several of the techniques discussed in this section.

3. *Nontranslational elicitation.* By "elicitation," of course, is meant "to draw out information from a person," but the term is most often used of the translational technique discussed in Chapter 6 whereby one gets utterances in response to the question: "How do you say . . .?" Here we are concerned with a technique which depends on only a few stimuli from the

field worker. All that he needs to do, unless he is using pictures, is to ask "Tell me about . . . (naming some subject or referring to some incident)" or "Tell me a . . . (giving the name for story, proverb, and so on)"; in the latter instance the field worker will get traditional material and in the former nontraditional. The material thus obtained will be either prose or nonprose. The second will be short, usually unconnected utterances. In this category (nonprose nontranslational elicited material, if one needs a name) would be included such things as personal names, proverbs, riddles, refrains from songs, curses, and prayers. Anything which was sentencelike would fall in this category. That Gbeya names belong here is seen from the following examples: *nam kɔ́ dɛ̌rá ná* "family does not like a crowd," *nam sió d'oŋ* "family retreated," *zɔ́n ŋgay ná* "do not admire male children." In the category of prose would fall connected speech in a monologue or dialogue, regardless of the topic or style of discourse; the principal feature here is length of speech, and connection is implied. Both of these categories are generally covered by the single term "text" and although it would be convenient to have a term to distinguish the first more clearly from the second, tradition will probably reject any neologism.

There is no better way of obtaining a large body of natural speech than by eliciting texts.[2] All that has hitherto been said about a good corpus should make this abundantly clear. Yet we can add one more reason for the importance of texts. If the linguist can train himself to go back to his texts for answers to problems, rather than running to the informant to test a hypothesis, he will not only find the answer to his problem—although perhaps at a little more cost in time and effort—but also learn other things about the language. The explanation for this is simple: until the day when the investigator knows the language as well as his informant does, he will continually be discovering unsuspected things in the texts. Problems should make him "go to the sources," an injunction that every historian learns early in his career. Translational elicitation is the handy-man's do-it-yourself solution.

Texts are recorded in three ways: written by the informant, dictated to the investigator who writes them down, and mechanically recorded.

Texts written by the informant free the field linguist for other work. The use of a text-writing informant also greatly increases the size of one's corpus. In this way Franz Boas obtained 4165 pages (as they finally appeared in publication) of Kwakiutl and Tsimshian texts from two native speakers (White 1963). Informant texts have against them two features: (1) They are imperfect representations of speech; a written account of an episode in one's life or of a folk tale is generally an abbreviated version

---

[2] Yet one scholar feels that ". . . the use of texts has declined in popularity in comparison to 'word-list' eliciting . . ." (Olmsted 1961:309).

of a spoken one. (2) They will need a great deal of editing for omitted words, inconsistencies of spelling, and so on. If these texts are then dictated to the investigator for immediate transcription (or tape recorded for eventual transcription), some of this editing will be cared for. Where the informant uses a traditional script, such as Amharic or Arabic, which does not represent the informant's pronunciation, it will be necessary for the investigator to have this reading. It should be pointed out that spelling inconsistencies, mentioned above as a disadvantage, can also be of some use to the field worker, for they may provide valuable clues to the language's structure (Sapir 1933).

Dictated texts were the principal constituent of linguistic corpora before the invention of the magnetic recorder (for example, Hans Vogt's grammar of Kalispel), and even today they are not obsolete. The great advantage of this technique of corpus collection is that it precludes further transcription, a step which is always required by mechanical recording. The summit of efficiency is demonstrated by the investigator of Jungle Quechua who typed out the texts as her informant lay dictating in his hammock! Usually the effort is more demanding than this, however. Vogt's work will serve as an example. The last 4 of his 11 weeks on the field were spent in taking down tales from one informant, the 85-year-old One-Eyed Tom. Vogt writes:

> [Tom] was almost totally blind and rather deaf, but mentally still alert. . . . As he did not talk or understand English, and also because of his physical handicaps, the contact between him and the investigator was not a very easy one. I had to a large extent depend upon Joe [16-year-old informant], who, in the beginning, helped me by repeating Tom word for word. This did not present a great difficulty for him, as he already knew most of the tales. I took down Joe's translation on the spot, and checked later in the same day both text and translation with him. . . . Most of the material was checked several times (1940:8).

There are some disadvantages to getting texts by dictation: (a) If the language has not been fairly well analyzed at the time of the dictation, the texts will certainly suffer from errors of transcription and segmentation. Voegelin's collection of Shawnee laws, dictated "pretty much word for word," must have had some such weakness, because another Shawnee informant could not make out the sense of the texts ten years later even though the texts were provided with "a sort of lexical gloss for the longer words" by the original informant (Voegelin 1954a). Even when texts are literally translated with the assistance of the informant, they will frequently contain passages which are unintelligible to the investigator (Vogt 1940:8). (b) Like informant texts (that is, those written down by an informant), dictated texts will also tend to be unnatural in some respects. The speech will be more deliberate, for example. An informant dictating a text will also have difficulty in maintaining the proper connection between the separated stretches of speech. The problem here is akin to that of speaking through an interpreter; as a person has to learn this technique, so does he to dictate. However, it may be easier for an informant to dictate some kinds of material (traditional, for one) than it is others. Certain kinds of speech are ruled out entirely, such as extemporaneous conversation.

Mechanical recordings today are synonymous with tape recordings, but the earliest ones were made on phonograph records. These had the disadvantages of being difficult to make on the field and of deteriorating in quality rather quickly, but some remarkable work was accomplished with them. Witness D. M. Beach's *The Phonetics of the Hottentot Language* based on work done in the early thirties. It was the invention of magnetic recording, first in the form of wire, which provided linguistics with a breakthrough in field techniques. Today a field linguist's equipment would be incomplete without a tape recorder. Sarah Gudschinsky makes the strong claim that recordings saved about two years in learning a language by providing repetitions of utterances and data on "higher level" phonology. Tape-recorded material also helps a person to understand better, which in turn accelerates his language learning. Even when one is not learning the language, mechanical recording is extremely important to the collection of a good corpus. It generally provides one with a quantity of natural, varied speech.[3] But the recordings are only as good as the original discourse; their quality is not enhanced by virtue of their being recorded. It has been said that linguistic materials recorded at random are utterly worthless for purposes of linguistic analysis (Voegelin 1950: 299). Therefore all that has been said about a good corpus must be kept in mind *before* the microphone is put before the native speaker.

How much and what the field linguist records is determined by the use to which the recordings are to be put and how much time is available for their study. The linguist who delayed his recording to the last week or even last few days of his field trips, getting only a few short texts as well as repetition of material earlier transcribed on paper, obviously had in mind a purpose which was different from that of language learning: he perhaps wanted to add just enough data to "round out" his description with comments on intonation or syntax (Voegelin 1950:298). Where recordings are

---

[3] Some investigators have reported difficulty in tape recording conversations, but this was not my experience in working with speakers of Sango or Gbeya. All I had to do was set up a situation, assign the participants their roles, and provide them with several topics they could talk about. Roman Jakobson seems to feel that tape-recorded discourses will tend to be less than natural: "When we elicit metalinguistic reactions [referring to language] from our informant we create a less unnatural situation than when forcing him to produce a monologue. For many natives this is a quite unusual or a uniquely ritual form of speech, particularly unusual when addressed to a recording machine and to a foreigner without command of the native's language" (Jakobson 1958:590).

meant to constitute the core corpus, to provide the primary data for language description, it will be advisable to obtain more than what can reasonably be processed. The reason for this is that it is far better to cull out the inferior recordings than to be forced to use just what one has. Recordings may be inferior in several ways: technically (volume too high or too low, mechanical noise, background noise), because of speaker's idiosyncracies (slurring, declamatory style, and so on), because a topic is uninteresting, because length prohibits inclusion as a sample of a single discourse. There are many other reasons why one-fifth of one's recordings, more or less, might be considered inferior to the rest.[4] I will illustrate just the topical consideration. When I was recording Sango speech in Berberati (Central African Republic) I had asked a woman to talk about her work around the house. Very soon after beginning, she launched into a tirade against her "lazy, good-for-nothing husband." As the crowd of women began to laugh, I noticed that they looked at a man seated nearby, who turned out to be the husband. Needless to say, a text such as this could not be played over and over without incurring the disfavor of the man.[5]

Getting people to talk or to talk on certain subjects can be a difficult and frustrating experience. This is where the field linguist's ability to achieve rapport with others must be used; as soon as one feels safe with another person, he also feels free to talk. The linguist who took the 12-year-old Badaga boy to the zoo was acting with this knowledge; whereas the lad had been almost mute before the "sahib," he returned with excited stories to tell to his friends and relatives, particularly of the ostrich which he had never seen before, much of which the linguist was able to record.

There are other devices that one can use, some of which are treated as techniques coordinate with this one on nontranslational elicitation. The field linguist, for example, can ask the informant to tell what he has been doing that day or week; he can ask the informant to explain the use of a certain tool. The presence of a concrete object seems to make talk easier for a frightened informant. This is why pictorial representation, made by

[4] The figure is much higher for my collection of about 40 hours of Sango recordings. Among the 311 transcribed texts only 159 are considered as having the highest priority for further processing in preparation for a volume of readings in Sango. There are 77 rated 2, 21 rated 3, and 54 rated X. Among the latter are texts so scabrous that their inclusion in a publication is ill-advised. There is no reason, of course, why they cannot be used for other purposes. While the question of propriety here is from the viewpoint of the audience for whom these readings are being prepared, one must also consider propriety in terms of the mores of the community being studied. A vulgar text may be narrated in the context of folkloristic storytelling, for example, with women and children around (as with my own Sango tales), but it may be embarrassing to the informant in daylight while sitting in the linguist's study.

[5] This is only one example of many ways that a repetitious use of a tape-recorded text can be embarrassing to people who speak the language. One American Indian informant is reported to have been brought to tears by having to hear her own mistake repeatedly (or what she thought was a mistake) before a group of students.

the informant or furnished by the investigator, often stimulates talk (Aitken 1955):

> The usefulness of either two dimensional stick-men or three dimensional doll-like figures is well illustrated by an experience . . . [in] trying to obtain words from a Salish informant who had not spoken her native language for many years. In response to requests for direct translation of English words, she appeared able to remember scarcely anything; when remembering the most common Salish words, such as those for *tree* or *house,* she spoke only in citation forms. However, as soon as she was presented with stick-men pictures, she gave not only citation forms but also context forms—forms embedded in brief utterances (Voegelin and Robinett 1954:94).

The informant can be asked to describe what he sees, but it is perhaps more effective to leave a well-illustrated book or magazine with a small group of people near a running tape recorder (Hayes 1954; Harris and Voegelin 1953; Yegerlehner 1955).[6] The difficulty with pictorial stimuli, however, is that they may not be understood by preliterates; long periods of silence during which the informant studies the pictures hardly seem to justify the effort when other techniques are available.

Another device is "interactive elicitation." Here the investigator must provide recurrent linguistic stimuli in the contact language or the language being studied. The first form is questioning; texts obtained in this way might be called "interview texts." Assuming that the informant is willing to answer questions, the following could elicit quite a variety of constructions:

> What is this?
> Who made it?
> What is this part called?
> What do you do with it?
> Where did you get the wood? (or other material)
> Where do you put it at night?
> How do you hold it?
> How do you stand when you use it?
> Can a woman (child and so on) use it?
> Can you use it for other things (for example, scooping up excrement)?
> Do you have to sharpen it?
> How do you sharpen it?

The questions here have to do with an African hoe, but questions about people can be equally productive if the social situation permits the interrogation ("Where is he going?" "Why is he walking fast?").

---

[6] The use of pictures has been suggested also as a means of assuring uniformity in linguistic responses, such as in the study of geographical dialects or of sociological correlates of speech. One pictorial handbook is the *Pictorial Linguistic Interview Manual* (also known as *PLIM*) developed for the American Library of Recorded Dialect Studies (Sapon 1957, 1958). Some linguists are not convinced of their usefulness (DeCamp 1959).

The "word-to-text" technique has been suggested for other difficult situations (Voegelin and Robinett 1954:98–99). One first elicits the names of objects and concepts in the area of the informant's competence and then asks him to talk about these things. This technique can hardly produce texts of any length, yet it avoids the difficulties of pure translation and has the value of illustrating the use of words in contexts. The artificiality which it produces can be somewhat overcome by providing the informant with a long list of words to choose from and giving him enough time, a whole day perhaps, to think about the discourse.

4. *Sentence completion.* Another technique for increasing variety in one's corpus and for obtaining parallel utterances is sentence completion. Hitherto it has been used only as a testing device in psychological and anthropological research, but there is so much in its favor that this programmatic discussion seems justified (Rychlak, *et al.,* 1957). The investigator starts with unelicited sentences; the texts are a good source for them. He then eliminates parts of the sentences and asks his informant to add anything he thinks is appropriate. For example, if one took the Gbeya sentence

1. *gan am zɔkaa ná wen kɔ́ mɔ nɛm gboá d'oŋ*
   I didn't see him because I arrived late

and stopped at *kɔ́* (with *wen kɔ́* "affair of . . ." which is used as a connective), he might get the following expressions:

2. *wen kɔ́m ᵖmɔná zaŋ-ré*   because I was home
3. *wen kɑ̃́ ɑ̃́ laŋgà tí*   because he had gone ahead
4. *wen kɔ́ zéré nɛ ʔmɛ̃rám*   because sickness prevented me
5. *wen kɔ́ zéré á ʔmɛ̃rámi*   because it was sickness which prevented me

From these he will learn: that (a) *wen kɔ́* following a clause always precedes a clause and that (b) this second clause is always in the perfective. The second observation can be tested by changing the first clause, resulting in:

6. *gan ném zɔkaa ná wen kɔ́ mɔ nɛ gan ném gbo sɛnɛ̀ ná*
   I won't see him because I won't arrive there.

The change in tense is observed as well as (c) that the original form of the connective has returned: *wen kɔ́ mɔ nɛ* "affair of thing and." It would probably be advisable to postpone the use of this technique until one has acquired some control of the language because of the possibility of mystifying the informants with unrealistic sentence fragments. I doubt, for example, that *gan am zɔkaa ná wen* would get any response whatsoever. Of course, one can not be sure in the early stage of analysis exactly what

the unrealistic segmentations are. If the investigator had identified *gan*
. . . *ná* as the mark of the negative, he might hesitate to stop after *zɔkaa*,
but the following sentence is certainly natural:

gan am zɔkaa zéɛ tɛˈfara nɛ wotóo ɾ̃kɔ́ ŋma wí-ré sɛnɛ̀ ná
I didn't see him yesterday at the place where an automobile struck a person
(literally, I see him yesterday at place and auto struck some person there not).

Care and Handling of Corpus

If the field linguist's corpus is anywhere like the ideal corpus described in Chapter 4, he has an invaluable possession. It will deserve his
utmost attention against destruction or loss. Since the longevity and usefulness of a corpus depends on how it is recorded, we need to consider
the equipment that will be used.

Paper supplies

Linguistic information is recorded on paper or on magnetic tape.
(These are the primary materials; some of the corpus may later be put
on phonographic disks or on microfilm for greater longevity.) Among the
paper supplied I would consider the following to be the minimum:

Pocket-size spiral notebooks
Composition books with sewn backs
3-by-5-inch file slips   ⎱   Be prepared for different sizes
8½-by-11-inch bond paper   ⎰   where metric system is used.

The spiral notebooks are handy for noting down words and phrases caught
on the fly outside the work session. The notes in this form are not permanent, since everything will be checked with the informant and written
down in the permanent notebooks. In Africa I carried mine in the hip
pocket of my shorts (since my upper garment was only a T-shirt). To
protect the notebook from perspiration I had a tailor make a case out
of cushion covering, which was the strongest cloth available at the time,
dividing it at one side for inserting a mechanical lead pencil; the pencil
with its retractable point has obvious advantages. The composition (or
copy) books should be of good quality; one does not want the pages to
become loose or the paper to become brittle with time. I do not recommend loose-leaf paper because of the danger of tearing, although high
quality rag bond is protected against the usual such danger. (A botanist
with extensive field experience under many adverse conditions, H. A.
Gleason, Sr., recommends paper and special binders available from John
C. Moore Corp., Rochester, New York.) The hard back of the composition
books makes it easier to take notes when no table is available. As they are

used, the notebooks will be numbered, as will the pages within them. It is also essential to include the date of the recording (no two dates on one page) and to number the entries 1–n for each page. Hence a reference to 1/5.10 will be read as "Notebook 1, page 5, entry 10." File slips rarely need to be larger than 3 by 5 inches.

Slips should be loose, not prepared in pads; "slipping" (the making of data slips) is by itself too much a drudgery without the additional effort of tearing off pages. If plans are made to cut the slips somewhere in the field, one is advised to use only a press-cutter and to prepare the slips in large quantities. Poorly cut clips greatly decrease efficiency in handling. Because of the uncertainty of having the job well done in the field, it is advisable to take one's supply from the home base. In one large Asian city a paper supplier could not be convinced that slips cut to size were more important than trimming waste. Commercial file dividers are bulky and inadequate for the many divisions one's file demands. One can make his own dividers by cutting white paper stock to size and cutting out whatever dividers one needs.

A little more needs to be said about the value of using high quality paper in the field. Climatic conditions can cause paper to become discolored and, more seriously, to become brittle. In the latter case one is prevented from handling the data as often and as carelessly as one would like. One might see the advantage of using good paper with permanent records but not with temporary notes. The reason that good paper should be used for all documents is that it is all too common for "temporary" records, things which one—with the best of intentions—hopes to redo, to remain the only records of data or analyses! The field worker should therefore treat his corpus with the care of an archivist.

A serious attempt should be made to record as much as possible in duplicate, sending copies to another place for safe keeping at regular intervals.

Typewriters

A typewriter adapted to the needs of the language under investigation can render inestimable service. One should therefore seek to ascertain the phonologic features which might require symbolization on the phonetic or phonemic level before equipping a typewriter for field work. No two manufacturers of typewriters have exactly the same assortment of type characters or styles, but typewriter repair shops can sometimes make up the necessary keyboard from their own stock or by ordering the missing characters. Such work is always more expensive than when it is done at the factory; some manufacturers allow a certain number of free exchanges. Poor workmanship must be avoided when diacritics are to be used. For example, one can make room for two extra keys by using a raised dot (for

TABLE OF DIACRITICS

[ ]	*square brackets:* phonetic notations.
{ }	*braces:* formulas and special symbols, such as the morpheme {Z}.
> <	*greater, lesser:* "becomes," "is derived from," such as Sango *sava* "to be restored to health" < French *ça va?* "How goes it?"
/	*diagonal:* phonemic units, /tayp/ "type"; mark the ends of syntactic units in texts.
*	*asterisk:* generally useful in marking classes of items in texts and lists; traditionally used to mark reconstructed forms in historical linguistics.
˜	*tilde:* nasalization (*ã*), special consonants (*ñ*), "alternates with" (/a ˜ o/).
~ ∞	*similar, infinity:* "alternates with."
+	*plus:* Sango *tála* "of them" < *tí* "of" + *ála* "they."
´ ` ^	*acute, grave, circumflex:* tones, vowel qualities, special consonants, *á, ć, č,* (grave + acute), ↑ (vertical bar + circumflex).
،	*cedilla:* nasalization (*ǫ*), special consonants (*ţ*).
ˇ	*klicka (wedge):* *č.*
ε	*Polish hook:* *ą.*
˘	*breve:* *ă.*
¨	*umlaut:* *ö.*
|	*vertical bar (single parallel):* special units or classes (|Z|), rising pitch (as above).
?	*dotless question mark:* glottal catch; the question mark is made with (.) + (ʔ).
#	*number:* juncture.
→	*forms* ⎫
↗ ↘	*arrow N.E., arrow S.E.* ⎬ : pitch contours.
√	*radical sign:* word roots.

length or for retroflexion: *t·* *ţ*) over a period for a colon and over a comma for a semicolon, but the spacing must be near-perfect. Similarly, a dead key with acute and grave accents is useful for making the wedge (*č*) only if they are properly spaced; the combination does not work on all machines. (A dead key is one which does not make the carriage move. It is convenient to have all diacritics on dead keys, preferably on the right-hand side.) If there are to be many diacritics, one is probably best advised to use pica type instead of elite. Pica has the added advantage of making more legible carbon copies.

Above is a sample of the kinds of special typewriter characters which one may find useful; exactly what the final keyboard looks like depends on the language being studied, the orthography which is chosen, and the major use to which the machine will be put (reading material for the speakers of the language or scientific publications). The uses are only illustrative. In some cases the names may be current for some typewriter companies only.

Several typewriter companies manufacture replaceable, "snap-on" type-bars under different trade names. Their use is in each case fundamentally the same; it involves selecting the type desired, inserting the bar into the

Use of a snap-on type-bar. (*Photograph of "Typit" by permission of Mechanical Enterprises, Inc., Alexandria, Va.*)

type guide, and then striking any key. (See the accompanying plate.) The bar holding the special symbol is then unsnapped and one continues as normally. The use of this device requires the installation of a special type guide (sold separately) which is appropriate to one's machine; the installation is a minor operation for qualified typewriter mechanics. The special symbols are sold individually from stock lists, and specially designed ones are made upon request. In at least some cases it is possible to buy the type unmounted. With the proper tools and skill one can reduce the cost of a set of special symbols by soldering the type to the bars.

The value of any such device is that it eliminates the need of having to hand-letter special symbols in a typewritten text, thus assuring legibility, uniformity, and neatness; it also reduces the chances of overlooking a symbol that one intends to letter-in after the completion of a whole page. The advantages decrease, however, in proportion to the frequency of use per page; it would be better to have the symbol on one's keyboard if one expects more than six or so occurrences per page.

Many people find note taking easier with pencil than with pen, but its disadvantage is that it smudges and fades with wear; but where moisture may make ink illegible, pencil still finds its advocates.

Moisture is clearly one danger which the field worker must be prepared to avoid. In the highlands of Mexico one is bothered by fog coming in through the paneless windows. Elsewhere there is danger from leaking roofs or waterlogged earth floors. Other dangers to paper documents are: mice, which make nests to their convenience with the 3-×-5-inch slips in the files; insects such as cockroaches and termites, especially the latter with their terribly efficient ways; and fire. Against all of these one can only advise the use of watertight tin or galvanized iron boxes, plastic bags, insecticide, and, above all, precaution.

Tape recorders

Recordings on magnetic tape are only as good as the equipment used and the care exercised in their making. Pains should therefore be taken in the purchase and maintenance of all equipment.[7]

The first step is one of investigation. Before any purchases are made one should determine what he hopes to accomplish with his recording equipment and what kind of field conditions he can expect to find. Obviously, an investigator who knows that he will have to walk three days in hilly, tropical territory will not go equipped as one who will travel by plane and train and settle down with AC current. One needs to get information about climatic conditions. Humidity, for example, is hard on certain types of microphones, on tapes, and on machines; wood casings will rot under some conditions, and fungus will work on electrical connections. It is important also to find out where the closest sales and servicing depot is and what makes of recording equipment it specializes in. An excellent piece of equipment will do the investigator no good if he cannot keep it running. Therefore, for some field conditions it might be advisable to purchase a simpler machine, one that is easily repaired.

The purchase of equipment is best done before one leaves for the field in order to make certain of the proper functioning of all components. This can be done only by checking out all mechanical and electrical parts by

[7] The reader is advised to consult works such as the following for more detailed information about the use of tape recorders. Information of a technical nature: Dyar 1959, 1960, 1961, 1962; Merriam 1954; Pickett and Lemcoe 1959. Suggestions for field work (anthropological, ethnomusicological): Karpeles (Ed.), 1958; Polunin 1965. Use of tape recorders in dialect studies: Pierce 1952; Hickerson, *et al.*, 1952; Wilson 1956; Zwirner 1963.

actual use. A manufacturer's guarantee or a dealer's assurance is no good to the field worker somewhere in central Brazil! Inexperience in this point almost cost me several weeks delay (out of a total of six weeks available) because of a poorly soldered connection on a microphone attachment.

The most expensive single unit will be the tape recorder itself. There are several good machines, both domestic and foreign, on the market, but none of them can be bought new at bargain prices. It would be time well spent to make one's own investigation instead of relying on the enthusiastic testimonials of friends and other field workers, remembering that what is good for one project may not be for another. The investigation should include experimenting with the machine, which one either borrows or rents from the dealer. Tape-recorder directories, such as the one produced by Audio Devices, Inc., are useful for this purpose. Almost as important as the make of the machine is the place where it is bought. One should avoid department stores and other establishments which depend on a large volume of business. Instead, one should deal with dealers who sell and service professional equipment. (At such a place, one can often find used, "checked out" professional equipment superior in quality but comparable in price to a "popular" brand.)

Because of the great improvement in the manufacturing of tape recorders in recent years, one can expect satisfactory work from quality portable, that is, battery-operated machines, especially since some of these are adaptable to AC (alternating current) as well. The more versatile machines are naturally preferred to the simpler ones. Their disadvantage is that they are more difficult to repair. The size of the machine is far less important than dealers would have us believe. Although a 6-pound machine is easier to carry than a 12-pound machine is, any machine becomes a burden when carried over long distances. It is unrealistic, moreover, to imagine that the recorder is the only piece of equipment which will be transported. Those same conditions which require foot travel will also require extreme precautions in the shipment of all equipment; therefore porters will be used.

POWER.   The two important sources of power are dry cell batteries and generated current, DC (direct current) or AC. Spring-drive ("wind-up") machines, although once made (for example, by the Amplifier Corporation of America), have been almost entirely superseded by battery-driven ones; some foreign models, however, are still available. Some machines take special batteries which are rechargeable, with the proper equipment, from a main supply (that is, generated current) or motor car battery. The difficulty with such special batteries is that they are sometimes difficult to recharge in the field and that when they are left permanently discharged, they suffer irreparable damage.

Some field workers will find the use of the ordinary flashlight battery

with a D cell giving 1½ volts the most satisfactory because of their availability the world over. (Some machines require two different sizes of batteries, one for the motor drive and one for the amplifier. It would be better
to avoid these.) Foreign makes are not always leak-proof, however, and
one should make certain that they are not left in the recorder's compart-
ment over a long period of time. Since the loss of power can be impercep-
tible, it is important to have some device for measuring the strength of
the batteries before recording. (Some machines have built-in battery
checkers.) It is important that this be done under load, for rested cells
can give the appearance of having more power than they do, and one
cannot guess at how many hours his batteries have been working. A simple
and inexpensive device is made by Shurite, New Haven, Conn. When a
cell is put in position, the light goes on, putting a drain on the cell. If, after
two minutes, the voltmeter still reads something close to 1½ volts, the cell
can be judged serviceable.

The availability of generated power will not eliminate all of the field
worker's problems. He must be prepared for several different kinds of
contingencies. In the first place, he must not assume that all current will
be alternating. In some countries direct current is used. Accurate information must also be obtained concerning the voltage and frequency characteristics of the electric power. The standard specifications for American
units are 110 volts (tending more and more to 120) and 60 cycles, but many
machines have built-in components which can be adjusted to other specifications. Other machines are so constructed that they will not be damaged
when run on 50 cycles and can be equipped with 50-cycle motors and
60-cycle adapter drive spindles. Accessories are also available for adapting
stable current of one type or another to one's needs, such as a step down
transformer for volt reduction or inverter for converting a specific low
voltage (6, 12, 28, or 32 volts DC) to 110 volts 60 cycles AC (as in using
an automobile battery with a recorder).

In some areas the problem may not be so much that of matching up
one's equipment to the available power as in getting a stable current.
Extreme variations can seriously damage machines which are ill-prepared
for them; at the least, they can affect the signal which is recorded on the
tape. Low voltage, for example, will be detected by an erratic or slow-
running tape. Unfortunately many of the effects of variation will not be
discovered until the recordings are played with stable current. A machine
with a high quality synchronous motor is designed to operate without any
difficulty over a range of 105–135 volts, but if the range is from 85–250, as
has been reported in some areas, particularly at the peak hours of power
consumption, one's machine is not protected. AC voltage regulators will
solve some of the problems.

The problem of variation due to diverse voltage and frequency conditions can be partly solved by the use of a 440 cycles per second tuning pipe (musical "A"). The procedure is to record this tone at the beginning and end of each recording, regardless of whether or not one suspects errors. In this way adjustments can be made during the making of copies where laboratory equipment is available. Tapes "tone-labeled" in this way also are more accurately comparable in pitch and tempo. Since they cost only a few cents, one should equip oneself with at least two such tuning pipes.

MAGNETIC HEADS.   The most expensive single unit in most recording machines is the magnetic head. It certainly is the most critical. What one records and what he hears is determined in large measure by this extremely sensitive instrument. Machines in the medium-priced range generally have only two heads, one for erase, which demagnetizes a tape for re-recording, and a record/playback head. (Cheap machines may even have a permanent bar magnet instead of an erase head. When not in function, it faces away from the tape. The obvious danger with this method is that the magnetic field eventually erases the material which is being played. Bar magnets can also lose their magnetism and hence not function as they should.)

The quality of the record/playback head is determined by many factors too detailed to go into here. Among them are the material used and the care exercised in their construction. Some idea of the quality of the head can be obtained from the specifications on the frequency responses; but even these, although not necessarily untruthful, can be misleading. For example, some machines have a high frequency response on playback but not on record. Other machines have fairly reliable specifications when new but drop considerably with age. One of the reasons for this degeneration is that with cheaper heads the gap in the head widens as the tape is passed over it again and again. This is possible, because such a gap is V-shaped and because the tape is covered with microscopic, sandpaper-like pieces of iron oxide. A high quality head has a gap with parallel faces which remain at the same distance from each other. As with any piece of electronic equipment, what is desired is high frequency responses at both ends of the scale, in the lows as well as in the highs. High fidelity is widely recognized for music, but it is also important in linguistic work, for example, in discriminating the fricatives. With a low frequency response one would have great difficulty in differentiating [s š ɬ x ç].

It is the construction of the recording head which determines how many tracks there are. (Some people have tried getting double play out of a reel of tape by recording on both sides!) The figure below illustrates the three types of tracks: full, half, and quarter. The arrows indicate the direction in which the recording is made, either by flipping over the reel (say, taking it from the right-hand side and putting it back on the left) or by recording with the feeder reel on the right-hand side—if the machine permits such

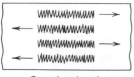
Quarter track

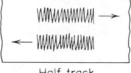
Half track

Full track

a process. Notice that there is or must always be gaps between the recorded signals. Full track heads are becoming uncommon on all but very specialized machines. Quarter-track machines are not recommended, because with them head quality and line-up are much more critical. It is also reported that they lose high frequencies. In any case the smaller portables are not yet equipped with quarter-track heads. A field worker is advised against using more than one track; by recording only on one track he will find it much easier to edit the texts and make copies of them. Admittedly, the investigator saves money in using the two tracks, since he needs half as much tape, and he has less material to carry around, but these considerations, I can testify from personal experience, are less important than those involved in editing. It should also be remembered that heads should be conveniently accessible for cleaning (more will be said about this below), and that they must be adequately shielded. Inadequate shielding can result in hum on playback and noise in recording.

SPEED.   The speed with which the tape is fed over the head is important for two reasons. First, it determines how much recording can be obtained on one track from the beginning to the end of the tape. Obviously, if, in one second, 7½ inches pass over the head, a 1200-foot reel of tape will be used up more quickly than if the tape moved only at 1⅞ inches per second. In the second place, it determines the quality of the recording: the faster the speed, the higher the fidelity. With one machine, for example, the frequency response at 7½ ips is around 50–20,000 cycles per second whereas at 15⁄16 ips it drops to 50–4,500 cycles per second. Another advantage of 7½, incidentally, is that it makes the editing of tapes easier, because there is twice as much tape for each word as there would be with 3¾. For critical recordings therefore—as when one is studying certain phonological problems aurally or with a sound spectrograph— one should record at the highest possible speed.

Recording time, mentioned under the first point above, is affected also by how much tape there is on a reel. This in turn is determined by the size of the reel and by the thickness of the tape itself. A 7-inch reel of half-mil tape, giving 2400 feet, played at 15⁄16 ips, will give 8½ hours of uninterrupted recording. If one is concerned with recording the whole of some ritual, the advantage of this combination is uncontested.

Having taken these factors of speed and time under serious consideration, one should be able to make an intelligent estimate concerning his tape needs for his project. It is certain that he should plan on taking his whole supply with him, for in many places the price of tapes is exorbitantly high, even three times as high as what one has been accustomed to paying; it is also very likely that it will be impossible to purchase quality tapes in some parts of the world.

CONTROLS. The minimum controls for any machine include record, play, rewind (going back to original position), fast forward, and stop. The record control should be so designed that one does not accidentally start recording (and thereby erasing something old) instead of playing. This is best effected by requiring the use of two hands in the manipulation of two buttons or levers. A pause control is useful too, because it permits a halt in recording without disconnecting the heads, thereby eliminating loud clicks on the tape.

Of considerable importance to the linguist, something dealers cannot fully appreciate, is ease of manipulating the controls. Because the field linguist will be spending hours upon hours at playing, stopping, and backtracking, he must be able to work the machine as easily as possible, preferably with the left hand. I find the single-knob arrangement of Machine 4 shown in the figure on page 94 I the best; one can find the knob after transscribing without looking. The others require going from one button to another. With Machine 1 it was too easy to press "rewind" or "fast forward" instead of "stop" when one was not looking at the controls. The stop control with Machine 3 is effected by simply raising the tabs: to play, one pushes down. Some problems can be eliminated by a foot pedal, such as typists use with dictating machines, which controls play and reverse. Not all machines are adapted for this accessory, however, although some portables can be rigged up for its use. A foot control speeds up transcription of texts to a great degree if one is using a typewriter for this purpose. The one problem I had with a foot control was with pick-up: I could not resume at precisely the place I had left off.

There are two other important things about machine control which the prospective buyer should consider. The first is the efficiency of rewind stoppage. By this is meant the ability to get back to a certain point quickly and accurately: there should be no gradual acceleration or looping of the tape; the machine should be able to go back ½ inch as well as 3 inches. Machine 2 was very inefficient in this respect because of its sliding control. The recorder should also make it possible to pick up right from the point where one left off, that is, without having lost several syllables or words during acceleration. It is an awful nuisance to be obliged to rewind after every halt during transcription. Machine 4 was bad in this respect, because it had no take-up device which maintained tension on the tape. In "stop" position, pressure was released from the tape and it fell from its groove, and not until tension was built up again on "play" was the recording

FOUR TYPES OF MACHINE CONTROLS

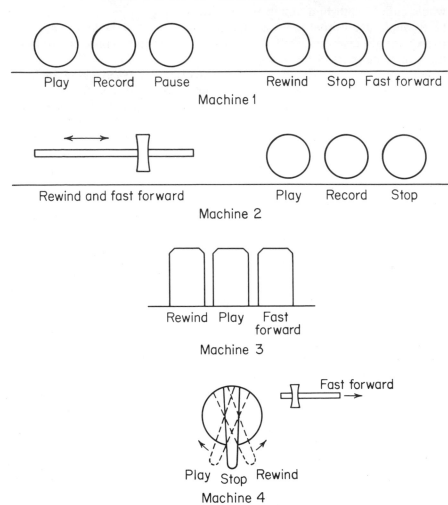

intelligible. All of this implies good braking, that is, stopping smoothly in any direction, either during recording or playing.

In addition to ease of operation, mechanical controls should also be tested for noise. This can be done by playing a tape of some unknown language and making a serious attempt at transcribing a short portion of it. At "stop" and "play" a noisy machine will distract the attention of the listener. This feature is increasingly noticeable as one listens to shorter and shorter bits.

INDICATORS.   A counter indicator, which does not indicate footage but approximate place on a tape, is useful. More important are record level indicators. These indicate the volume at which the recording is being made, a factor which figures significantly in the quality of a recording. The best device is the vu (volume unit) type meter. It is critical and reliable. It is identified by the numerated calibrations between which an arrow fluctuates during recording. Less reliable are the magic eye, where the faces of two colored areas approach each other proportionate to the volume, and the level meter, where an arrow fluctuates between a black and red area. One should also remember, in connection with volume, that the tolerance for overloading is lower with cheaper machines.

Microphones

Microphones generally come with medium-priced tape recorders, but only in a few cases are they equal to the demands of scientific work. It therefore pays to be suspicious of all such microphones until their specifications are checked out, for a microphone, like the lens of a camera, determines what is going to be recorded.

The type of microphone most strongly recommended for linguistic field work is dynamic and directional with low impedance. Dynamic characterizes the kind of pick-up element which converts the sound waves into electrical energy. A dynamic type mike is superior to one with carbon, crystal, or ceramic elements; condenser mikes are good but too expensive for the average field project. The better dynamic mikes (for they are available in cheap versions also) are rugged and comparatively resistant to environmental influence. The reason that crystal mikes are not recommended is that they are easily damaged by heat, shock, and humidity. They will inevitably suffer from at least one of these. Directional characterizes the pick-up pattern. A directional or cardioid mike as it is also called is more sensitive to the sound it is pointed at than to what comes from other directions; other sound will be picked up, but it will be fainter. Other pick-up patterns are: omnidirectional, which picks up sound from all directions; bidirectional or cosine, which picks up sound from the front and back, but is very insensitive to the extreme right and left; and hyperdirectional whose other characteristics do not make it useful for most field work at all. These sentences too briefly characterize the various types of microphones. A close study of the instructions and specifications which accompany a microphone will be rewarding.

Low impedance refers to the electrical characteristics of the microphone. Its chief value is that it reduces the amount of hum that will be picked up by the mike lines from stray magnetic fields such as are in the earth and elsewhere. This is especially important when the microphone is extended over some distance (say, 200 feet) from the recording machine. (If one has a high impedance mike, he must therefore remember that he should reduce the distance from machine to mike as much as possible,

certainly never over 20 feet.) What is most important is that the microphone be matched to the recording machine, low for low, high for high.
Home-type recorders usually have a high impedance input, but some
dealers will install a low impedance input upon request. If this is not
possible, one must have a matching transformer. This is a unit to which is
wired a low impedance input and a high impedance output; the first is
connected to the low impedance mike by some kind of multiple con-
nector, and the second is simply inserted into the recording machine's
input. (It is equally important to match impedances when making copies
of a tape on a second machine. It is not enough that they can be connected
with a patch cord; their impedances must be matched or, as with microphones, a transformer must be used.) Cable to extend the distance from
the mike to the machine must, of course, match the demands of low impedance. When the tape recorder is run by generated power and one wants
to increase the distance between the source of power and the machine,
it is wise to use a cable with number 16 wire. This is especially important
when DC is used because of the higher power drain over long distances.

When buying a microphone to replace the one with which the tape
recorder was provided, one should make certain that it is compatible with
the machine. One will not get the quality he wants when the microphone
is not matched to the machine's characteristics. It will be sufficient to alert
the microphone dealer of the use to which the unit will be put.

Several other items should be included in the microphone kit: (a) A
leather case with soft inner lining is needed to protect the mike from dust
and dirt. Protection from excessive humidity is assured only by a metal
container. It is unwise to put the mike into a plastic bag because of the
danger of the condensation of moisture inside the bag itself. (b) Equipment is also needed for the support of the mike. It should, of course, never
be placed on an object which carries sound. If the mike is put on a table,
it should at least be supported by a cushion of cloth or other soft material.
A plastic or foam-rubber sponge, for example, can have a trough cut into
it for the placement of the mike. Lavelier attachments for hanging a mike
around the neck of an informant are convenient. One can also obtain
collapsible tripod microphone stands, adaptors for using a standard
camera tripod, clamps for attaching mikes to convenient objects. (c) A
wind shield (or screen) can be made or purchased. It is placed just behind
the mike to prevent the recording of the humming or whistling of breezes
which the undiscriminating mike "hears" but one's own ears do not hear.

Magnetic tape

Magnetic tape chosen for the field project should have high fidelity
and durability under much use and bad environmental conditions. The
quality is determined by the material out of which the backing is made,

the thickness of the backing, and the oxide coating. The three common base materials in the United States are cellulose acetate (popularly called "plastic base"), polyvinyl chloride (used by 3-M Inc. in its "Tenzar" brand) and polyester (made by Dupont as "Mylar"). Acetate should be avoided, because it tends to break easily, to become brittle with age, and

Length in feet

Reel Size	1.5 Mil	1 Mil	.5 Tensilized	.5 mil Tensilized	100' of tape plays minutes at I.P.S.	
3"	150'	–	300'	600'	10-2/3	1-7/8
5"	600'	900'	1200'	1800'	5-1/3	3-3/4
7"	1200'	1800'	2400'	3600'	2-2/3	7-1/2

Length in meters

Reel Size	1.5 Mil	1 Mil	.5 Tensilized	.5 Tensilized	30 meters of tape plays minutes at CM per second
3"	45m	–	90m	180m	10-2/3 at 4.75
5"	180m	270m	360m	540m	5-1/3 at 9.5
7"	360m	540m	730m	1100m	2-2/3 at 19

Playing time of recording tape measured in feet and meters. The thickness of the tape is measured in mils.

under certain climatic conditions to become sticky. Although triacetate tape is better than the older diacetate, it still is somewhat inferior to Mylar-backed kinds. The most common thicknesses are 1.5 mils (0.0015 inch), 1 mil (extra or long play), and 0.5 mil (double play), but even thinner tapes are manufactured. With thinner tape one can get more footage per reel, hence more recording time, but the thinner tapes are more liable to stretching and print-through, that is, the picking up of signals by contiguous sections of tape when wound up on the reel. The safest choice would be 1.5 mils.

The kind of oxide coating a tape has will determine the frequency response it gets. Inferior grades of oxide coating can also damage the heads. Coating grades are not so frequently published on the cardboard reel containers, and one will have to ask about this matter. A safe rule to follow is that no inexpensive tape can be expected to have grade A coating. One should also remember that some manufacturers produce a variety of grades of tape; one should therefore not rely on a product because of the name of its manufacturer. Since specifications for tape are available, one should ask for them and buy accordingly. Incidentally, one is assured more uniformity of quality if one avoids splicing different brands of tape together.

Tape can be bought on reels suited to one's machine, but if the reel size is less than seven inches, one should consider buying the larger reels of tape and putting it on smaller reels. In some cases one can thus considerably reduce the cost of his tape. Before buying tape—even before buying a recording machine—one should also consider the adaptability of various sizes of reels to one's machine. It is obvious that a larger turntable will take a smaller reel but not vice versa; what is less obvious is the fact that some turntables are not entirely flat. A hollowed-out basin will therefore not accept larger reels at all.

Accessories for the proper use of tape should include the following items:

Tape splicer and splicing tape
Leader tape
Empty reels
Adhesive labels, felt-tipped pens
Plastic clips
Stop watch

The splicer is a tool for cutting diagonally through two tapes which are to be joined and then, with a different blade, for trimming the top and bottom edges to remove the edges of the splicing tape. Special splicing tape must be used to prevent the adhesive material from becoming attached to the adjacent layers of tape. One should never use packaging tape for splicing; some of it has reportedly attacked the glue between the laminations of the heads. Leader tape should be spliced on to the ends of all recording tape, which tend to fray with use. (In any case, the first two feet of any new reel should be cut off because of the adhesive tape which was used to fix down the end.) Leader tape, which comes in different colors, can also be used to separate different texts on a reel and in other ways identify certain sections. They can be marked with a felt-tipped pen. (Special leaderlike tape can also be marked with low frequency [for example, 40 cycles] tones for text identification; see Krones, Sawyer, and Grosjean 1964). Empty reels are useful for the temporary storage of sections of tapes. One might want to invest in reels of different colors, coded for different categories. Metal reels as well as plastic ones are available. Adhesive labels and/or felt-tipped pens are needed to mark the reels. This is a necessary precaution, because reels never seem to stay in their original containers. The labels are preferable because they can be easily replaced. Plastic clips are useful for keeping the tape from unwinding. This can be a nuisance when the reel is not fully loaded with tape. A stop watch is valuable at the editing stage for timing the texts. Its cost is generally proportionate to the maximum time it can measure.

Recording procedures

The highest quality of recording equipment is no substitute for poor recording procedures. Any one of a number of details can ruin what could have been an extremely good and valuable recording.

VOLUME.   One should determine what is the best recording volume for the machine and microphone being used under different conditions: the volume will be different if all the recordings are made outside instead of within an office with plastered walls. In general, the volume should be rather low in the recording to reduce the level of background noises; recording at a high volume also overloads the machine and produces distortion. Once the speaker has begun, it may be necessary to lower or raise the volume, depending on whether he is talking unexpectedly loudly or softly, but the operator should avoid a constant modulation of the volume, for this makes for nonuniform recordings.

ACOUSTICS.   The physical environment figures importantly in the recording of sound. Dominant echoes must be particularly avoided. These will be produced in enclosed spaces with little or no furnishings; a metal roof under most circumstances will also create some echo effects. To avoid producing a recording which sounds as if it were made in a barrel, it is important to make certain that there is some damping in the immediate vicinity of the recording; damping is the absorption of sound waves. Blankets, cushions, and even a wall of persons are suitable for this purpose. One of the best recording rooms in the field from this point of view is the grass-roofed house. In any case, one should test-record at different places in a room. The differences can be astounding.

NOISE.   One should make certain that there is no internal noise, which is produced by the machine itself. (Much of this is assured by having the proper equipment in good running condition.) Ideally, one should test-play the tapes on another machine, because one can become accustomed to some low-level squeaks and hums of one's own machine. A sample recording air mailed to a colleague from time to time can be used for this purpose. However, if the recording head of either machine is not properly aligned, the playback will be far from satisfactory. External noises cannot be eliminated if they are of the accidental type (like the crowing of a rooster), but some can certainly be avoided. Such continuous noise as that of a running engine (as from a power-generator) or continuous automobile traffic are extremely detrimental to recording. One must also see to the possibility of paper rustling, chairs scraping, doors slamming, and so on.

MICROPHONE PLACEMENT.   The microphone should be around 8 inches from the speaker's mouth and about 4 to 6 inches down. In this way one avoids recording strong aspiration as puffs or pops. On the other hand, if one is having difficulty in distinguishing aspirated or glottalized sounds from others, putting the microphone in the direct path of sound might be helpful.

I would also advise giving a summary description of the recording process to the informants and bystanders. This includes explaining the signals for "start" and "stop" as well as the function of the microphone, the recording level indicator, the turning of the tape, the reason for having to glance at the machine occasionally. I have found that if their curiosity was satisfied at the outset, they were much more cooperative as audience or participants. This kind of explanation will avoid one of the frustrating things about recording, having the speaker start when the operator is still talking or when the machine has not yet been put on "record." It is both embarrassing and wasteful to have to redo a recording.

As a final check before the recording, the operator of a machine might ask himself these questions:

Are the tape spools on properly?
Is the tape properly threaded?
Is the volume at the right setting?
Is this virgin tape or am I recording over something?
Is there enough empty space between this and the last recording?
Is there enough power in the batteries?
Was the "record" button pressed and not "play"?

Maintenance of equipment

The proper selection of one's equipment is extremely important, but the proper maintenance of one's equipment is equally important. The field worker alone must be responsible for the condition of his tools. There is much that he can do even though he may not be an electronics specialist.

The first step is to know one's machine. One should make an arrangement with the dealer from whom the equipment is being bought to be shown how to clean the machine and replace those parts which usually go out first: belts, idlers, tubes, transistors (if they are the plug-in type). One may have to pay the dealer for the hour or so which is needed, but this is money well spent.

Once the machine is put to use, it should be regularly cleaned. With methanol or isopropyl alcohol (or lighter fluid in an emergency) one should clean the heads, the capstan, and pressure roller—in other words, everything which comes in direct contact with the tape. The cleaning fluid should be applied with a cue-tip, cotton on a stick. No metal should be used for fear of scratching the head. In the same way one should clean the idlers, since a collection of oil can make the rubber slip. Once a week or before any critical job, one should also demagnetize the parts which come in contact with the tape. This is done with a special unit which is powered by an AC supply. The facing edge of the demagnetizer should be covered with a plastic or electric tape so as to avoid scratching the magnetic head. The demagnetizer should be turned on about two feet away from the machine (to avoid inducing magnetization on the head) and brought in to the machine slowly and in a direct line. Without directly touching the parts, the demagnetizer is moved in several directions and then finally drawn away before being turned off. One must make certain that tape recordings are not lying around in the vicinity when demagnetization is done.

One should also be equipped with spare parts and tools. Here are some suggestions:

Rubber belts
Springs
Critical screws and bolts
Fuses
Replaceable tubes or transistors
Rubber idlers
Pressure roller and screw
Factory service manual (difficult to obtain but valuable)
Patch cords and adapters
Adapters for foreign type outlets
Allen wrenches
Miniature screwdrivers
Phillips screwdrivers

In addition to the factory service manual, one is advised to purchase a Sams Service Manual (Howard W. Sams and Co., Indianapolis, Ind.) which is appropriate for one's machine and which can be purchased from the dealer. Written for professionals, these manuals often give information which is not found in the factory manuals.

Many problems can be avoided by careful handling and storage of equipment. Even before going to the field, if a great deal of humidity and heat are to be expected, one should have his recorder "tropicalized." An antifungus material is brushed or sprayed on those parts where fungus can induce poor connections or even break connections. It is common, for example, for fungus to attack rosin-core solder. This work can be done at the dealer's or, upon request, by the manufacturer. On his own, the prospective field worker can rub liquid silicone on the outside of wood or leather-covered equipment to prevent the development of fungus.

All equipment must be protected against shock, dust, and moisture as much as possible. Dust, for example, is extremely detrimental to a machine when it gets into "oilite" (porous bronze) bearings. For some conditions one should construct a special padded crate for the recording machine. This precaution preserved my own machine from harm even though it was stored in the back of a pickup, along with the rest of the baggage, and was driven over hundreds of miles of bumpy, dusty African roads. Tapes are best protected in some ferrous container whose edges can be sealed with waterproof tape. Some will find it too expensive to put each reel in a metal can. They should therefore use a suitable chest in which several reels can be stored and transported. In areas of high humidity it is advisable to put a desiccant into the tape container; this precaution is especially important with any tapes that have been handled, for it is these which are most susceptible to the development of fungus. The storage material should always be impervious to stray magnetic fields. Many a tape has been completely erased from inadequate protection. Another protective device is the use of weather-proof packing material which can be obtained from commercial packing establishments. This consists of a bag having one layer of Kraft paper, one of aluminum foil, and one of vinyl. The open edge is sealed shut by simply running a hot iron over it.

Some technicians recommend against the storing of tightly-wound tapes for several years, believing that print-through may develop. If they are correct, one should not wind tapes at the highest play-back speed. In any case, it is advisable to rewind tapes every few years to avoid print-through. The tapes which deserve the greatest care are the masters or originals; these should be used for no other purpose than making copies.

Text processing

The usefulness of any collection of recordings depends to a great extent on the thoroughness with which it is catalogued, yet one of the most common sins of field workers is procrastination, saying "I'll make a notation later on."[8] Each reel of tape should be numbered and each text identified by topic and speaker. This is the least that one should be satisfied with; more complete cataloguing will always repay itself several times.

The cataloguing of my Sango texts will serve as an example. My first attempt at getting predetermined information about the speaker and the recording failed, because I tried to fill out forms which I had duplicated for this purpose. Under the strain and confusion of getting people to talk, making a good recording, and leaving on good relations with the speakers, I often failed to complete the forms. More successful was a new technique: I attached to the tape recorder the list of topics I wanted to cover and

---

[8] In a well-executed field project an investigator will also keep records of such things as: place names, distances measured in miles, kilometers, or by hours of travel (by foot, horseback, boat and so on), names of people (with their titles or offices) who rendered some service or from whom information was obtained, conditions under which work was done. Many people have found that these records are kept most easily by jotting the information down during the day and then summarizing everything in a daily journal. A carbon copy of these daily reports should be mailed away for safekeeping. Some people combine field reports and letter-writing in "diary letters" (Boas, for one; see Yampolsky 1958), but the two can also be used complementarily.

TEXT DATA

[1]Code **N4/29** [2]Master **12. 1. 3** [3]Topic **Anecdote about fishing**

[4]Date **6/21/62** [5]Place of recording **Berberati**

[6]Speaker's name **Doungoulou Gabriel** [7]Language **Gbaya**

[8]Sex **M** [9]Age **14** [10]Married **O** [11]Birthplace **Gamboula**

[12]Languages of parents: Father **Kaka** Mother **Gbaya/Berberati**

[13]Knowledge of other languages **Sango, French, Gbaya, Kaka (a little)**

[14]Religion: Prot. **+** Cath. ___ Other _____ [15]Occupation(s) **student in Cours Moyen**

[16]Where and how Sango was learned **in Bossangoa, at 12 years of age**

_____ [17]Reads Sango **+** [18]Writes Sango _____

[19]Amount of education in French **Cours Moyen**

[20]Conditions of recording **in classroom**

[21]Time **6.35** [22]Number of words _____ [23]French words _____

Evaluation: [24]Recording **good**

[25]Topic **fairly interesting**

[26]Speaker's voice **good, but quite high**

[27]Other features _____

[28]Recommended transcribing: Early ___ Late **+**

[29]Noteable linguistic features **says 'après' a lot, class laughed when he said 'ensuite'**

[30]Other comments _____

Sango project 1962

interviewed the speaker either at the beginning or at the end of the session. This informaion was then recorded at the time of the tape editing. Since the original recordings were on five-inch reels on both sides, I made a copy of the master set on seven-inch reels, using only one side. (One should never use master tapes for repeated hearing in any case.) This operation consisted also of adding leader tape to both ends, to prevent tearing of the recordings, and between the texts for easier location of the texts. While the texts were being copied, I filled out for each one the form illustrated above. The topics have the following significance: (1) It had already been decided to classify texts as to whether they were Anecdotes, Conversations, Fables, Interviews, and Narratives, in addition to material from Radio Centrafrique and Letters: N4/35 would be read "Narrative, Reel 4, 35th text of this category." (2) Since the master tapes contained unclassified material, they were identified by number and side: 12.2.9 would be "Reel 12, side 2, text 9." (7) "Language" referred to the native language of the speaker (since Sango is a lingua franca). (17) and (18) were answered with (+) or (0). (21) Each text was timed with a stop-watch: 5.00 would be "five minutes." (22) and (23) were never used. (28) was to guide the selection of texts which should have priority for transcription. Since the copying was done with the loud-speaker on, it was possible from time to time to make observations about various linguistic features.

The next step in the processing of texts is transcription; without it a recording constitutes just raw material. Transcribing should generally be done with the assistance of a native speaker, because anything short of native control of the language will make transcriptions a long and tedious task. One linguist reported that after months of intense and careful work on recordings of a Chadic language, he learned that there were errors on the average of one for every ten words. He had the good fortune of checking the transcription with the original speaker. Had he used a different speaker, the average might have been higher, for people have difficulty in identifying things in the speech of others. (Even the original speaker can fail to understand his own recordings. This is presumably the reason why experienced field workers emphasize the importance of transcribing soon after the recording while the material is still "warm.") However, an assistant other than the original speaker should be used when the latter refuses to allow the investigator to write down what was said and insists on substantially editing the text. Such an informant can make transcription an extremely slow and painful experience.

If the transcription is done early in the field work, that is, before much analysis has been achieved, it is good advice to transcribe and then analyze, transcribe and then analyze again. The reason for this procedure is that the more one knows about a language, the easier transcription becomes. The simplest procedure is to play back the recording, waiting until the informant gives the signal to stop or stopping wherever there is a marked pause, and having the informant repeat what he had said on the tape. One can write down this deliberate utterance or else record it on a second machine which runs continually at slow speed. It is often possible to transcribe from this dictation recording even without the assistance of the informant. The value of this second recording lies also in the fact that it records the informant's comments on his discourse, changes suggested by him, and so on. In fact, it is good practice to encourage the informant to "change" ("criticize," "comment on," "improve," call it what one will) the utterances, if this can be done without unduly slowing down the transcription.

Transcription is a long and incredibly laborious chore. The simple redictation of 2 hours of conversational text in Dakota took approximately 5 hours (Stark 1962). Careful records of the transcription of my Sango texts show that at least 22 hours were spent on each hour of recording. Half of this time was used by a native speaker who transcribed in longhand and the other half by myself; my own part was to check for verbal accuracy (scribal errors) and identify the most interesting phonetic variations. We were not, however, writing tone or using a narrow transcription. The assistant's average covered a period of 5 months, during which time he worked 40–48 hours a week. A trained linguist might produce more in 11 hours than he did, but certainly only at short periods of time; the strain of concentration quickly leads to a point of diminishing returns.

The transcription of a text should have a considerable amount of space for subsequent corrections; there should be ample margins and space between the lines. Some field workers have used composition notebooks for their texts, leaving the page opposite the transcription for observations of all types.[9] Before typing up an extensive collection of texts, the field worker is advised to duplicate a good supply of forms with places for coded information at the top and numbered lines at the side. The text mentioned above was entered in this way:

Subject __Anecdote about fishing__ Code __N29__ Page __1__(__4__)

The number within parentheses indicates the total number of typewritten pages. The lines are numbered at the right side, rather close to the edge of the paper. There is plenty of "editorial space" with wide margins and triple spacing for the lines.

---

[9] For other suggestions concerning *text establishment* see Preston 1946 and C. F. Voegelin 1953, 1954*a*.

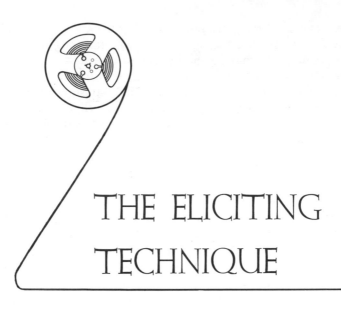

THE ELICITING
TECHNIQUE

6

It is purposeful eliciting as much as analytical or linguistic virtuosity which makes it possible for an investigator to attack a language
he has never before studied and to come up in a short time with a description that accounts for a large body of facts, if not all linguistically significant ones. To the layman the linguist's success is truly phenomenal. What
the layman does not realize is that the success is due to a skill which has
been developed by much practice. This is not apparent as the linguist
works with the informant, now asking for a certain noun, now for an apparently unrelated sentence, and now again for the meaning of a form
which was previously obtained. But there is a reason behind everything
he does. We now want to make explicit what is only implicit in his methodology.

The Nature of Eliciting

Several factors make eliciting distinct from every other technique
used in linguistic research: (a) The utterances obtained in elicitation are
short, generally not longer than a single sentence, and usually out of context. They may be related to other utterances which have a linguistic or

nonlinguistic context, but they bear no real or logical relationship to each other. (b) The elicitation is motivated toward analysis of some aspect of the linguistic system. All the utterances have value only insofar as they contribute to enlightening the investigator concerning this system. (c) Finally, eliciting is defined by the intimate human relations established between the investigator and his informant that affect the nature of the data which are obtained and their interpretation.

The Work Session

Elicitation as a technique for corpus collection and language analysis will be most successful if properly *scheduled*. This involves work sessions in appropriate environments with informants for prearranged periods of time. This is not to say that eliciting cannot be done under other circumstances. Because one helpful Mazatec, for example, hardly ever left her store, the investigators of this language had to sit behind the counter with her and pose their questions only when she was not busy with her customers (E. V. Pike 1958:61). But another investigator working on a Canadian Athapaskan language made the mistake of trying to get verb paradigms from his informant after a long day of hunting together. He obtained very little on that occasion, and what there was contained many errors; the informant obviously did not have his heart in the work: either he was tired or he considered the time and place inappropriate for such work.

The *place* for the work sessions should be to the greatest advantage of both the investigator and the informant. This means a place with adequate lighting and good acoustics without too many distractions and where the language files are accessible. The latter are quite important, because there is frequent need to consult the lexical or grammatical files in the course of elicitation. Privacy may be important to some field workers. But one must beware of the danger of alienating oneself from the community by a reclusive manner.

A field worker must further make certain that he does not put a strain on his informant by isolating him within a room whose interior may be very strange to him; the researcher should therefore try to determine what are the distracting features of the environment and either eliminate them or satisfy the informant's curiosity about them. By taking some time out regularly with an unsophisticated informant to introduce him to the oddities of our own material culture, the investigator also wins his appreciation and heightens his interest in the work sessions.

It will be to the advantage of the investigator to have a regular *time* for the work sessions. There are no prescriptions concerning the most fruitful hours: Pike's 5 A.M. session and my own post-lunch session were at unlikely hours, but they were both successful under the circumstances. What is more important than the hour of the day is the amount of time spent with the informant. If for any reason the work sessions must be protracted, it is essential that the investigator interrupt them with major breaks, for example, by getting up, walking about, and changing place. Even during a 45 to 60-minute period of work, it is advisable to change one's approach, pace of work, and so on. It is remarkable how much is accomplished with a yawn, for example, and "Say, I wonder what caused that dog to bark so much last night? It kept me awake for quite a while." After the informant has had a chance to make his remark, he is led back to work with "Let's see now . . . I was asking you how to say . . ." The boredom has been broken, and the investigator may even have thought of a more ingenious way to get what he wanted.

Two extremes must be avoided in the work sessions. The first is working at a breakneck speed, and the second is dawdling over analysis. Both of these err in leaving the informant at the periphery of the investigation, and both of them produce disinterest in the informant. There is, besides, hardly ever any justification for pell-mell investigations, because it is not so much the quantity of material that is important as the quality. If the neophyte feels that he is not accomplishing enough during a work session, he should be reminded that analytical elicitation is always slow moving. Under most circumstances 20 to 30 utterances can be considered normal for an hour's work.

Finally, we must remember that the informant is a human being whose feelings deserve the same attention as ours. A work session should therefore never begin abruptly. It should begin with an appropriate amount of time in the social amenities. The informant should be treated as if he were doing the investigator a great favor in coming once again to his help. Proper attention should also be given to his comfort, such as what he is sitting on, exposure to cold or direct sunlight, and other factors.

Where does eliciting start? About what is the investigator to get information? These are questions which the neophyte addresses himself before and even after he has collected a list of nouns and other odds and ends. The initial thrill of coming in contact with an exotic language has somewhat worn off, and he asks himself: "What now?" How he proceeds depends on how much he already knows about the structure of the language. The elicitation techniques will be either "scheduled" or "analytical."

Scheduled Elicitation

Scheduled elicitation starts with relative or complete ignorance about the language under investigation, but it proceeds from a knowledge of what can be expected in language universally.[1] One will expect to find, for example, two major classes of words which will very closely compare with our own nouns and verbs. One may be surprised to find in some languages that nouns are affixed with some of the morphemes which generally accompany "verb" stems or that other "nouns," like some Wiyot kinship terms, are really verbs. For example, *kučk-* "grandmother," *kučkad-* subordinative theme, *kučkadihy-* subjunctive theme, *kúčkadihyam* "your deceased grandmother" (Teeter 1964:38; see also Suttles 1965:160–161 for Halkomelem). But even here the distinctions between "nouns" and "verbs" will be maintained. He will also find many utterances which are identified as "sentences" and which consist of a "subject" or "actor" part and a "predicate" part, a language universal which generative grammarians symbolize as S $\longrightarrow$ NP + VP (Sentence is to be rewritten as Noun-phrase + Verb-phrase). One will also find some words which are modifiable, others which are modifying, and still others which are neither modifiable nor modifying (such as various types of connectives). When it comes to phonology, a list of assumptions might well run up to 100. For example: ". . . a language never has a greater number of phonemic contrasts in the vowels of unstressed syllables than it has in stressed syllables"; "extensive voiced-voiceless neutralization in a language takes place most commonly in final position and never inter-vocalically" (Ferguson 1963:42–43); and ". . . the frequency of any C_1C_2 would be a function of the difference between C_1 and C_2 with both extreme similarity and extreme difference tending to be avoided" (Saporta 1963:52).

One should prepare himself with as much explicit information about the languages of the proposed field of study as possible. There is published material of some kind on every language family of the world. However, very little of this is immediately usable in field work. There is therefore a desperate need for "standard elicitation instruments" ("schedules" or

---

[1] In view of the function of common-sense understanding of what is possible in human speech in language-structure discovery, it is surprising to read that "The student of an entirely new language will have to throw off all his prepossessions about language, and start with a clean slate. The sounds, constructions, and meanings of different languages are not the same: to get an easy command of a foreign language one must learn to ignore the features of any and all other languages, especially of one's own" (Bloomfield 1942:1).

Imagination and daring will probably figure prominently in the establishment of a set of language universals, but one should not imagine that he can predict language structure on the basis of cultural traits. Yet the claim is made that because "sexual functions of man and woman . . . [seem to] have their counterpart in linguistic forms possessing similar functions," one can hypothesize that "verb symbolizes woman" and "noun symbolizes man." It would follow "that (1) verb-based languages symbolize matricentered cultures and (2) noun-based languages symbolize patricentered cultures. . . . If a society is centered about females . . . there should be a comparable clustering of the linguistic elements about the verb and/or greater verb complexity and enhancement" (Altshuler 1956:106).

"protocols") for specific areas of the world. These would consist of the following: lists of noncultural and cultural words, some in isolation and some in context, sentences for eliciting the most characteristic features of grammar (like the ergative construction of Iranian languages or the "definite noun" of West African languages) as well as a text (as in answer to the question "How is palm wine prepared?").

Occasionally one will be able to find an appropriate research guide of the type produced by A. Capell for Australian languages (Capell 1945; see also 1952, 1962). It discusses the kinds of sounds one may expect to find, general and characteristic vocabulary (for example, "current of river or sea," "cooliban," "kookaburra," "hairbelt"), and sentences which will elicit particular features of the grammar (such as, "I hit him once," "I hit him hard," "I kept hitting him," "I hit him often"). Most often, however, one will be fortunate if he finds only word-, stem- or affix-lists or questionnaires of one type or another in the personal possession of investigators. See also Cohen 1950–1951.

The following list of word-lists and research guides, undoubtedly far from complete, may be useful. Since word-lists are passed around among linguists rather informally, it is difficult to be certain who deserves being credited with original authorship. (A word-list designed for world-wide use is to be found in the appendix.)

Africa
West Africa Languages Survey Word-List (Joseph E. Greenberg).
International African Institute Questionnaires (used in connection with the Linguistic Survey of the Northern Bantu Borderland and the *Handbook of African Languages*).
List of Words, Phrases, and Sentences for a Survey of African Languages (William E. Welmers).

India. See Grierson 1903–1928.

Malayo-Polynesia
Tri-Institutional Pacific Program (TRIPP) Linguistic Questionnaire (William C. Sturtevant and George W. Grace), as used, for example, in Dyen 1962.

New Guinea
A Manual for Eliciting and Recording New Guinea Linguistic Materials (S. A. Wurm 1959, ms.). Also Bee and Pence 1962.

Philippines
Lexical Check List for Philippine Languages (Harold C. Conklin for the Human Relations Area Files, 1951).

Western Hemisphere
Check List for Uto-Aztecan Comparative Data (Summer Institute of Linguistics).

The predecessors of the elicitation instruments were the "phrase books" of merchants, missionaries, and colonial administrators of the last 150 years. That they went out of style particularly in the U.S.A., whereas directed interviewing became intensive in the other social sciences, can only be explained by the desire of modern linguists to avoid the determinism of the categories of their own languages. But there is no need to go to extremes: using our knowledge of the best studied languages of an area, we can certainly produce elicitation instruments of great usefulness.

One can create his own questionnaire, and it would be advisable to do so. Some words of counsel are in order: (a) Make certain that the number of sentences is large enough. One will probably need as many as 400 for most languages. (b) There should be different sentences (located at different places in the list) for eliciting each grammatical feature. The purpose of scattering the sentences is to give greater freedom to the informant in the construction of the responses. (c) Each grammatical construction should be elicited with different lexical items: "I told him to go" and "my father is going to tell his brother to come," both elicit a verb ("go" or "come") in a construction which is dependent on another verb ("told" and "is going to tell"). (d) Each word should occur in as many different contexts as possible: such as "he entered the house," "they repaired the roof," "the house is burning," and others. The reason for this repetition is that it facilitates analysis of the material when there is no informant available. (e) Prepare the questionnaire in two or three languages to take advantage of polyglot informants: for example, in the Central African Republic it would be foolish not to have French and Sango equivalents for each entry. (f) It would be useful to have an index of each item, lexical or grammatical, which is included in the questionnaire. One of its values is that it serves as a check on the number of occurrences of each item as well as its various contexts. One characteristic that the questionnaire need *not* have is extremely simple sentences. Since simple sentences are so often (i) uninteresting, (ii) repetitive in some measure, and (iii) increase the size of the questionnaire, it is rather advisable to put as much as possible into each utterance. "Two men repaired the roof" could elicit the following: "roof," "repair," "men," "two," "plural," some tense or aspect indicator, noun determinant, objectival use of a noun which is usually in construction with another noun (that is, Gbeya *zúa* "the roof" instead of *zu-tuwa* "roof of house").

One of the limitations of such instruments is that there is no way of eliciting features which are always embedded in larger-than-sentence contexts, such as the consecutive verb prefixes of Kikuyu and other sentence-linking devices in languages. Moreover, the instrument can be only as good as the sources on which it is based. For example, although C. M. Doke's grammar of Zulu does not indicate it, this language does use the verb *-dlula* "pass" in making comparisons in a manner typical of so many other African languages. One would be misled by Doke if he did not try to get comparative constructions which might have "pass" in them, such as "I know things pass him" = "I know more than he does."

Analytical Elicitation

Analytical elicitation, in contrast with scheduled elicitation, always begins with data in the language being studied. The linguistic datum, whatever its size might be, stimulates investigation in a particular direction:

(a) There may be a need to get more examples of a morpheme or a particular construction. Thus, if someone studying English had discovered the apparently anomalous use of *were* (which had been previously found only with plural subjects) in the expression *if I were President I would . . .*, he would try to get *if I were Mayor I would, if I were Senator I would.* (He might elicit in this direction under the assumption that there was some connection between a prominent personage and the form of the verb. He would soon discover that this was not so.)

(b) Analytical elicitation can also be considered a probing device, comparable in some ways to open-ended questions in interviewing (such as "Could you tell me more about that?" "Could you explain that a little more?"). The investigator does not know the significance of what he has, but he uses it to acquire further information, some of which he hopes will prove valuable. If we had the Nyanja expression *wandipangila cakudya* and the meaning identified as "she has fixed food for me," we should like to answer the following questions at least: What part marks the subject? What is the word for "food," for "fix," for "me"? How is the completed action expressed? More grammatical structure may be revealed by this expression than we at the moment imagine, but we begin by giving it a good shake to see where the "seams" are to be found. That is the first task, to discover the pieces and the points at which they are joined. So one elicits for expressions like the following:

> she bought food
> she bought maize
> she bought me food
> she bought us food
> he has fixed food for me
> they have fixed food for me
> she has not fixed food for me
> she is about to fix food for me
> she fixed food for me (referring to yesterday)

In this way one determines the meaning and function of the Nyanja pieces:

w	+	a	+	ndi	+	pangila	+	cakudya
third person, singular		marker of completed aspect		first person, singular		to prepare food		food

The elicitation did not, however, reveal breaks in *pang-ila* and *ca-kudya*; these would eventually be revealed only by the careful comparison of verblike and nounlike words. Further analysis would reveal breaks in *il-a* and *ku-dya*.

(c) Elicitation is also experimental in nature. An experiment serves to test the relationship between classes of units by controlling one set and rigorously replacing (or modifying) another. For example, if in addition to the Nyanja utterance above we also had *wakupangila cakudya* "she has fixed you (sg.) food" and *wamupangila cakudya* "she has fixed him food," we should guess that whatever the other person markers would be, they would occur in the slot *wa——pangila*. On the basis of this hypothesis we ask for "she has fixed us food," and we indeed get *watipangila*. Looked at in this way, elicitation is a technique for proving whether one's analysis is valid.

(d) The final use of elicitation, in the determination of meaning, will be taken up in connection with field lexicography in Chapter 9.

There may be another use of elicitation, although I do not know to what extent it has figured in the experience of field workers. It seems that even in a large data-collecting project where analysis was going to be postponed until later, there should be some spot-checking of the grammar, rather deep probes at various points in the corpus, somewhat in the way an archeologist may sink trial-trenches at various points at a dig site. Such exploratory elicitation might reveal areas of the language which would need more copious documentation or it might lead the investigator to reschedule his project in some practical manner.

There is more than one way to get information from an informant. Which eliciting technique one uses will be determined by at least three factors: the stage of the investigation a person finds himself in, the kind of data he is working on (as well as the purpose of the analysis), and the aptitudes of the informants.[2] In general the first of the following techniques is most serviceable, but this does not mean that it is always the most advisable.

---

[2] Implied in this sentence is the influence of one's approach to linguistic analysis (one's theory) on field work. Field workers of both tagmemic and generative persuasions have reported in conversation and correspondence that the problems they worked on and the way they handled these problems were conditioned by the linguistic models they operated with. We should hope that they will discuss this matter in print. A beginning has already been made: see Hale 1965.

1. *Reverse translation elicitation.*[3] This is the technique implied above in working out a preliminary analysis of the Nyanja expression. The procedure is that of starting with forms in the contact language and having them translated into the target language. (The term is restricted by the addition of "reverse" to contrast it with other uses of translation in linguistic field work.) What should be noticed in particular about this method of obtaining information is that it is not the ordinary kind of stimulus for a linguistic response. The ordinary kind is illustrated by the question "Where are you going?" which would elicit "Out for a walk," or "Oh, down to the corner for a package of cigarettes," or innumerable other utterances which would be appropriate, some said in all seriousness, others humorously, but all normal in the language of the respondent. This is not necessarily the case with reverse translation. Here the stimulus gets back a response which is a more or less correctly mirrored image of itself.

There is an ambiguity with this technique that cannot be resolved. The investigator both wants and fears the reflection of his stimulus in the response. He wants it, because it will help him to decipher the response (as in assuming that *wandipangila cakudya* somewhere will have a marker for "third person singular" and perhaps "feminine"). He fears it, because of the danger that the response will be determined by the stimulus in the contact language. But is the danger so great that this technique should be eschewed? [4] Certainly not. With proper precautions, some of which are mentioned here and others in Chapter 7, the possibility of error can be kept to a minimum.

Another difficulty with this type of elicitation is that it cannot anticipate what is of grammatical importance in the language (unless the investigator has prior acquaintance with it or a similar language). For example, one will quickly discover in Hindi the construction known as ergative. In this and related languages sentences in the past tense having transitive verbs and direct objects are formally different (and are called ergative) from the same sentences in another tense or with intransitive verbs. The ergative is seen in example 2 below where the form of the noun for "boy" is different from what it is in 1. Notice also that whereas in 1 the subject and verb agree, in 2 it is the object and verb which agree. Examples 3–6 illustrate agreement with a transitive verb; its stem is irregular:

---

[3] Others call it simply translation eliciting or shared morpheme eliciting (C. F. and F. M. Voegelin 1957:2–3).

[4] L. Bloomfield is one field worker who is supposed to have done so. According to Voegelin, Bloomfield "preferred being corrected, when he made an error as a child-like speaker of Menomini, to asking a direct question on how do you say so-and-so to a bilingual Menomini—for fear of obtaining a false analogy. During the three summers Bloomfield and I recorded Ojibwa texts together at Linguistic Institutes, he never once asked a 'how do you say' question. . . ." (Voegelin 1960:204).

1. *lərka   lərki   dekhta hæ*
   boy   girl   seeing

The boy sees the girl.

2. *lərke ne lərki dekhi.*		The boy saw the girl.
3. *lərka jata hæ.*		The boy goes.
4. *lərki jati hæ.*		The girl goes.
5. *lərka gəya.*		The boy went.
6. *lərki gəi.*		The girl went.

But in this language there are a few intransitive verbs which take the ergative construction and a few transitive verbs which do not take the ergative. Unless these anomalies occurred in the corpus, the investigator would have no way of knowing that they occurred at all, nor would he be able to elicit information to learn about them. And in Idoma, a language spoken in Nigeria, there is a subjunctive—rather unusual in West Africa—which was discovered only after the study of the language was far advanced. The reason is that the forms which make up the subjunctive differ subtly only by the tones of their subject pronouns from the indicative affirmative and negative. Moreover, they occur in intricate syntactic constructions, not the kind that an investigator is likely to invent independently (Armstrong 1963).

2. *Substitution elicitation.* Working either in the contact language, and using reverse translation, or in the language being studied, one elicits a considerable amount of information by manipulating linguistic elements within frames. (It can also be called the "paradigmatic" or "frame and substitution" technique.) This has already been partly illustrated with an utterance in the Nyanja language. Here is an even clearer illustration of its usefulness. Having already observed that various elements in a sentence are in agreement with nouns, we are eager to discover precisely what these elements are and how the agreement is realized. We are particularly interested in getting examples of agreement in unelicited sentences; and when we have them, we use them to the fullest extent. Thus, having obtained the pair of sentences *Mazila onse ndi abwino?* "Are the eggs good?" and *Ena ndi abwino* "Some are good," we ask: What would happen if we substituted *cimanga* "corn," *zinthu* "things," *nyama* "meat," and *cakudya* "food" for *mazila* "eggs"? And this is what we get:

Cimanga conse ndi cabwino?	*Cina ndi cabwino.*
Is all the corn good?	Some is good.
Zinthu zonse ndi zabwino?	*Zina ndi zabwino.*
Are all the things good?	Some are good.
Nyama yonse ndi yabwino?	*Ina ndi yabwino.*
Is all the meat good?	Some is good.
Cakudya conse ndi cabwino?	*Cina ndi cabwino.*
Is all the food good?	Some is good.

This technique can also be used in ascertaining the limits of distribution of an element. Having obtained in English *that's a girlish thing to do,* one can experiment with replacing *girl* with other words. Thus, one gets *childish, bullish,* and *piggish,* but not *cattish* and *ladyish.* There might be some doubt about *mannish* and *boyish* in this sentence, however. As any speaker of English can testify, there are some *–ish* constructions which seem to be perfectly normal, others which would be outlandish, and still others about which no certain opinion could be given. This kind of indecision must be expected in speakers of other languages as well.

In phonological studies substitution is used in several ways. In all of them particular environments are used as frames through which to run a set of phones. One can, for example, in this way learn that in Gbeya certain sounds like [l b d g] never occur following a nasalized vowel. If we put [bã] and [da] to an informant, we will get [baⁿda], and if we put [bã] and [la] to him, we will get [bãr̃ã], where the intervocalic consonant is a nasalized voiced lateral flap. Even more useful is substitution in those languages where morphemes, particularly those of content words (noun-like and verblike), are primarily monosyllabic. Many field workers have been able to guess at the existence of words by simply adding consonants and vowels together in the ways which are permitted by the language (Lugg 1952). Thus, in Sango we get *lá* "sun," *lé* "seed," *li* "head," *lo* "third person singular pronoun," *lɔ* "to gather up," and *lú* "to plant." The only vowel not represented is ɛ and we would obtain it if we went on to disyllabic words, namely *lɛkɛ* "to fix." With an imaginative informant one can even go on to experimentation with disyllables. When one is in need of words of certain phonemic shapes for working out the rules for certain morphophonemic changes or when one wants to enlarge his lexicon when full meanings are still not terribly important (for example, to have a large variety of different kinds of words for substitution elicitation), this device for discovering words can be quite practical.[5] However, one must realize that the informant may fail to recognize perfectly good words which are given out of context and in random sequence.

It is with substitution elicitation that the investigator finds himself asking "Can you say . . . ?" In theory there is nothing wrong with this manner of obtaining information. The error comes in the practice. In the first place, since the field worker will be making an attempt to say something in a language which he only partially controls, he must be fairly certain that he is correctly articulating the form; if he is still having great difficulties with the phonology, he should depend less on this technique for checking forms. It may be necessary sometimes to give the informant

---

[5] In some societies there are games, as among the Thai, where children vie at thinking up words (that is, those already in the language) when their turn comes up (Haas 1957).

an idea what it is one is trying to say: "When a person wants to find out who stole his food, can he say . . . ?" When using this procedure, one must be aware of the possibility of the informant's rejecting or accepting the utterance on the basis of a meaning different from the one intended by the investigator. For example, if one were to ask a Kikuyu, "Can you say *maretoa mare manana*?" the answer will be an unequivocal affirmative. He would take the expression to mean "the names are eight" or "there are eight names." Now if the investigator had been working on the various demonstratives and their concord with nouns, he might have intended the phrase to mean "those eight names," but it cannot mean this. One must always know to what his informant is saying yes or no. Furthermore, if his answer is no, he should be asked to correct the expression. This procedure will not only validate his response but also provide additional information.

3. *Corrective elicitation.* When an investigator knows what linguistic elements he is dealing with but does not know how they function, he will often find it advantageous to put constructions to the informant for correction. Some of these will by accident be correct, and others will be hopelessly incorrect. How the informant restructures them (what the new construction is) and what he observes as he does this may contribute valuable clues to the analyst. This was done, in working on Ata clause-marking particles. One such problem was to distinguish between the functions of *ka* and *ko*. It turns out that *ko* marks a subordinate clause to which it is phonologically bound, meaning something like "if, when." In the following examples the first three were excerpted from tape-recorded texts, and of the a–b paired sentences the first were put to the informant by the investigator, the second were his corrections:

1. *Madoqot ka qigqodok to homoy* "Using it to plant rice is bad" (literally "bad the plant the rice")
2. *Pila ka imboli sikan?* "How much did it cost to buy that?" ("how-much the buy that")
3. *Soqoyoq ka inautan* "There is the mountain" ("there the mountain")
4a. *Nakalogon si Boyboy ka tanoq*
4b. *Nakalogon si Boyboy to tanoq* "Boyboy was able to lift the earth" ("able-to-lift the Boyboy the earth")
5a. *Baagad ka mananoy kid ogquliq*
5b. *Baagad ko mananoy kid ogquliq* "Never mind if we're late in returning" ("never-mind if slow we-now return")
6a. *Woy nowgbayadi ka ogquliq kid*
6b. *Woy nowgbayadi ko ogquliq kid* "Wait until we get back before you pay them" ("before you-pay if return we-now")

4. *Ancillary elicitation.* This technique is used particularly with texts and is especially recommended when analysis has to be done away from the field. In going over his texts, a person may find, for example, several

score occurrences of the first and third person singular substitutes but none of the first and second person plural. What he must do, therefore, is to "ring some changes" on those morphological and syntactic constructions which seem to him of significance. Likewise, he elicits from the informant supporting sentences, more sentences of the kind that are found in the text. We can illustrate this procedure by using the first sentence from a Gbeya text of ethnographic nature, one relating to marriage customs. It is freely translated as follows: "While he (the young man) is doing the bride-work, he cannot sleep with the girl for whom he is doing the bride-work." In literal translation:

tɛ	ꞌ	*wesé - kɔfɛ*	*nã*	*ã*	*dɛ́i,*	*nɛ*	*gan ã*	*rɛ́m*
body	day	in-law	and	he	do	and	not he	can

ɔ	*ín*	*kóoi*	*nã*	*ã*	*dɛ́*	*kɔfɛ́ai*	*ná.*
sleep	with	the girl	and	he	do	the in-law	not

This literal translation is possible only because the language has now been fully described. A field worker whose principal task was the collection of texts would hardly be able to get all this information, although he might get the Gbeya words for "sleep," "girl," "bride-work," "be able," and "he." In any case, ancillary elicitation stimulated by this sentence would include sentences like the following:

1. While he is working, he cannot eat.
2. While he is building a house, he cannot go hunting.
3. When he eats, he sits on the ground.
4. When he goes hunting, he takes five men with him.
5. He cannot speak to the girl for whom he is doing bride-work.
6. He cannot eat the animal which he killed.
7. He is afraid of the man whose gun he stole.
8. He is doing the bride-work for the girl.
9. He slept with the girl for whom he was working.
10. During the time that he was working for the girl, he slept with her.

If these sentences were obtained by reverse translation, the investigator would have an experience that is very common. He would find that instead of other occurrences of *wesé* + noun where the English has a temporal dependent clause, there are other ways of expressing this idea, such as *wesé nã ã dɛ́ tuwa* (literally "day and he do house") or *bã́ ã́ dɛ tuwa* both of which translate "when he builds a house." But such variation must not be considered unfortunate. Variety is what we want in the corpus. It is only unnatural sentences that we are trying to avoid. And since these elicited sentences cluster around the text sentences, the probability of naturalness is rather high. To assure this naturalness the investigator needs only to keep the informant thinking about the text: "Here you said . . . So how would you say . . . ?"

Another practical point to bear in mind is the necessity of cross-referencing to the texts all material that one obtains by ancillary elicitation. Without such identification one might later assume that a particular utterance could occur in isolation whereas it was originally given by the informant with another utterance clearly in mind. For example, a person eliciting on the basis of a Kikuyu narrative text may get utterances with the verbal prefix *ke-*, because its function is to mark sequential action. But such an isolated instance of *ke-* could not be interpreted as meaning that *ke-* was normal outside of a particular linguistic context.

5. *Paraphrasing.* For the purpose of linguistic field work paraphrasing can be simply defined as "saying the same thing in a different way." What it seeks to do is collect a set of sentences which are related by a common meaning and by sharing the fundamental lexical items. How much one succeeds depends in part on how similar the investigator wants the sentences to be and how well he can train the informant in paraphrasing. At a later stage in his analysis an investigator might want the maximum of rigor (especially if he is interested in a generative description; see Chapter 9). However, if he is at the stage when he is concerned most with getting a well varied corpus, he can be satisfied with almost any degree of paraphrasing. The kind of results he will obtain can be illustrated by the following variations of the sentence used above, assuming for the moment that English is the target language: *While he is building a house, he cannot go hunting.*

1. *During the time that he builds a house, he cannot go hunting.*
2. *While engaged in house-building, he cannot go hunting.*
3. *House-building prevents him from going hunting.*
4. *He cannot go hunting while building a house.*
5. *He is unable to go hunting while building a house.*
6. *Because he is building a house, he cannot go hunting.*
7. *Hunting and house-building cannot be done at the same time.*
8. *He cannot build a house and go hunting at the same time.*

The chief value of this technique is that it is likely to bring to the investigator's attention syntactic structures of which he is entirely unaware. Moreover, because the lexical items remain more or less constant, he is freed from having to determine the lexical meanings of new words and can focus his attention on structural matters. Moreover, if there are complex morphophonemic changes in the language, these somewhat controlled sentences permit him to view the changes with greater accuracy.

6. *Covert elicitation.* From time to time the investigator may find it productive to stimulate his informant in less structured ways than those already described. Thus, should the investigator be working on Gbeya interrogative sentences, he might say—almost to himself—*zaŋám yŭm* "my stomach hurts" and then wait for the informant to say something. The response might be *ge a dé mé ge ndé* "What ails you?" or *dɛà ré ge*

"What in the world?" or *yŭm dɔ́ka wéndé* "Does it hurt much?" In any case, the investigator obtains the kind of utterance he sought to elicit (a query) and one which is linguistically and socio-culturally relevant. Similarly, one can mutter certain words or phrases under one's breath, ostensibly ignoring the informant, when there is some question about its accuracy or when one wonders if similar forms occur in the language. Thus, if one would like to know if there is a form [ba] as well as [pa], he might play with the syllables in a pensive sort of way: [pa pa], [ba ba], [pa ba].

Each elicitation procedure has its own particular limitations, and some are more dangerous than others because of the greater possibility of influencing the informant's responses. Inherent in them all is one difficulty which deserves special attention. It can be called the assembly-line syndrome. What happens is that the investigator becomes preoccupied with, say, a set of sentences he is trying to elicit, and because of this preoccupation he fails to see the significance of new material which turns up in the elicitation session. What the field worker must learn to develop is presence of mind; the ability to see significant grammatical features when they arise. An adept field worker immediately records them and does a superficial investigation. This takes skill. A person must have a pretty good idea of the structure of the data he has already obtained. And he must not become so engrossed in every new feature that he can never follow the original analytical problem through to the end. This presence of mind and the ability to take advantage of the unforeseen linguistic datum are among the most distinctive characteristics of the proficient field linguist. Another person may know what to do with data when these face him alone at the study table, but the agile investigator responds imaginatively and creatively to every new stimulus.

Steps in Eliciting

Part of the success of the field worker depends on how he conducts his informant sessions. By taking certain precautions and following certain rules he can assure himself efficiency in his sessions and accuracy in his data. For the sake of convenience we shall assume here that we are primarily concerned with grammatical analysis.

PREPARATION.   There is no more important ingredient of successful work sessions than preparation. The investigator must have done his homework well if he expects the session to be profitable. This involves, first of all, an analysis of the data which have already been obtained. The analyst should have filed away the preceding day's material. The next thing is to select several matters as targets for investigation. One is sufficient, but it is not uncommon for a person to discover during the work session that he has been barking up the wrong tree. Unless he can switch over to some other problem with ease, the investigator· runs the risk of embarrassing himself before the informant or of floundering around for the remainder of the hour. If the investigator lapses into silence and stares at his material, the informant's attention is soon lost and it might not be regained in what time remains in the session. One should therefore observe the rule to refrain from doing in the presence of one's informant what one could have done before the session.

The problem to which the investigator addresses himself should be conceived in the clearest of terms. At times it is of considerable value to state both the problem and the manner one proposes to attack it in the form of a memorandum to oneself. This memorandum should not be looked upon lightly, for it constitutes a form of preliminary description.

This is an appropriate place to emphasize the importance of periodic progress reports or sketches of various aspects of the grammar. A rigorous handling of the data one has reveals how much is already known and what remains to be learned. (Almost as valuable as discursive write-ups are charts, diagrams, formulaic statements, and lists of problems which deserve attention.) The linguistic neophyte finds this hard to believe, since he contends that any description during the early stages of analysis will have only the remotest resemblance to the final one; to him these experiments at description are nothing but a waste of time. But Malinowski, who contributed so much to ethnographic field work, underlined the value of in-the-field preliminary analysis. His own published account of the *kula* institution among the Trobriand Islanders was the ninth description. Undoubtedly Malinowski not only came to understand the institution better as he wrote each description of it but also became more skillful in executing the description. The field is where the linguist serves his apprenticeship. If he hopes to be a competent journeyman, he must take advantage of the opportunities that are his.

The next step is to work out the forms in the contact language which will elicit the desired ones in the target language. The linguist must thoroughly understand the strengths and limitations of this elicitation instrument. If he does not, he will be unprepared for the informant's difficulties and unexpected responses. In other words, one's expectation awareness must always be as high as possible. It would be difficult to imagine all of the problematic areas. We can only suggest a few examples. The concept of "being" is difficult in elicitation, because one generally does not understand all that is implied by the English verb *be* in its various forms: to illustrate, *he is a teacher* (identification), *he is over there* (location), *he is sick* (characteristic). A more serious mistake is to misunderstand the function of nouns in such expressions as "grass house," "smoke-hole," or "honey bee." Taking these nouns for adjectives or modifiers in an attempt to get equivalent forms in the target language can only lead to puzzlement on the part of the informant. Notice also the subtle differences between the following two sentences: "If they ate that, they would die" and "Had they eaten that, they would have died." The investigator might think that in going from the first to the second he was changing only the time, future in the first and past in the second. But there is also a significant syntactic change in the protasis:

> If they ate: If they had eaten
> Had they eaten

When the investigator is not conscious of differences like this one, he cannot expect his informant to perceive them either. The result will surely be distortion somewhere.

Should there be any possibility of the informant's not understanding an expression, it is a wise practice to prepare him for it. This can sometimes be done covertly. For example, a person may want to get the expression "short leg," but he realizes that if it is understood as referring to a human leg, it will sound somewhat bizarre. The investigator therefore asks the informant what he calls a table leg (pointing to it). If the same word is used of table as well as human leg, the investigator can then proceed to ask for "short (that is, table) leg." This ability to visualize a speech context is one of the marks of a skillful field linguist.

This procedure might be included in a more general one which perhaps deserves being set apart as another step in elicitation: *enlighten the informant.* (See also Chapter 3.) The informant will cooperate more intelligently and efficiently if he understands what it is the investigator is doing. How much he can be told depends on how much he can understand. In addition, an informant who knows that the investigator is concerned with a special problem is more likely to be sympathetic and cooperative. There are times, on the other hand, when the investigator wants the informant to be thinking of something else to prevent his distorting the data. And it is always important to have him think about the content of expressions rather than the form.

Because the investigator can always expect a number of the expressions in his elicitation instrument to be unusable, he should come prepared with a good variety of material, far more than he could possibly use in one session. For example, if one is doing nothing more than testing nouns in a sentence frame in objectival position, it would be foolish to select only "I bought a ———." He might end up with sentences like:

> I bought a hoe.
> I bought a knife.
> I bought a shirt.
> I bought a house.

But in a society where everyone built his own house, buying a house would be culturally irrelevant. At times like these it is surprising how difficult it is to think of alternate forms to use.

In this connection it should be added that for certain types of grammatical studies it is good to have a list of concrete, well-understood, and simple words. Most of the words in the Lexicostatical Word-List (in the appendix) will serve for this purpose, but one should add to them words which have a very high cultural relevance, like "rice" or "manioc" in some areas. One reason for increasing the size of the list is that some words may have to be temporarily set aside, because they pose phonological difficulties which the investigator cannot yet cope with. One class of words which might also be ignored for a time consists of kinship terms. It is a naive field worker indeed who asks for "my brother went to town" if he is not prepared first of all to conduct a preliminary investigation of kinship.

In preparing for the work session, the investigator should balance off the unknown against the known. It is not generally prudent to elicit for completely new information. At times this is unavoidable, but when the investigator has advanced to a point where he is examining matters of grammatical significance, he should not overload his stimulus sentences with lexical items or other features he has not yet encountered. If, for example, he is primarily interested in studying the aspectual categories of verbs, he should not ask for "his wife went to town to buy corn," unless he has (i) obtained the nouns for "wife," "town," and "corn"; (ii) examined the possession of nouns; and (iii) learned what formal relation exists between a primary verb ("went") and one dependent on it ("to buy").

BUILD-UP.   Until a person has become fairly familiar with the language—that is, until he can transcribe rather rapidly and accurately—it would be advisable to build up toward the sentence that he desires to get. For example, if he wanted to elicit a sentence for "his wife went to town to buy corn," he might first elicit for "his wife," "his wife went to town," and "his wife bought corn." Such a procedure is certainly preferable to having the informant repeat a sentence several times until the investigator is satisfied that he has recorded it accurately. It also serves to alert the investigator to problems which might exist in the sentence. When words in a language look like these from Kutenai, an American Indian language, one does well indeed to use the build-up technique: *qake·ʔne· / cxałqaqaʔne· ʔinʹinya·qake·ʔke· / hucukate· kincxa / hucxałłitqʔatiłqʔakpame·k ʔinʹinya·qakłapke·.* "(The chief) said / Will be thus it the way you said / I take your saying (word) / I shall never forget it the way you told us" (Garvin 1953:305).

This procedure also avoids having to ask the informant to speak slowly, something that one should hardly ever have to do. The reason is that compliance with the request may result in unnatural speech, for the expression "speak slowly" is a very ambiguous one. In ordinary speech it means putting more pauses into one's stream of speech or making the pauses of longer duration. But when an utterance is as brief as a single sentence, there may be no linguistically appropriate place to put pauses, and the informant can only think of inserting them after syllables or of stressing certain syllables.

TRANSCRIPTION.   By this term we refer to the recording, as linguistic data, of all that the informant says in his own language. It will be put down in a composition notebook, never directly on individual slips. Each expression will be on a different line, with enough space between lines for comments to be written at a later date if necessary. The tendency will be for the field worker to write down the translation before he gets the target language form; but because he may have to reject the stimulus sentence, or because the meaning of the sentence he finally gets will be considerably different from the stimulus one, he should write down the target language sentence first. The field worker should always be looking into the face of the informant when he gives the stimulus sentence and when the informant makes his response. The reason is that he must observe the external physical features which accompany speech, such as lip position and throat musculature, as well as the nonlinguistic cues to comprehension, appropriateness, and others (matters that are discussed in the next chapter). This is also the way he can get a better understanding of the articulation of the utterance. The field worker should train himself to record as much as possible after the very first articulation. He must rely on his own ability to perceive the finest of phonetic differentiations, not on the informant's successive repetitions, for in spite of his failure to fully comprehend the utterance, he will be able to recall some part of what he has heard. As various kinds of tests with mature speakers have shown, recall will be highest for the beginning of words, then for the end, and finally for the middle (Brown and McNeill 1965). (Because of this phenomenon, one should so organize data that is being checked so as to favor the initial or final parts.) One then asks for repetitions, each time adding as much as possible, until the full form is recorded. There is more to say about transcribing an informant's responses, but it is reserved for Chapter 9.

There is more to write down than just the translation of the stimulus sentence. The most important thing is the meaning or use of the sentence. It is not sufficient to have the stimulus sentence opposite its response. This is in fact a bad procedure. Very often the meanings of the investigator's stimulus and the informant's response are substantially different. One should therefore find a variety of ways to elicit the meaning of the informant's response: "And how would you translate that?" "Would you translate that differently for me?" Such back translation is an effective control of the data that one acquires. Everything that seems to elucidate the utterance should be recorded but with the proper recognition of how the information was obtained. It is wrong, for example, to add just "used only with elders" in the English gloss when it was the informant who contributed this information. It should certainly be recorded if he volunteered it, but the field notes should make a clear distinction between what the informant says and what the investigator infers.[6] The adoption of a few unambiguous symbols might be adequate for this purpose. Another kind of information that is too often omitted in field notes is contextual information provided by the investigator. When he asks, "How do you say 'she was in the house'?" he immediately adds, after a pause or in a different tone of voice, "that is, a few minutes ago." What he tries to get is an utterance which implies the immediate past. After having transcribed the response, however, he writes down only "she was in the house." It may be that the language makes no distinction between remote and immediate past, but until he learns this, the investigator is obligated to write down precisely what he asked for.

One of the things that the investigator must check on, especially when he still is in the "What is this?" stage, is the possibility that ingenious descriptive phrases are being given him. He may think that he is getting the distinctive name of a certain basket, but what he records is nothing more than "little basket"; he may want to know the generic term, and the informant will give him the specific name. But these are misunderstandings that can sometimes be cleared up quickly with on-the-spot analysis and further elicitation (by asking for contrasting terms, for instance). It is certainly better to catch the errors at that time than it is to return to the forms for checking at a later date. A classic set of examples illustrating this kind of error is the following taken in translation from an important dictionary of the Toba language (Argentina):

Elicited	*Given*
excrement	Damn it!
tree	algarrobo tree
forehead	our forehead
dog	I pet

When the informant produces the utterances in two or more ways, these variations also must be recorded. (One reason for training the informant to restrict himself to a single articulation at a time is to reduce

---

[6] Compare the various indications used in the preparation of the *Linguistic Atlas of New England* (Kurath 1939:143–145): observed in the informant's unguarded conversation; offered by the informant as a spontaneous correction of his first response; repeated by the informant at the field worker's request; secured by "forcing" (by repeated questioning); suggested by the field worker and recognized by the informant as his own usage; a hesitating response, uttered with signs of amusement; doubt as to the pronunciation, the meaning, or the naturalness of the form; reported by the informant as heard from others but not used by himself; characterized by the informant as "old," out of date, obsolete; characterized by the informant as recently introduced or used only by a younger generation, offered not by the informant but by someone else (an auxiliary informant) who happened to be present.

the amount of variation. If the Marathi informant uses [šaela] and then immediately [šalela], the field worker's uncertainty about the utterance is greater.) Once again there should be adequate documentation of the variations. Notice how ambiguous the following entry is:

ti šaela tsalət zai literary
šalela   (zat ase) spoken
"she used to walk to school"

The variation between [zai] and [zat ase] is explained, but not between [šaela] and [šalela]. Going over his notes several months later, the field worker might assume that [šaela . . . zai] was literary and [šalela . . . zat ase] colloquial.

In recording variations one must pay considerable attention to the informant's feelings. If one set of variations represents informal speech, where there is some kind of difference between formal and informal, or if the speech community represented by the informant is entirely unconscious of the changes which occur in allegro speech, the informant may resent their being recorded. People also resent the recording of "errors" where there is a strong tradition of correct speech.

Even where the stimulus elicits no equivalent response some record should be made of the fact. These negative responses ("We can't say that" or "We can't say it that way") may very well lead to information of grammatical significance. Like the impossibility of saying *mans* (where *men* is appropriate) in English, the rejected construction may indicate the limitation of some grammatical rule.

An informant will quickly learn the significance of the rhythm of the interaction between himself and the field worker, and soon he will become very much at home with it. He will wait patiently, with some pride undoubtedly, as his exact words are being recorded. In time he will be puzzled by the investigator's failure to transcribe what he has said. He may interpret it as a criticism of his own performance or may see it as an indication of the linguist's incompetence. It is therefore wise to write down as much as the informant gives and never to ask for something that will not be recorded—advice to be followed within the bounds of reason, of course.

REPETITION.[7]   Getting repetitions of an utterance is an explicit part of the elicitation procedure, and there are good and bad ways of

---

[7] Some investigators have found the use of tape-recorded repetitions helpful. A simple device is arranged with a tape loop (made by joining the two ends of a tape) and a soft-drink bottle. The loop is fed over the heads and plays around the bottle, avoiding the spindles, which maintains sufficient tension for easy operation if properly placed. After the recording is made—only one articulation is needed—the tape can be played as many times as desired. Special cartridges of various sizes are made by one manufacturer, but it is reported that the tapes do considerable damage to the playback heads.

doing it. Involuntary repetitions are made either by the informant or the field worker. Those of the informant are important for reasons already given. Those of the investigator, on the other hand, must be eliminated —as long as they are involuntary. If the investigator is in the habit of repeating what the informant says, he cannot assume that the informant's assent (for example, some affirmative interjection) is full approval for the manner and content of his own utterance. When the investigator wants the informant to critically evaluate his own performance, he must be very explicit as to what he wants done.

If the investigator is uncertain at all about the grammaticalness of his own utterance—and this can happen when he fails to repeat all of what the informant has said—he can test the validity of the informant's "That's good" by asking him to repeat what he, that is, the investigator, has just said. If the informant cannot do so, the other can assume that there was something wrong with what he had said. This procedure is based on the assumption that a naive native speaker of a language will have more difficulty repeating a nongrammatical stretch of speech than a grammatical one (Feigenbaum 1961).

The dangers inherent in getting repetitions become apparent when one realizes how far they are from normal speech. First, speech is usually engaged in as one interacts with other people, but translating sentences outside of a meaningful context is abnormal. More possibilities of distortion are introduced by the function of repetition: it means "What I said was . . ." With each repetition that the investigator requests the informant may alter its purpose. For example, he may imply "Didn't you understand that I said . . . ?" Sometimes such changes can be particularly disconcerting. For example, even without repetition distortions in Wishram Chinook, an American Indian language, the working out of the patterns for the placement of stress was apparently quite difficult. Although there appeared to be one phoneme of stress, it was also observed that the place of the primary stress seemed to move around, and then in some contexts there also appeared secondary stress. It turns out that in addition to the strictly linguistic factors, there were rhetorical considerations which played a part, that is, where the informant's feelings were involved during speech; repetitions for the benefit of the investigator are clearly included here. Thus, there is *wítʔa* "again" in isolation and in *wítʔa dáukwa galíxux* "again thus he did," but also *wìtʔa dáukwa gàlixùx* and *dáukwa wìtʔa gàlixùx* meaning the same thing (Dyk and Hymes 1956).

Repetitions should always be obtained in the same conditions which prevailed for the original utterance. For certain kinds of problems it does little good, and perhaps much harm, to ask for a word in isolation when it was just heard in a sentence. This would be true in Wishram Chinook where sentence rhythm is one of the factors affecting stress placement.

It is for this reason that both *tgwíwalal* and *tgwiwálal* "they are dancing" occur in the language. A more mystifying phenomenon is said to occur in one African language where nouns are tonally different depending on whether one wants to say "(the noun . . .) has not been mentioned before" and "(the noun . . .) has already been mentioned." Not knowing that such a difference existed in the language, a field worker would almost despair of ever working out the tonal analysis. In any case, one should always be exceedingly careful to observe the intonational features which accompany repetitions.

From time to time an investigator finds it necessary to hear certain words or parts of words several times. For example, he may want to listen to the quality of a certain vowel first, then the palatalization of a certain consonant, then the tone or stress, and so on. Rather than having the informant repeat the form again and again, one can put it in a different context or pretend to be interested in a different part of the sentence, taking the informant's attention from the word in question. Sometimes one may even have to wait for another day.

Very frequently an investigator will want the informant to repeat something he said earlier in the session or on some preceding day. If the linguist wants to hear the utterance in exactly the form he first heard it, or thought he heard it, it will be necessary to give both the meaning and the form: "Would you again give me the expression for 'he is angry'? I think that it was something like *dã dέ ã*." But he should be neither surprised nor annoyed in getting an altogether different form. The informant is not an automaton, nor should he be one.

Analyzing and Checking for Elicitation

It has been very difficult in this chapter to avoid talking about the analytical aspects of linguistic field work. All that we have done is declare the interdependence of the two by setting up the category of "analytical elicitation" (page 112ff). It is by daily processing one's data, that is, collating and analyzing it, that one learns what more he needs for his corpus.

There are other practical values in carefully going over and collating one's data. The first is that a person becomes familiar with his material. It is inefficient, if not embarrassing, to elicit for the second or third time things which are already in the file. In the second place, the investigator observes how his transcription varies. Without the collated occurrences of a particular word, he may be unaware, for example, that he has vacillated between [ɪ], [ï], and [ə].

A regular part of informant sessions will be checking. This may involve nothing more than determining whether the original transcription is correct. When one is still working on the analysis of the phonology, checking may loom large in one's work sessions. (Specific suggestions are given in Chapter 9.) But even after he has begun morphological analysis, he will have to determine, for example, if the variations of a particular morph are linguistically significant. The most important purpose of checking is to test the validity of analyses. This can be carried out by elicitation or by seeing how adequate the provisional analysis is in explaining the forms which occur in the texts. Checking is therefore an important part of field work, but it is one of its dullest parts.

There must be a systematic approach to checking. Very little is accomplished when one rummages through one's field notes looking for those places where a problem is indicated by a question mark. The items to be checked should be collated, taken from the slip file (where their absence should be noted), or written down in lists. It is not economical to recopy all of the original notation if most of it is irrelevant to the problem at hand, but there should be some notation where all of this information could be found.

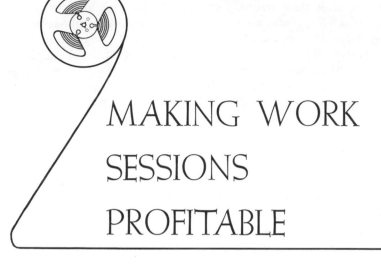

MAKING WORK
SESSIONS
PROFITABLE

7

Linguistic work sessions, like battles, depend on much more than material and manpower. There must be strategy: understanding the nature of all the problems and contingencies and effectively coping with them. There is never all the information that is needed; so one decides what is needed most and devises ways of getting it. Men are never adequate in number or competence; so one arranges for their greatest potential by proper deployment. It is a matter of wits and wisdom. Good linguistic data and willing informants do not automatically result in sound descriptions. That depends on the way the investigator uses them both.

We have already touched upon subjects which relate to personal factors in field work, and we shall have more to say in succeeding chapters. In this one we want to look at only four of the crucial aspects of the work session, all of which are integrated by a common feature, a concern with effective communication.

Language Problems

The chief tool in informant work is language. Whether the investigator uses his own, the informant's language, or some other one which both he and the informant know, language serves as a means for analyzing data.

Ideally, informant sessions should be carried on in the language of the informant. In this way the investigator obtains more data than just what he tries to elicit. He also is one step removed from the categories of his language, therefore reducing the possibility of influencing the responses on the part of the informant. But it is illusory to imagine that by the use of a language other than his own the investigator thereby automatically frees himself from the bias imposed by his native tongue. Only by conscious effort can he hope to accomplish this.

Monolingual approach

Working monolingually—entirely in the language being studied—is so effective an approach to language investigation that many field workers have made it their explicit goal from the very beginning of their projects, even when a contact language was available to them. Some have chosen to accomplish this goal by weaning themselves as quickly as possible from the intermediate language, and others have taken the more difficult alternative of pretending ignorance of the intermediate language and refusing to speak it. The choice between the two alternatives cannot be an entirely personal one; circumstances will figure significantly in the decision. In some communities people do not want an investigator to speak anything else but the more prestigious contact language (as in many parts of Latin America); in other communities the investigator has no choice, since no bilingual is available to him. (From here on we deal with this obligatory monolingualism.)

Initiation into a language monolingually is relatively easy. The researcher can soon discover, for example, the expression for "What is this?" or "What is it?" as people ask each other the identity or function of some of his belongings. The acquisition of this question makes possible the elicitation of names for many visible objects. From here on the travel is all upstream, and his work demands peculiar efforts:

(a) The investigator must obtain most of his data "on the fly," snatching phrases and sentences spoken to him or to others. At this stage even the most rudimentary elicitation is extremely tiresome and disagreeable to native speakers; the field worker's knowledge of the language is so incomplete that they get little satisfaction from verbal exchanges with him. They very quickly become impatient with his ignorance.

(b) The investigator must fully account for as much of the linguistic and extralinguistic context as he imagines might condition the meaning of each utterance: preceding or following statements, person speaking and person(s) spoken to. This information is all the more necessary since much of the original glosses will be incorrect. Thus, it was a long time before one worker learned that he had been saying "Adam's apple" when speaking of himself! Apparently he had raised his hand to his throat when trying to get the form for "I," and the informant, knowing only that he was trying to get the name for *something,* gave him the name of the object to which he pointed! Another person, trying to get the words for "thick" and "thin," made a paste of flour and water only to get an expression which later turned out to mean "like phlegm."

(c) The monolingual approach requires the investigator to be both ingenious in his use of the words and phrases he has acquired and also sensitive to the responses they stimulate. Knowing the words for "water," "tree" and "body," for example, one might be able to get words for "sap" and "blood": by asking for "water of tree" and "water of body." (The dangers inherent in such ingenious circumlocutions should be obvious. In addition to the possibility of getting a perfectly strange construction there is the more serious possibility of being indelicate in one's speech, for the informant might understand "water of body" as semen or a menstrual flow.) Even when one is not asking for explicit terms, one can obtain corrections or alternative ways of saying the same thing, because people seem to have an irresistable impulse to translate unnatural speech into natural speech, and some of this—unless the society's etiquette forbids such behavior—is verbalized. In other words, one should pay close attention to what others may mutter after one has spoken. They may be saying the same thing in a corrected or alternate form.

Using interpreters

Where bilingual informants are not available and one does not have the time to undertake a full-scale linguistic investigation monolingually, it will be necessary to use an interpreter. This generally is a person for whom the target language is a second language.[1] His chief function will be to act as intermediary between the investigator and the real informant. Although much useful information can be gained from him, he can never be considered an informant in the technical sense because of his nonnative control of the language.

The principal difficulty in working through interpreters is that one is very much at their mercy. It is the interpreter who presents the field worker to the community. The investigator may want to assume the role of learner, but the interpreter may present him as an authority on languages or at least as some "very important person." In any case, the

---

[1] He may also be a person for whom the contact language is a second language, for example, a native speaker of Badaga who interviews another Badaga speaker in Tamil. This procedure may be followed when one does not want the informant's responses to be influenced by an interview in his own language.

interpreter cannot be expected to understand the linguistic project as the investigator does nor can he always be expected to be equally concerned about the subtleties of human relations (although his sensitivity may sometimes far exceed that of his employer). Sometimes an interpreter will even use his temporary relation with the investigator to increase his stature in the eyes of the people or to take advantage of them (by requiring gifts and services). If the investigator remains entirely dependent on his interpreter, his only knowledge of the poor rapport established with the community will be a vague feeling that "things are not going too well."

Because of the potential difficulties in this area it is important that the interpreter be selected with care. Inquiries should be made as discreetly as possible concerning the nature and extent of his relationship with the people whose language is being studied. His behavior among them under different circumstances should be observed. Finally, the investigator should become personally acquainted with the interpreter in other areas of life.

There are two fundamental rules which the interviewer and the interpreter must follow. The interviewer must formulate his statements in the clearest and most concise terms. He does not, in other words, speak about the topic that interests him and then ask the interpreter to frame a statement that will be appropriate. (Yet the interpreter should not be discouraged from making his own intelligent contributions: pointing out ambiguities in the original statements, for example.) The field worker should therefore address his statement directly to the informant as if the latter were going to understand it in the other's language. In addition to being efficient, the concise statements of the interviewer are also useful as a measure of the faithfulness of the translation. If the original statement was a relatively short one and its image was twice or three times as long, the investigator can assume that either it was not clear or that the interpreter was interjecting too many of his own opinions into it. If the translations are regularly longer, however, the investigator should assume that something is wrong; perhaps the statements he puts to the interpreter are not culturally relevant.

The informant and interpreter should never be seated in such a way that the investigator is psychologically cut off from them. If their linguistic solidarity is reinforced by a spatial one, they will inevitably be talking amongst themselves, with the interpreter only *reporting* to the investigator on their discussion. The problem, although potentially quite dangerous, is easily eliminated. One simply puts himself between the informant and the interpreter. To avoid gradual changes in position which will be corrected at the danger perhaps of insulting the other participants, everyone might be seated at a table, illustrated by the diagram below. The advantage of a long table is that it keeps the interpreter and informant physically away from each other and that it permits the investigator to create dyadic relations with his assistants. By turning to one or the other of the participants he creates a momentary solidarity with him. Thus, he can choose to watch the informant's face while the interpreter is putting a statement

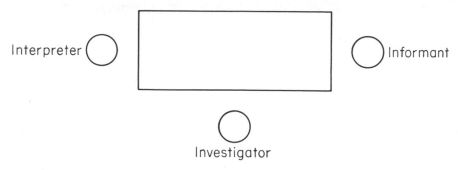

to him. He can smile, act as if he understood the statement in translation (he actually does, having stated it first in his own language); in short, simulate a realistic dialogue.

Instructions

It is with language that the linguistic investigator dominates the informant session. In seeking to obtain information from his assistant, he gives commands and asks questions. How the informant responds depends to a considerable extent on how the directives are given. If they are clear and explicit, the probability of his giving what the investigator wants is much higher. Stated in just that way the preceding sentence is a truism, something any sensitive adult would know. But the investigator's verbal relationship to his informant is not normal; its apparent similarities with ordinary dialogue are deceptive. The field worker must therefore recognize the part his own verbal activity has in the work session and improve the art of efficient interviewing.

The chief obstacle to acquiring this art is the difficulty an investigator has in viewing his own participation objectively. He is not fully aware of the way he puts his questions and commands; and because the informant is usually able to make some kind of a response, the investigator may continue in his illusion that all is going well. Only at specific junctures in the session—when the informant does not understand or gives an utterance that is obviously different from the one the investigator wanted—is the interviewer made aware of his failings. He should learn from these episodes and improve his technique.

Instructions and requests for information must be clearly understood by the informant. It is confusing to the informant to have the field worker somewhat absentmindedly ask "Would you repeat that please?" if he has had two or three different linguistic expressions before him. Wherever possible the investigator should establish explicit steps in the elicitation procedure. For example, the following can be used in getting a list of nounlike words:

> Linguist: "What is the word for 'house'?"
> (He looks at informant, meaning "Go ahead.")
> Informant: [tuwa]
> (Pause while linguist listens or writes.)
> Linguist: "Again please." (Or he nods, a signal which they have agreed on.)
> Informant: [tuwa]
> (Pause)
> Linguist: "Once more." (It might be agreed that this phrase elicits the final utterance whereas "Again please" elicits all others.)
> Informant: [tuwa]
> (Pause. The linguist looks at his transcription, repeats the word to himself, thinks.)
> Linguist: [tuwa] (In mimicry of the informant's pronunciation, it being understood that the informant will approve or disapprove of the utterance, not repeat it.)
> Informant: [mm] (In approval.)

Misunderstandings also arise, because the field worker and the informant may be talking about different things. For example, in eliciting the noun "fat," an investigator put the following question to a Kikuyu speaker: "How do you say 'fat'? You know, not a 'fat man' but 'fat'." The informant's response to this was: "The one you would use for grease? The one we use for frying?" In response to the investigator's "Yes," the informant gave a phrase that literally means "fat for frying" and not just "fat, grease." Another person, working with a Marathi informant, wasted much time, because he did not make it clear that when he asked for "the women won't stand," he wanted only the negative future and not "the women refuse to stand." (The misunderstanding was due to the informant's interpreting *won't* as "wills not to.")

It should be clear that the informant must fully understand what his response is expected to be. The linguist can help him by being aware of the potential problems. He words his stimulus statement or prepares for it in ways that make clear what is desired. For example, rather than simply asking for the equivalent of "What are you eating?" the investigator might first say: "Suppose that I am walking through the village and come upon a group of men sharing an evening meal. They haven't finished yet; I see that there is some food still in the bowl. If it were polite to do so, how would I ask, 'What are you eating?' "

The best corrective to poor "informant technique" (which is the term that covers the whole gamut of the investigator's interaction with an informant) is listening critically to tape-recorded work sessions, paying careful attention to the form and context of each directive given to the informant and the kinds of responses they elicit—immediate verbalization, pauses, clearing of the throat, questions for clarification, and so on.[2] There will be many surprises. The first observation that the investigator will make is that many of his stimuli are barely more than cues to the informant, the kind of thing that is normal in face-to-face verbal encounters of a casual nature and that facilitates the communicative exchange between the participants. The following somewhat edited transcript of a classroom "field session" with a university-trained Marathi informant is probably typical of most such sessions. The asterisk indicates that some intervening material has been omitted.

PORTIONS FROM A WORK SESSION IN MARATHI

Elicitor	*Informant*
How do you say "He swam yesterday"?	[to kal pohəlá]
And what does that mean?	He swam yesterday.
* How do you say "He swam every day"?	[to roz pohot ase]
And that means?	He swam every day *or* He used to swim every day.
How do you say, "The letters will come tomorrow"?	[pətre udea yetil]
"The letters will come tomorrow, eh?"	Yes, that's right.
* "The letters will *not* come tomorrow."	[pətre udea yinar hahit]
* About the same letters	
"They will come *some* day"	[ti kədhitəri yetil]
* Can we say something like, "Let's go"?	Yes.
"Let's go!"	[apən zaoya]
Would you say "Let's be brave" again please?	[apən šur ho'oya]
And now, "Let's go"?	[apən zaoya]
* This sentence, "If I were brave." Now if one was praying to a deity, and he wished to ask the deity to make him brave, would he use this?	No, he would request the deity to make him brave.
Let's get that one.	"Make me brave," that would be the translation. [məla šur kər]

---

[2] My own observations of classroom performances are supplemented by those of Bernard J. Covner who made disk recordings of counseling interviews to check the accuracy of reports. He found not only that less than one-third of the original material was included in the final report but more significantly that from one-tenth to as much as one-fourth of the information (as compared with the original interview) was inaccurate (Covner 1944).

Elicitative metalanguage

It is very clear from transcripts of informant sessions that there are different styles of interviewing, each person having his own particular repertoire of expressions and nonlinguistic communicative signals, such as grunts of assent. The following is a sample of those used in classroom sessions:

> How would you say, "Before he went on his way he did that?"
> What would "He arrived yesterday" be?
> Would this be correct: . . . ?
> Would you say: . . . ? (*Meaning:* Would it be grammatically correct to say)
> Say the whole thing again please.
> Would you repeat the verb please?
> May I have that again?
> Now once again please.
> Is there any other way that you would normally gloss this?
> And that would be glossed: . . . ?

The availability of these expressions is quite convenient for the English-speaking investigator when his informant understands this language. But one must make certain that this way of talking about language is perfectly understood, for every language has its own (though often rudimentary) metalanguage, and the overlapping systems between different languages may conceal important differences. Notice how in English we can speak of verbal forms as if they were tangible objects which could be passed from one person to another, by the use of verbs "give" and "have," illustrated above. For some second-language speakers of English it might be less ambiguous to use only the verb "say."

The field linguist is responsible for the repertoire he uses, even though its development is not obvious to him. During the first stages of field work he unconsciously experiments with several different eliciting expressions, finally settling on those which seem to produce the desired forms with the minimum of effort. This trial-and-error method actually works. This has been demonstrated by the experience of all field workers. However, what the learner may never realize after the habits have been adopted is that some of the expressions are less efficient than they could be. For this reason the beginning field worker should try to be aware of the choices he makes and should strive to select those which are maximally efficient.

This repertoire of words and phrases used by the investigator in elicitation might be called an *elicitative* (or *field*) *metalanguage*. The examples we have looked at are taken from English. A field linguist will have little difficulty in developing (if one is not already available) such an "idiom" in the literary languages of the world. But if he works in a preliterate language, he may find himself handicapped by a severely restricted metalanguage.

There probably is some way in every language to talk about speech in general. In most preliterate languages there seems to be, however, only one word to designate any meaningful and isolable stretch of speech, ranging from a "word" in our sense to a lengthy discourse; sometimes it even includes "language" (as in Machiguenga, a language of Peru, or Brôu, a Mon-Khmer language of Viet Nam). There is much more diversity in dealing with the concept of "meaning." Some languages use only the verb "say" (as in Machiguenga: *tatoita onkantakera* . . . ? "What will it say . . . ?"); More uses a word for "hole" (. . . *võre ya bwẽ* " . . . hole is what?"); Bilaan (in the Philippines) speaks of a "place of throwing something (target)" or "place something is dropped on"; similarly Colorado of Ecuador uses the verb "fall" ("Do . . . and . . . fall the same?"); Brôu uses the same word which means "name" (*cú'q tau' sâng ramú'h* . . . "I don't understand the meaning of . . . [lit. I don't hear the name of]"); and in Ata (Philippines) when one asks for an explanation of meaning, he says *lituka nu ka kagi no* . . . "tune the word . . . ."

It is when one begins to segment speech and talk about its parts that difficulties arise. Since many languages do not make a distinction between "discourse" and "word," it is hardly likely that they would identify affixes, syllables, or sounds. Yet surprising discoveries are occasionally made. Brôu, for example, has a word to designate "rhyming" syllables (those with identical vowel and final consonants). (One can also have "near" or "close" rhymes, namely, *radau't cheq ra cheq*.)

The absence of these technical terms hardly hinders progress in linguistic analysis, and there is no need to mirror in the language being studied the grammatical metalanguage of a literary language. On the other hand, an imaginative use of a language's lexicon, on the part of either the informant or the researcher, should not be discouraged. Words can be extended in meaning or new constructions coined to the great advantage of discussion about the language's structure. It was a Brôu informant, for example, who distinguished first from second syllables of words. In this language there are never more than two syllables per word, the first of which are characterized by being unstressed and having both very little vowel contrast and few consonant types: that is, there is greatest phonological contrast in the second syllable. This informant, perceiving the difference, named the first syllables *nau'm* "trunk (as of a tree)" and the second syllables *coiq* "branches and leafy canopy." In the Ata language it has proved possible to designate homophones by the term *lalaud* "friendship name," for among the Ata, as among some other Philippine peoples, the custom prevails that two people institutionalize their friendship by sharing the same name; each calls the other by a name that they have agreed on. Tagbanwa has a word for "example" which is used natively in an utterance like "An X of a good-for-nothing person is . . . (here a person is named)." Because of the morphology of this language, this word could be predicated in asking for illustrations of how words could be used. Even when isolated words were presented to the informant, he was able to describe the referent and give sentences in which it could be used or whole stories which would illustrate its meaning. (This field worker was fortunate. It is very often difficult, as it was in Gbeya, to say: "Use this word in another sentence [or, in a different way]." The closest equivalent I found for Gbeya was *tó ŋma mbé wen nɛ é wen nɔɔ sɛné* "Speak a new speech and put this word in it."

Terms for which the investigator was more responsible are in Twi: "big voice" for low tone, "join" to refer to permitted morphological and syntactic sequences, "free" and "slave" to designate "free" and "bound," and "assistant words" (key words which serve as models in making phonological comparisons). In Amharic it was possible to talk about "tight" and "loose" (geminate and nongeminate) consonants with the informant working in the English language. It proved more convenient to use a general English term with a specific meaning than to use a technical term. Other workers have found it useful to introduce the few terms they needed from the intermediate language and teach their informants their use.

One must be extremely careful with all neologisms. In my work on Gbeya I thought that *nú* "month" and *dod'i* "end" would be convenient terms for distinguishing the first and latter parts of utterances (*nú* is commonly used to speak of the edge of a knife, the end of a pencil.) Some time had elapsed—and a bad habit had been acquired (partly because of an indulgent informant)—before I realized that *nú* means "end" only when the point is away from the speaker and could therefore be used only of the end of the utterance. (It probably acquires its meaning "edge" in terms of orientation from the center.)

A person might be able to discover the language's own grammatical terminology by observing what is said to children when their speech is corrected. (This is not to say that adults or parents in all societies take an interest in the verbal performance of children.) One can also try to get puns and word-plays and determine what was funny or interesting with the utterances.

Ultimately, the task we have been talking about in this section is that of seeking some common ground for talking about language. We can expect *some* success, but there is no more reason for having complete success here than it is in expecting the Aucas of Ecuador to have words for "camel," "book," "market-place," and so on. But with patience and persistence it is surprising how much communication can be achieved.

Fortunately, field linguistics can be carried on with only the lexicon available to the preliterates since time immemorial: "say," "again," "fast," "slow," and so forth.

Nonlanguage Problems

Working with informants, an investigator may have difficulty obtaining linguistic information because of personal, societal, or situational restraints. Some of these problems are peculiar to the informant session, but others are confronted elsewhere in field work.

The *personal restraints* are psychological ones which prevent an informant from cooperating harmoniously with the investigator or from producing accurate and natural speech. Tension because of nervousness or fright is one of them, and it can result from several factors: a feeling of inadequacy for the task he has undertaken, embarrassment in the presence of others who may be critical of his performance, and intimidation by an overbearing field worker. Anxieties on the part of the investigator can incite the same emotion in the informant. One may resent the fact that the informant was late to the work session, that he brought others with him, that rain had just begun and work would be hampered; one may be embarrassed at not knowing enough of the vocabulary and may think that the informant considers the investigator's control of the language far from adequate. I clearly recall that on one occasion I had determined to be much more demanding of myself in making phonetic distinctions. About one half hour after having begun the session with the informant I became conscious of the fact that his pronunciation was somewhat artificial and that there was a look of concentration on his face. As I leaned back to suggest that he relax and not pay so much attention to my problems, I realized that it was I who needed to relax. (What added to the strain between us was my own physical condition that day; several flu symptoms had already begun to make me feel ill.)

Boredom and inattention also must be coped with. The reason for boredom may be the apparent irrelevancy of linguistic investigations and the hopelessly illogical and uninteresting content of the utterances which are elicited. A series of possessive forms might be extremely important at a certain point in one's study, but an informant can hardly expect to stay alert saying "my father, my dog, my machete, my corn field." Boredom can lead to inattention, and inattention to sleepiness. The caricature of the sedated informant is the Mazatec girl, half asleep, leaning forward with her chin on the table, her arms dangling at her sides, and her eyes shut! When she responded, the words had to force their way through clenched teeth (E. V. Pike 1956:26).

It is paradigmatic interviewing, which is very often responsible for inducing inattention and even confusion. When the Mazatec informant mentioned above was giving the equivalents for the following:

The girl sold beans.
The girl sold beans for the first time last Sunday.
The girl sold beans in the market frequently.
The girl had sold beans since she was a little girl.
The girl sold only a few beans today.

she substituted the verb "sold" with the verb "bought" in the last sentence. Her mind had simply wandered; perhaps she had thought of a real-life situation for which the sentence "The girl *bought* only a few beans today" was more appropriate.

Informant confusion is illustrated by the experiences investigators have had in holding informants to paradigmatic forms of the same series. Thus, when Yupik verb forms were being elicited in a study of subjectival and objectival affixes, the Yupik informant would get so muddled that he would mix them up. And in Philippine languages, one can have a difficult time in getting the full range of differently focussed elements of a single sentence—that is, at one sitting. Usually, "focus" (the linguistic topic of the sentence) is marked by the juxtaposition of the focus morpheme, but sometimes there are concomitant changes elsewhere. But it proved impossible, at least with an Ata informant, to go from one "focussable" element to another in a mechanical way; the informant would inevitably change the original sentence.

If the problems with the paradigmatic method become acute, one can prepare the paradigms beforehand but elicit the forms in a variety of contexts, by interspersing other expressions amongst them, for instance. It is also useful to offset the mesmerizing effects of paradigmatic interviewing by the deliberate introduction of error or something humorously absurd, making certain that neither the informant nor his society is being ridiculed.

Another restraint on an informant's performance is a failure of memory. Under ordinary circumstances it is a momentary phenomenon, and the most important thing is not to aggravate it, not to allow it to embarrass the informant. The investigator must immediately pass on to something else or modify his question in some way. More difficult to cope with are those cases where informants have not spoken their languages for many years. One might say that they have virtually forgotten their native languages. The most dramatic such case is that of Dayuma, the Auca woman who had fled her homestead at about the age of 15 following a raid which left her father and grandfather dead. For about 17 years she had lived among Quechua-speaking Indians, repressing her knowledge of Auca in fear of her life. In this environment, and before she had resumed normal

contact with her former life, Auca speech was elicited with extreme difficulty. It was, moreover (as comparisons with early and later tape-record-
ings show), very much changed in phonology and reduced in lexicon and
morphology. The extent of this simplification is described as follows:

> . . . the verb suffixal system was impoverished, but supplemented by oc-
> casional Quichua affixes. The native pronominal set (apart from the honorific
> and the first-person exclusive plural forms) seems to have been complete.
> Most of the tense or aspect group was found, but only three occurred with
> normal frequency. The modal system was impoverished. Modal suffixes
> indicating uncertainty, doubt, probability, intention, negation, and obligation,
> were used so rarely as to be outside her effective control. Modal enclitics
> indicating derision, disgust, satire, extreme emotion, and emphatic negative
> seem to have been completely missing. Of the imperative system, only one of
> several suffixal combinations was used (Saint 1962:28–29).

Similar difficulties have been experienced in the study of moribund
North American Indian languages, but the investigators were unable to
return their informants to their native speech community as was done with
Dayuma. However, recall can often be stimulated by devices such as
pictures, writing, and reminiscing. (See Chapter 5.)

Societal restraints are primarily the sanctions of taboo or etiquette.
These can affect almost every aspect of field work. In some societies one
can expect the posing of questions, or the posing of certain kinds of
questions to certain people, to be rude. Some people consider it crude to
raise one's voice in speech. Hence among the Zapotecs it was difficult to
get an informant to speak loudly enough for easy hearing (K. L. Pike
1948:36fn.). But among the Ata, quiet speech is viewed as an attempt
to conceal secrets or slander. Even when working in their own houses, the
investigators and their informants had to talk loudly enough for everything to be heard in the neighboring houses. If not, someone would cry
out, "Friend, you're learning the wrong way; speak louder!" Among the
Ata it is even difficult for a researcher to repeat what has been said to him,
a procedure the field linguist ordinarily follows in making certain that he
has heard correctly. The reason is that the Ata consider mimicry equivalent to mockery and both are classed as *saoq*, that is, an offense against
the dignity of a person or deity. The field workers were delivered from this
predicament by having a woman informant willing enough to review
conversations during which she was present and to point out new words
and their meanings.

Much more common than the restraints just mentioned are those on
topics of discourse. In Muslim societies it would be considered in very
poor taste, if not revolting, to talk about dogs except in a very derogatory
manner. In Tongan there is a rather long list of things which one avoids
mentioning in polite speech, some of which are: the body and its parts,
fire, food or its preparation (Churchward 1963). Among the Manobo
people of the Philippines a whole area of discourse is restricted by the

anit taboo. The *anit* seems to be a supernatural force which brings down retribution for violation of certain restrictions. Among the Ata, who belong to this group, the punishment takes the form of electric storms whose thunder is said to break people's backs. These restrictions involve "human behavior toward living things, animate or inanimate, which departs from the accepted norm of 'natural' or 'logical,' " for example, talking to a dog or "making nonsense statements ['butterflies weave,' 'monkeys build houses'] which ascribe to non-human creatures human-like faculties or abilities . . ." (Elkins 1964:188, 186). Among the Ata the field linguists had to particularly avoid the names of insects for which the taboo was especially strict. The mention of one of these creatures invariably brought out a violent cry of *Ayow!* "Taboo!" It was therefore difficult to check the stress and vowel qualities of a word like *langow* "fly." Quite common also are taboos restricting the use of personal names. In many traditional Amerindian societies, for example, it was considered rude to ask a person his name, for this was interpreted as having an evil intent. Even where names can be obtained, say, from relatives or close friends, the field worker may not be at liberty to use them freely.

It is not only what one says but where and when he says it that is regulated by society. One may have difficulty in getting riddles in some African groups during the day, for these must be asked at night. In other words, it may be difficult or nearly impossible to elicit folklore of certain types outside of their appropriate settings.

Another type of situational restraint imposed by society is that which determines how folklore is to be transmitted. Some lore is the property of certain families and is passed from older to younger generations in prescribed ways. Elsewhere the lore is considered the property of the "tribe," and an outsider, regardless how good his relations might be with the members of the group, cannot acquire a knowledge of it, although he might be permitted to hear it. Some such restriction prevented a field worker from getting traditional lore from an Uscarira shaman acting as informant. The latter even denied the existence of such a body of oral literature. It was not until about 18 months of close contact with the investigator that the shaman said that the friend should be called by a kin term, that is, be adopted. The foreigner was given the status of "younger brother" of the shaman, and only after this had taken place did the informant begin to divulge the information he had been concealing, even against the protests of other shamans.[3]

There is an unquestionable element of delicacy when one begins to

---

[3] Because a field worker often finds himself becoming a collector of folklore, one is well advised to familiarize himself with this area of investigation (genres of folklore, categories of tradition bearers, collecting techniques). Goldstein's *A Guide for Field Workers in Folklore* (1964) deals with "folklore which has passed the peak of vitality" (which is not generally true of preliterate societies), but it would be a good beginning.

probe into the life of other people with the harmless intent of studying their language. The foreign investigator is probably exempted from some of the sanctions which govern the natives, but this is not to say that he will be the less shocking for flaunting, even ignorantly, the circumscriptions of etiquette or taboo. Sometimes native reaction to bad manners will come violently and without premeditation, as when an American was struck and almost knocked off an Ata house-ladder for unwittingly breaking the *anit* taboo.

Psychological Factors
in Interviewing[4]

An investigator and an informant sitting down for the first time for language study experience considerable discomfort. Each one realizes that he is confronting a human being in a situation which is abnormal. Eventually they become habituated to their relationship. For the investigator this may be unfortunate. If he has become familiar with the crude techniques of linguistic interviewing without having learned its subtleties and pitfalls, he will end up having difficulty in obtaining what he needs while ignorant of the causes. It is necessary therefore that the person embarking on linguistic field work understand the nature of the linguistic interview. (The term "interview" is employed here, because what is said applies to brief informant sessions in surveys as well as to regularly scheduled, "formal" elicitation sessions.)

Linguistic interviewing must be distinguished from other forms of speech behavior, because it seeks to obtain information under peculiar circumstances and for unusual reasons. Getting information from others by the use of language is, of course, normal between humans. We regularly ask such questions as "When does the next plane leave for London?" or "Who won yesterday's ball game?" But the characteristic features of such inquiries are that they are casual, randomly scattered in the discourse and that they have relevance to the immediate linguistic or nonlinguistic context. The interlocutor understands the reason for the inquiries. Linguistic interviewing, on the other hand, is prolonged and one-sided.

Sustained questioning (or what we call in English interrogation) is probably restricted in all societies to a limited number of settings. In our own we can imagine being questioned by a physician, highway patrolman, income tax controller, census taker, personnel manager, bank mortgage

[4] Important insights can be obtained from the experience of psychiatrists in interviewing. Sullivan's *The Psychiatric Interview* (1954) can be read with profit without previous technical training in this field.

representative, and so on. This list of interrogators points out a significant fact about these settings: that the person opposite us is in some official capacity: his role is formally defined within a legal, occupational, or other context. In this setting we are passive and vulnerable. This is no less true when the questions are put by those with whom we are otherwise on intimate terms, our parents or our spouses, for example. A university student finds little pleasure in being asked a long series of questions by members of his family about his year away in school. In our society one therefore avoids every semblance of a formal interview, either by loading discourse with the cues of informal speech or by breaking up the interrogation, if there must be one, into bits and spreading it over a period of hours or days.

The only interview which people truly tolerate is the one that they initiate or view as possibly being of benefit to themselves. This can be called the assistance interview, for the person goes as a client to the expert for help—medical, legal, mechanical, and so on. He understands that the expert must ask questions to achieve his—the client's—own goal, the solution of a personal problem. Little embarrassment is experienced by the "suppliant," because he does not feel truly passive in the situation; he will go away healthier, wiser, or happier for the help that will have been given him. It may be that he thinks he understands his situation so well that he will "field" the questions by answering (more or less frankly, as he understands frankness at the moment) those which will help him and by dodging the others. People come to this kind of interview with preconceived notions of what kind of help they really need.

The research interview is of a very different nature. It is the expert who has the problem. He has a subject about which he wants to make generalizations. For this purpose he needs a large body of data obtainable most directly, and in some cases, only, by eliciting them from people. The interviewee is therefore the source of information. His involvement with the problem, as conceived by the interviewer, is practically nil. In fact, he probably has little idea what the problem is. Much of this kind of interviewing goes on under the rubric of "consumer research," but in psychology, sociology, and anthropology there is also a large amount of pure research which employs this technique. In both cases the interview is a relatively recent innovation.

With this ethnographic understanding of linguistic interviewing, the field linguist can be more sympathetic with his assistant. But in order to steer a straight and safe course through the interview, he must also appreciate what constitutes it. We shall therefore look at the *relationship between the participants* and the *nature of the encounter*.

The participants have already been identified: one is the interviewer (the field linguist) and the other is the interviewee (the informant). The roles they play have also been alluded to, the first has the dominant and the other the secondary role. This is probably true for most linguistic investigations where the informant is not linguistically sophisticated. Unless he is in part responsible for the statement of the investigatory problem, he can only help when called upon to do so. He is in somewhat the same position as the mechanically naive person who is in an automobile when it develops engine trouble. Not knowing the interrelationships between the fuel and electrical systems, he cannot anticipate his friend's mechanical needs—a certain sized wrench or a screwdriver. A truly helpful person is one who understands what can go wrong, what steps must be taken to determine where the problem lies, and what tools will be needed as each point is checked out.

The nature of the encounter between the investigator and his informant is extremely complex. It helps to see it as a communicative event structured in several different ways. The participants are not merely engaged in searching for certain kinds of linguistic utterances. They are also telling each other what they think of the problem at hand, how their behavior is affecting each other, and what their attitude to some utterance is.

Some of the information is verbal: for example, protective mimicry and slips of the tongue. Protective mimicry is what an informant resorts to in order to avoid, it seems, the shock of the investigator's unnatural utterance, in phonology or in grammar. Thus, a Marathi informant imitated an investigator's stress pattern as the latter repeated each utterance after transcribing it. Slips of the tongue are important, because they may indicate how the informant looks upon a particular line of investigation. Thus, after having given one utterance in response to a source language model, he may change it on a repetition or in talking about it later on.

In addition to the purely linguistic information, there is paralinguistic information, such as speed of utterance, pauses and pitch level. What any sudden change in these features signifies may be difficult to determine, but by being aware of them the investigator is better armed to control what is going on.

Nonverbal information can also be diagnostic, whether it be psychosomatic (perspiration, breathing rate) or kinesic (body position, change in position). One investigator used such information in deciding what contextual styles of speech his informants were using (Labov 1964*b*:167–168).

Since the encounter between the informant and the investigator is made up of a network of signals, it is important for the communication to go on unhindered between them. Free communication will be possible only if the participants properly understand their relationship in the linguistic investigation and respect each other. These requirements set the stage for the relationship and have long-lasting effects. Immediate attention must be given to the elimination of anxieties, for anxieties constitute a substantial obstacle to effective communication. By anxiety we mean anything, conscious or unconscious, which prevents a person from fully expressing himself. In this sense, anxiety can be identified with a person's preoccupation with a speck of food on another person's chin, because it distracts his attention from the primary concerns of their encounter. But the more serious anxieties are those which block the informant's performance by activating his security system. The forms it takes are numerous, but its function is always to protect the ego from exposure and vulnerability. A person who feels ill at ease in some situation is one who is not certain if he can handle himself to his own satisfaction.

There are a number of types of behavior on the part of the investigator which can destroy the informant's feeling of well-being, for example, laughter, silence, or "tone" of voice. Anxieties can also be induced by making the informant believe that he is being tested or that he is inferior by comparison with the investigator.

The effects of anxiety are not always evidenced by an immediate "freezing up" of the informant's behavior, for there may be a period of time, several hours or days, between the first stimulus and the informant's resolution (perhaps only unconscious) of his inner problem. An accumulation of negative responses can seriously limit the usefulness of an informant.

Having looked at the investigator-informant encounter in terms of communication, we can view its dynamic aspects. There is nothing static nor mechanical about the informant session; the two participants are involved in a never-ceasing process of adjusting to each other. The important characteristic of their relationship is change. The members of this encounter in dyadic relationship to each other constantly modify their performance in response to the behavior of the other. We can see this illustrated in the varying heights of interest displayed by the investigator and his informant. Only rarely are their interests of the same intensity (or nearly the same, for we cannot measure it). The linguist comes to the work session with a specific problem in mind; his interest is high, but the informant's is low. As the study of the problem progresses, the informant's interest increases, although not perhaps for the same reasons which motivate the linguist. At some point there will be change. Perhaps a particular line of investigation is proving unfruitful, so the linguist's interest drops while the informant's interest is maintained until he perceives the change; perhaps the lin-

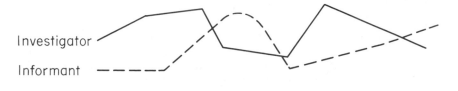

Investigator

Informant

guist's interest is maintained because of the appearance of a new line of investigation, but the rapid switch of focus may not be followed by the informant, who loses interest temporarily. The dynamics of this situation are illustrated by the figure above. A good field worker seeks to control his own and the informant's interest levels. That is, he makes an attempt to camouflage the sharp drops in his own interest to prevent their adversely affecting the informant's. What we want in a work session is an absence of frequent, sudden, and drastic drops. This ideal can be approximated with some success by the interjection of interest-catching topics, and by changing pace of work.

Truth and Error

A field worker, as we have already seen, must always be alert to the possibility of error being introduced into his corpus. Let us review a few ways in which this can happen:

1. The informant may misunderstand the investigator's request in elicitation (see Chapter 7).

2. The informant may give some illegitimate form because of embarrassment (see Chapter 3). For example, naive informants often try to improve their language in the direction of the more prestigious contact language. If they do not find a natural equivalent to what the field worker requests, they may translate literally.

3. Another source of error is the informant's accommodation to the ignorance of the investigator. He does this by either simplifying his speech (by reducing the number of affixes used with verb stems, for instance), or introducing distinctions where there are none in normal speech (see Chapter 4).

4. When an informant introduces into an utterance a form which would have been appropriate in an earlier one, we have errors from paradigmatic feedback, illustrated by the way an informant interpreted stimulus sentence number 10 in the following. (Four sentences following number 4 are omitted, because they are irrelevant here.)

1. He eats.
2. He eats an orange.
3. He gives.
4. He gives me an orange.
9. He bites.
10. A dog bites a boy.

Because of the appropriateness of the meaning "chew" following sentences 1–4, the informant replaced it for "sink teeth into" (implied in "bite" asked by the student). The result is a grammatically correct but culturally unacceptable form, which means "A dog chews on a boy."

5. Error can be introduced by a misunderstanding on the part of either the informant or investigator, or both, of what is meant by same and different in the identification of linguistic units. If an informant says that *dogs* in *he dogs my footsteps* and *two dogs* are not the same, the investigator must find some explanation for this judgment. Whereas native reaction of this type has been assumed to be part of a speaker's psychological response to internalized grammatical structure, it is too easy to forget that such a response is also culturally determined. We cannot expect speakers of two different linguistic backgrounds to understand the concepts of same and different in the same way. The informant's response to a question about identification must always be interpreted and cross-examined.

6. Information about frequencies of occurrence are sometimes necessary and at other times useful in linguistic studies. When the information is based on an identified corpus, there will be no reason to doubt the statistics. Only the interpretation will come under judgment. The real problem lies with field workers who uncritically use their own or their informants' observations. Such subjectivism is especially misleading when frequencies constitute some of the criteria in linguistic analysis. It is clear that when faced with having to decide between two analyses, linguists will opt for the one that accounts for the more normal utterances. Such a procedure is prejudicial, because the final description never records the historical facts of the investigation; only one analysis is presented. We must recognize that most individuals are inexperienced in averaging out an activity which occurs sporadically.[5] An informant's comment that a certain linguistic form "does not normally occur" must therefore be evaluated with caution. This is not to say, however, that we should turn a deaf ear to statements about frequency. They too constitute data which can lead to significant discoveries. It is important, for example, to know that people *think* that "the old folks use that term" or that "the word ain't used as much as it used to be" even though they might actually be wrong.

7. Another kind of error can be called expectation error. Its source is the investigator's expectation of what form an utterance will take. This is unavoidable. No human being can possibly give equal attention to every part of an utterance at one time; he can only focus his attention on what

---

[5] This statement must be modified in two ways. Because there is a correlation between frequency of occurrence and style, one might be able to learn about frequencies by asking informants about the appropriateness of a certain form under certain conditions. Secondly, although individuals may not be able to give useful (that is, more or less accurate) information about frequencies, it might be available by averaging out the responses of many individuals. Thus, John B. Carroll has found a surprising agreement among speakers of English in the estimation of word frequencies (as reported in a Linguistic Forum lecture at the Linguistic Institute, Ann Arbor, Michigan, 1965).

he expects to be new. The rest he is likely to identify as being the same as what he has already observed in the language. This can best be illustrated for phonology. When one has identified a certain vowel, which is transcribed as [ɑ], he may not at first notice that in an environment hitherto absent from the corpus, there is a vowel which is both more forward and higher than [ɑ], one which is really in the region of [ɛ]. The ease with which this kind of error is made is the reason why dialectological field workers must have special training; if they did not, they would probably not hear all the variations in a word like English *bird*.

8. Even without the interference of an investigator an informant can make mistakes. Yet some field workers seem to have operated as if their informants, like customers, were always right. This view is the result of the emphasis by early field workers on describing languages in terms of their own structures and on the insistence that there *was* structure, that what the foreign observer considered exceptions would invariably turn out to be perfectly regular within the system. But we must also realize that the informant is no more privileged with linguistic infallibility (in his own language) than the investigator (in his). We all make mistakes. All that one needs to do is to observe his own speech or the speech of others in his own community for examples of linguistic fallibility.

Because texts are generally tidied up before publication, we rarely are provided with information about kinds of errors which were made. One study, unusual in this respect, indicates each instance where the Sranan (Dutch Guiana) informant later did not know what he had originally meant to say and where he had modified or corrected the text (Voorhoeve 1962). Here are a few of the mistakes:

> *e-ko ala man* "come all men," but the informant thought he had meant to say *te ala man kon* "when all the people came"
> *den bogri boi* "the naughty boys" should be *ogri boi*
> *da wan witji a fesi* "then a week before" should be *fosi*
> *want da den wan* "for then the men" should be *man*
> *d ê-srot e in kupu* "they shut him in (a) cage" was corrected to *d ê-srot en n in kupu* (in fact every *in* was corrected to *n in*) but *d ê-srot in kupu* "they are locked in cages" would be even more appropriate in the context

What is disturbing about the possibility of such errors is that they can occur so frequently. One field worker, using a questionnaire and a number of carefully selected Liberian informants who on different occasions gave Gio equivalents to the same English sentences, found that there was an average of one discrepancy in every ten sentences.

The informant therefore is not always right. But it is assuring to know that he is more often right than the investigator. This is one thing that linguistics has taught us about unlettered informants.

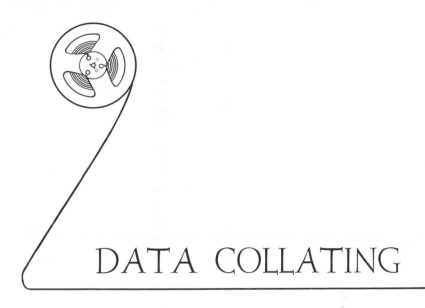

DATA COLLATING

8

As there is no eliciting without some concomitant analysis, there is no analysis without the collation of data. Bringing together a large body of data and classifying them according to similarities and dissimilarities is characteristic of any rigorous investigation. If one wanted to determine, for example, if women drivers were really worse than men, he would have to obtain information about their ages, driving experience, types of vehicles they drove, number and kinds of accidents they were involved in or traffic citations they received. Then, having defined "worse" by some arbitrary set of criteria, the investigator would apply his findings to answering the question. It is this putting together and sorting of data that we are concerned with in this chapter.

Need for Extensive Storage and Processing

For studies such as the one on women drivers people readily admit the need for storing mountains of data. They cannot imagine a person, even one gifted with the most phenomenal of memories, who can retain all the information and produce it whenever necessary. As for language,

151

laymen commonly (a) discount the need for systematic collection of information while (b) trusting their memories to supply whatever is relevant to the solving of problems. People seem to believe that if they speak a language, they control all the facts *about* it.[1] This assumption exists only because of the shallow knowledge people have of their own languages. When asked to produce as many different uses of English *just* as are permitted by the language (*just the man, just he came, he's just a little better, he just came, he just wants an apple*), native speakers quickly recognize their inability to do so. Is it any wonder, therefore, that a foreign speaker of More had never been able to understand the use of the *-se* suffix? He had simply never collected examples. Let this be clearly understood: when we say in linguistics "Analysis must be based on facts," we mean facts whose sources we can incontrovertibly document, not those drawn out of our memories. The only certain way of accomplishing this is to file away data. In some disciplines a scholar is loathe to reveal his "filing cabinet knowledge," but a beautiful language file is the linguist's pride.

Every utterance which enters the corpus must be dissected and its parts distributed through the files. Some utterances will be taken from conversations, others will be obtained during the work sessions (whether isolated or in paradigms), and others will come from the texts. Not all the raw corpus needs to be processed; but if the processed corpus is not identical with the raw one, published descriptions of the corpus should make this fact clear. It is only what is processed, what is used for the analysis, that counts. Texts are not part of the analytical corpus unless they have been used, that is, used in the same way that other utterances were used. One cannot claim to have used his texts when he simply scans them in search of certain kinds of information. We therefore need to know as much about what the analyst *does* with his corpus as about what constitutes it.

When to Begin Collating

One can begin processing data almost as soon as it is collected. Since the first hours of language contact will be devoted to familiarizing oneself with the phonology and some immediately useful vocabulary, there will be little grammatical analysis to do; but there will be sufficient work with sorting out the sounds and classifying the environments. The investigator should not be dissuaded from this undertaking by the realization that the

[1] This is one reason that grammars written by linguistically untrained people are as bad as they are. If linguistics is to have the assistance of those who are not professional linguists (Pierce 1965*b*), the first thing that they must be taught about methodology is the careful collection of data.

transcription is phonetically inaccurate. He must remember, first, that phonetic accuracy is going to come gradually. If he waits for the day when he is sure of what he hears, he may have to wait too long, for accuracy may in some areas of phonology come late. Besides, what bothers him most early in his work may after analysis prove to be relatively unimportant structurally. In the second place, the investigator must realize that he cannot properly elicit without analysis, which means that he will not know how best to use his time without having analyzed. There is no more embarrassing and discouraging experience in field work than coming to the work session planning to "play it by ear" because the last session's material was not processed! Of course, one can blunder along, but when one is caught up with one's material, having filed everything away, he is at the cutting edge of his investigation.

One can proceed for some time without processing the data and then come back to check the transcription for accuracy. There is no disadvantage in this procedure unless one has accumulated too much material. The investigator must realize that going over a lot of old material will be extremely tiresome to both himself and his informant, unless he has somehow systematized the checking; but this is itself a step in data processing.

Ways to Process Data

It has been difficult in the foregoing discussion to avoid the word file because for the field worker slip filing is the most common and the most convenient method of processing one's material; but at least two other methods are used, each with its advantages: namely, charts and punch cards.

The principal function of any data-processing system is to store up information in a systematic way. The best storage device has the following characteristics: (1) it can accommodate a large quantity of data; (2) it permits the data to be used in several ways; (3) it contributes to the ease with which data can be retrieved. These features do not appear naturally in any storage-and-retrieval system; they must be built into it. In the creation of the "machine" one asks himself: what must I do to recover this (or that) information when I want it? The more information there is to process, the more thought must go into the creation of the machine. If a million words are to be processed, 48 hours of preparation is far from extravagant, but 24 hours would be too much for studying 100 words. It is consideration of economy which is the deciding factor in choosing between the various systems for processing data.

(1) *Charts and lists.* Compiling information in the form of charts or lists (so-called flat filing) facilitates comparisons. Similarities and contrasts are

always more apparent in the paradigmatic presentation of lists than they are on slips stacked vertically one after the other in the file box. But the great disadvantage of lists is that they tolerate so little change. A second disadvantage is that they cannot serve another purpose. Once the structural pattern is seen from the data so presented, there can be no redistribution of the utterances. To use them again one must recopy them. Charts are presentations of data designed for special purposes. While they can play a useful role in the collating stage of linguistic analysis, they figure more importantly in the discovery and the description of linguistic structure. For this reason they will be taken up in Chapter 9.

(2) *Slip files*. By slip file (or plain card filing) is meant a collection of slips of paper each of which contains a significant bit of information. That is, each slip represents an "entry" attesting to the occurrence of a linguistic form or its meaning. The slips will document the occurrence of nouns, affixes, verb phrases, words which occur at the beginning of utterances, particular instances of a rising-falling pitch contour—whatever the analyst considers significant to the description of the language structure. Because the entries are grouped in some orderly fashion, the file also represents an analysis of the data. By looking at the headings in a well-labeled file, one can get a good bird's-eye view of the grammar-in-the-making. A rational ordering of the slips generally indicates a growing awareness of the language structure whereas a disorderly file reveals uncertainty or confusion. This truth can be stated in the dictum: know *what* to file away, *where* to file it and *how* to modify the file (if necessary) to accommodate new data and new analyses.

The value of a slip file is that it so easily adapts itself to the exigencies of day-by-day analysis. One day we will have all of the occurrences of verb affixes in the Verb section. Next day these will be taken out, divided according to Derivational or Inflectional functions and placed in a section devoted to Bound Morphemes. All that is required is to introduce a few more properly labeled dividers. A file is therefore very much like a fitting room: one can try out all kinds of combinations and arrangements with no obligation to appear in public until the proper selection has been made.

From the very beginning one should begin to collate data in three principal files: phonological, grammatical, and lexical.

The *phonological file* can have the following divisions:

Words that sound alike (for determining the nature of phonological contrasts)
Dialectal or free variants of words
Regular phonological changes (morphophonemics)
Phones
Jokes, puns, plays on words (because of the possibility of providing clues to phonologically marked distinctions)

Only the section on phones will be extensive. These can be grouped according to "consonants" and "vowels" or according to "syllable initial" or some other category. Those sounds which are unambiguously identified should be specially marked, or even separately filed. For example, if one is having difficulty in distinguishing between [e] and [ε] but hears an unmistakable [e] in one word, this should be put aside as a measure with which to test other instances of [e]. The same can be said of suprasegmental features such as tone: hearing a string of high level tones as in Sango *lo mú kété kóngbá ní* "He took the small luggage" is important when one tries to determine whether the tones of *wále* "woman" and *kóli* "man" are high-high, high-mid, or high-low.

The organization of the *grammatical file* will be largely determined by the investigator's approach to analysis. One person might begin with a classified collection of sentences: for example, declarative, interrogative, imperative—with subdivisions for affirmative and negative; transitive, intransitive; sentences with preverbal subjects, sentences with postverbal subjects, and others. Such a file might pretty well ignore details of affixation if there was a lot of it in the language. Another person, on the other hand, might begin by largely ignoring sentence structure, although he would get considerable help from his general impressions about sentences. He might prefer to seek to isolate and classify all the morphemes in his corpus. He would assign each one to some category. The main headings might be "nominals," "verbals," "modifiers" (of nominals or verbals), and "function words." As various patterns of distribution emerge from the data, the classification becomes more refined: for example, one needs to distinguish nominal themes from nominal affixes; the affixes must be distinguished for position, as prefixal or suffixal; some affixes are inflectional and others are derivational. Some of the works mentioned in the section that is concerned with grammatical analysis (Chapter 9), give more detailed help in organizing one's material.

The *lexical file* will consist of two sections: one for source language (the analyst's) to target language (informant's) and the other in the reverse direction. The TL to SL file will at first be hardly distinguishable from the grammatical file, and if two identical sets are not being made, the lexical file can be thinned out from time to time, leaving only what is necessary to identify the semantic range of each word. The SL to TL file has other purposes and must be handled in a slightly different manner.

A lexical file is indispensable if one of the goals of language analysis is the compilation of a dictionary, but it has other values too. (a) It provides a check on grammatical analysis and meaning identification. One may, for example, find that a particular morpheme or construction is being translated in several different ways, as "at" and "in" as well as "on." Or one may discover there is a formal distinction in verb forms which is concealed by the identity of English past participles: to illustrate, along with "dead" of "that dead goat" one will at first file "dead" of "Is it dead?" only to see that the latter sentence should really be translated "Did it die?" (b) It makes more convenient the selection of words which will be used in elicitation. Whether he wants several nouns or verbs of particular phonological shape or representing specific lexical domains, the analyst can easily find them by thumbing through his file. Finally, (c) the file provides a check on what has already been obtained. Since the field worker cannot possibly remember all the utterances he hears, he will save time if he can verify a previous recording rather than re-eliciting the form he wants.

The keeping of a lexical file is not at all complicated, but certain procedures must be followed to increase its usefulness.

(a) Collate the material thoroughly and consistently. As a check on himself, the field worker can mark each selection from the field notes with a red-pencilled dot.

(b) Underline in a conspicuous way only the English word which is to be filed. If the target language form is to be identified, a different symbol (perhaps a check) should be used.

(c) Separate the slips from each other by inserting a colored slip at the beginning of each batch of slips illustrating the use of a different word and write that word in one corner: Sango *bá* N, *ba* V, *báa* V. On this slip or one which replaces it, one may eventually want to write its definition; the other slips would constitute its attestation.

(d) Ignore morphological changes and file according to a basic meaning, as shown here:

"came" with "come"
"flies" with "fly"
"feet" with "foot"
"am, is, was, were, been" with "be"
"I, me, my, mine" with "I"

(e) File according to some of the grammatical categories:

"possession" ("of," "cat's," "his")
"numerals"
"negatives" ("not," "never")
"future" ("shall," "going to," "about to")

(f) File all the various uses of a word under one heading, using cross-referencing ("stomach, belly, abdomen, womb"). It will be necessary to go through the file periodically to eliminate unnecessary entries. In this way one can also check on statements which are made by the informant. He may on one occasion insist that a certain word means only "garment" whereas on another occasion he translates the same word as "cloth."

(g) Do not file:

(i) English words which are required by English grammatical categories: e.g. "the, a, does, to" in "The boy takes a jump," "Does he feed you?" "He used to eat there"; also "will, shall, would" etc.

(ii) Descriptive terms which are part of the gloss: if a TL form has been identified as "red (hot) coals" one files "coals" but not "red."

(iii) Words which are part of English idioms: "at" in "look at the goat"; "own" in "He washed his own hands" (which differs from "He washed himself" only by the inclusion of the object "hands"); nor "was" in "An orange was cut by him" which is "He cut an orange" + "passive."

In short, file only what is grammatically marked in the informant's language, systematizing the English entries so as to bring all relevant material together under single headings.

The SL to TL file can be entirely alphabetical, or it can be differentiated by word classes: Nouns, Verbs, and Other Words. One can further classify the entries according to lexical domains (kinship terms, names of animals, and others) which are most useful in elicitation. There should also be a Problem section in which are filed words which cannot be defined with accuracy, as in "a certain edible root the plant of which has a single large leaf."

In addition to the phonological, grammatical, and lexical files which have just been described one should also keep a record of the language-learning material which he has produced. It might also be instructive to keep a record of the unacceptable utterances made by the field worker. A file of such utterances which for the time being can be accounted for, neither by the informant nor by the investigator, may very well contain clues to grammatical patterns. Although the nonpermitted constructions on a morphological or syntactic level are always more numerous than the permitted ones, it is nonetheless true that as learners of languages we register and remember what cannot be said. We learn, for example, that "I used to going" is wrong but "I used to go" correct.

The storage material consists of individual slips of paper of whatever size is most convenient. On this slip are recorded at least two bits of information, namely, the linguistic form and its source. The linguistic form should be included with some of its linguistic environment. If there is none, or if it could not be recorded, this fact must somehow be indicated. For example, it should be apparent from the slip that a single recorded word was obtained in isolation. This is why the source of the form must be carefully noted, whether from the elicitation notebook, from some connected text, or from overheard conversation. It is valuable also to distinguish, especially for utterances obtained during a work session, between those which translate sentences put by the investigator and those which are volunteered by the informant. To this minimum one should also add the gloss, unless he is thoroughly familiar with the language. But one should avoid indicating more information than is necessary. Notice the redundant features of the first slip when compared with the second, each illustrating the subjectival use of the Gbeya word wa^2.

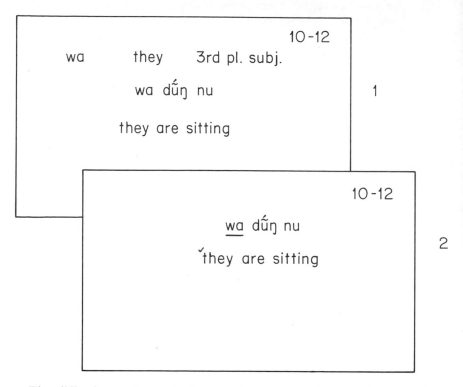

The difficult question which every investigator faces is: how much to file? He may have a fairly good idea as to *what* he should file, but he is uncertain about *how much* is adequate. When one must go through one's corpus selectively, laboriously making slips by hand or with a typewriter, he will put the question to himself again and again. This kind of *selective filing,* as compared with complete filing to be described, has several disadvantages. First, the assumption of knowing what to file is never fully justified in the early stages of investigation. The true significance of information becomes apparent only as the analysis takes shape. Therefore when one decides to ignore a particular instance of a morpheme, not seeing its function in a general pattern, he is unwittingly postponing the day of reckoning with it. Secondly, selective filing is uneconomical with time, because a decision is required for each item which appears in an utterance.

---

[2] The notation 10–12 indicates the date of the original transcription. When slips are to be prepared in mass, efficiency can be increased by using a date stamp and pad.

The *complete filing system* is free of the disadvantages inherent in the selective system and enjoys other advantages.[3] It is simply this: one takes a particular corpus and files away every conceivable bit of information. While it can be used for phonological as well as grammatical analysis, it is the latter use that we shall describe here. It should be remembered that complete filing can also be done with manual punch cards or electronic computers, but we are using the term exclusively for slip filing. The complete coverage of the corpus is made possible by duplicating machines, for it is the making of slips that largely determines how much filing is done. Once the slips are made, the collation proceeds as with any slip-using technique. In describing the process we must therefore pay greatest attention to the preparation of slips.

One begins with the preparation of the master. Any duplicating process is adequate: spirit-duplication, mimeographing, offset. The first process is the least expensive and the simplest to operate. It can also be used for original transcriptions in the work sessions, in this way one can do all his work directly on the masters. Its disadvantage is that it produces a restricted number of legible copies. When working with texts, it is preferable to use the mimeographing machine: time and labor are saved by the use of the longer stencils; stencils can also be re-used if more slips are required. When properly cared for (between absorbent sheets or water-washed—if the proper kind of ink is used), stencils can easily be used after several months even for long runs. They should be clearly labeled. Incidentally, proof-reading of the stencil can be easy if one uses carbon cushion sheets which are sold by the larger distributors.

The master is divided into "frames" of whatever size is most convenient for storage and handling. With an 8½-x-11-inch stencil one obtains 8 frames 2¾ x 4¼ inches in size. With a 14 inch stencil there are 10 frames of the same size, leaving a ¼ inch strip of waste. Onto these frames sections from the text are typed in such a way that each frame has material of more or less the same length, and no sentences are avoidably left incomplete. All the frames are numbered serially for each text, and the source of the data is clearly indicated. If someone other than the investigator is going to complete the preparation of the slips for filing, the material has to be coded for filing. For those working on the Sango grammar project, for which the following slip was prepared, the instructions were: underline everything separated by a hyphen or word division; underline words marked with an asterisk twice (that is, make two different slips for them). The drawing below illustrates a single frame from which a slip has been prepared for the word *tongaso*. (The orthography in this illustration is

---

[3] The technique has been rather widely used by linguistic investigators. H. A. Gleason, Jr., made many practical contributions to its use on projects undertaken at the Hartford Seminary Foundation (Fula, Hausa, Nahuat, Sango).

different from the one later adopted and which is used for all citations in Sango in this book.) The next slip prepared from this frame was for *to-ngana*, the next for *a-*, and so on, until all words had been underlined, one to a slip (and **tãsɔ̃* was marked twice), making a total of 45 slips. Then a duplicate set—another 44 slips—was made for the dictionary project (see Taber 1965). The slips which were left over—and extra ones were deliberately made by running off the stencil more than 89 times—were stored away for other uses.

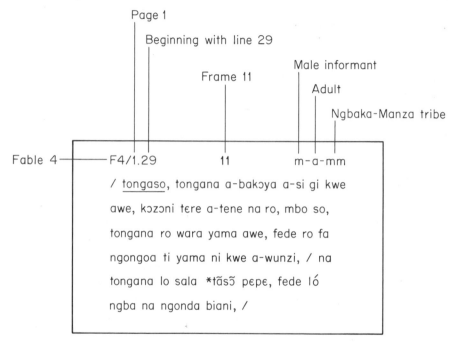

The hyphenated syllables were prefixes (plural marker in *a-bakɔya* and subject marker in *a-si*) and the words with preposed asterisks were French words of which a special study was going to be made. To reduce the number of slips we decided to write some words "solid." Although *so, ni,* and *na* are separable words, they were written solid in *tongaso, kɔzɔni,* and *tongana,* because we knew that these forms were extremely common. If we wanted to recover these occurrences of *so, ni* and *na,* we could go to the files for *tongaso,* and so on. The commas and diagonal slashes indicated short and longer pauses respectively. They were not used in the processing of data but were necessary for the syntactic analysis. This was principally a word and morpheme file. We could have coded the text for syntactical analysis easily enough, but this was not necessary. All noun phrases were recoverable from Nouns; verb phrases (as predicate, complements of other verbs) from Verbs; dependent clauses from *tongana*. For example, we had all the data we needed under Verbs to study the structure of two-verb constructions which are so common throughout much of Africa: namely, *fede ro fa ngongoa ti yama ni kwe a-wunzi* "he will *cut off* (and) *destroy* (the) seed (descendants) of the animal completely."

Underlining has been suggested as the means to code the slips, because it is the easiest operation to perform: one simply fans out the handful of slips and then makes a line under each bit of information. This coding will be done neatly and unambiguously if there is sufficient room between the segments and between the lines of material on each frame. This is why it is advisable to segment at the time of preparing the frames. Notice how much clearer is the coding of the Kikuyu verbal root [mbɛrɛr] in A than in B; the latter represents segmentation done after the frames have been prepared:

A	B
ma-ge-ke-a-<u>mbɛrɛr</u>-ia	ma|ge|ke|a|<u>mbɛrɛr</u>|ia

It is obvious that the slip markers will have to exert more care, and therefore take more time, in marking the second utterance.

To determine how many slips are needed for each stencil one simply tabulates the total of every item which is coded (that is, underlined) for filing. For this purpose it is useful to have stencil record sheets of the type which is illustrated below. It is wise to have some extra slips for contin-

STENCIL NO. 1   CODE NO. L1/1

Frame No.	Words	Morphemes	French	Sentences	Total
1	26	0	1	2	29
2	28	2	2	2	34
3	33	1	1	2	37
4	29	1	1	2	33
5	23	6	2	2	33
6	22	4	0	2	28
7	24	0	3	3	30
8	24	2	0	2	28
9	19	2	0	2	23
10	19	1	4	2	26
Total	247	19	14	21	301

gencies, such as inadequate duplication and unforeseen filing needs. It is obvious from the figures above that frame 3 will require the production of more slips than is necessary for the other frames (14 more than frame 9 requires). This is the reason for attempting to make the contents of each frame as much alike as possible. But the extra slips do not constitute a great waste. Each slip costs only a fraction of a cent, an insignificant factor when compared with the efficiency of the technique. (Incidentally, the stock of unused slips should be well labeled and stored away near at hand. In the United States large quantities of shoe boxes of the exact width of the slips were easily obtained for this purpose. Specially cut but unmounted cartons can also be ordered commercially for this purpose; they can be sent flat to the field.) One colored sheet should be run off to be cut up into dividers for separating each set of frames after they are cut. There should be a few sheets left uncut. These are useful in the study of prosodic and other features where a connected text is needed. After the slips have been cut, being careful to make them of uniform size, they are ready for underlining. It is this underlining which identifies the piece of information which must be filed. Unskilled labor can perform this task. Among the more than 74,000 slips underlined for the Sango project by a group of housewives, duplications and omissions were rare indeed.

When many different texts are being processed in this way, it is wise to keep complete and up-to-date records of the progress being made on each one, especially when there are assistants who are responsible for some of the work. But even when one is working alone, it is easy to lose track of what one has been doing. A progress chart of the kind shown below is strongly recommended. In each cell one adds the date of completion.

This is an appropriate place to emphasize the importance of the keeping of records of various types, although the subject was touched upon earlier in Chapter 5. The purpose of these records is to permit the correct interpretation of one's field observations one, ten, or even twenty years later. This means that one records, in general, what was done, how and why it was done, and when (and why) changes were made. Thus, one might begin by using the symbol ž at one point and then switch to ẓ; one might first write a glide as [kʸ] and then change to [ky]. These changes should be noted in a log with the date and the place in the notebook where they took place. (The log can take the form of a notebook or a section in one's file where notations are stored on slips.) In the process of going over his data the investigator will also alter the meaning, the form of the transcription such as changing [kɛ̃ɛ̃] to [gɛ̃ɛ̃], and so on. It is generally advisable to add the new information without obscuring or destroying the older form. Here too it is important to note the date of the modification.

Among the many advantages of complete filing the following can be mentioned:

(a) It can be initiated at any stage of the field work. It is as useful in working with material still poorly transcribed and inadequately analyzed as it is with material at the later stages of analysis.

(b) It can be done under rather primitive conditions with untrained help.

(c) It can be used for several different projects at once (dictionary and concordance filing as well as phonology and grammar).

	F1	F2	F3	F4	F5
1 Transcribed					
2 Typed					
3 Marked for stencil					
4 Stencil prepared					
5 Text run off					
6 Slips cut up					
7 Slips underlined					
8 Slips alphabetized					
9 Vocabulary filed					
10 Grammar filed					
11					
12					

(d) It provides the analyst with a large portion of linguistic context for each bit of information.

(e) It is economical with human labor and in terms of the equipment and materials used. In processing anything up to around 50,000 words it therefore has much more in its favor than the next technique, edge card. For a larger corpus electronic computers are probably advisable.

(f) It can be used with a small corpus as easily as with a large one. For example, a Temne fable of only 500 words was filed in this way in teaching linguistic analysis to a student. It is in fact advisable to process some data experimentally at first. This analytical experience might reveal the need for coding the texts in more, or less, elaborate ways.

Punch card systems are fundamentally code devices for designating when particular categories of information occur or do not occur. They answer only "yes" or "no" to the question "Does X occur?" (For example, "Does the suffix -*a* occur?" or "Does the suffix -*a* occur when the predication is negated?" Where the categories have already been identified and it is necessary to determine the interrelationships between several of them, punch card sorting can be of considerable utility.

The most practical system for the field worker is the use of *sorted punch cards*. This works on the principle that a previously designated slot is punched out to indicate the occurrence or presence of a bit of information. The selecting device, finding some slots punched and others intact, divides the cards with the occurring item from those where the item does not occur. The cards come in several shapes and sizes and are sorted either manually or by high-speed mechanical sorters. There are several devices for manually sorting the cards, but the one most convenient for the field worker is the needle-sorted edge-punch-cards. Its practicality is due to the ease with which the slots are punched and "needled."

Before looking at the system in general it will be convenient to see how it was used in a specific project, the study of Bambara ideophones. The purpose of the investigation was to determine what, if any, correlations there were between certain phonological features (consonants, vowels, length, tone, nasalization, reduplication) and certain semantic categories. The semantic categories were provisional, having been arrived at inductively from an examination of the 200 ideophones collected from a group of native speakers of the language. (The examples were provided by the informants, but the meanings and the pronunciation were verified by myself. By examination of the literature on the language, the present phonemicization proved to be adequate.) The application of the semantic categories to the ideophones was made by myself on the basis of the translations and discussion with the informants. It was assumed that all Bambara ideophones could be classified under at least one of these rubrics, some by several of them. The figure below duplicates the original card except that the semantic categories have been translated into English: *aye flẽ ti ka mɔnyɔ mɔnyɔ* "he broke the calabash into pieces" (my note adds "very small pieces"). One of the assistants was charged with notching everything but the semantic divisions. A slot for low tone proved to be unnecessary: anything not notched for high tone was thereby designated as having low tones.

All that is required for edge-card filing is a set of suitable cards, a device for cutting out (designated as "slotting" or "notching") the card's edge, and a needle. The *card* must be durable enough to withstand considerable handling. The commercially made ones meet this requirement. There should be enough blank space on the faces for whatever material is to be recorded, but this depends on the amount of information which will be retrieved; the attestation of the presence of some item by the notching must be in evidence on the citation. How much ancillary information is given depends on the nature of the study. However, since this system is designed only to bring together various bits of information, the ultimate source of the citation must always be indicated.

Notching is facilitated by previously drilled holes which come 3, 4, 5, and so on to the inch. They also come in one row (called shallow punch)

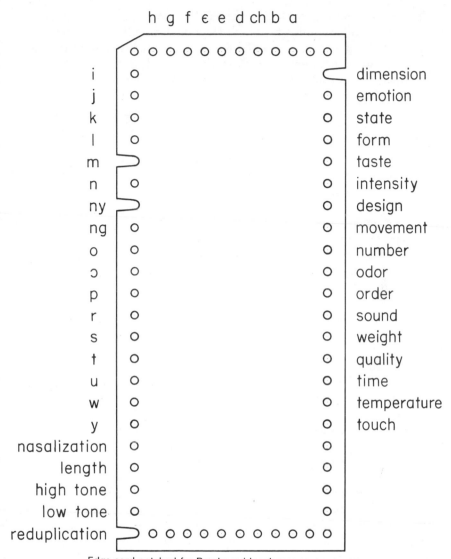

Edge card notched for Bambara ideophone: mɔnyɔ mɔnyɔ.

or more (deep punch) around the edge. Obviously, the more holes there are and the greater depth there is, the more versatile will be the card, but smaller holes will also demand greater care in the notching. The cards used for the Bambara project were obtained from Remington Rand (number P–11782) at a very reasonable cost. Generally, however, cards are extremely expensive. One firm advertised 5-by-8-inch cards at $50.00 per 1000.

The *notcher* most suitable for the field worker is a hand punch, but a platform (or table) punch is faster. The punch should be sturdy enough to go through several cards at once without too much strain on the hand. It should also be adapted to the card being used. Some punches make slots which are too wide for the number of holes per inch; the result is a weakened edge which tears easily. Because even the best of punches becomes dull with use, it is advisable to use one which has removable blades: punching with a dull tool can make notching a painful chore. This is a job which must be done accurately and neatly. The most common error in notching is the failure to remove enough of the edge to permit the needle to slip out without hindrance. To prevent this error some punches have locator tips which are drawn down (the card edge facing the floor) until it engages the lower ring of the hole. Errors in notching can be corrected with gummed paper, various types of which are sold by card manufacturers.

The *sorting needles* with handles are also sold commercially, but knitting needles (either 10 or 14 inches in length) are satisfactory for most needs. For the ⅛ of an inch hole a Number One needle is necessary. Two needles can be used simultaneously but with somewhat more awkwardness than a single needle. When two needles are used, a *sorting tray* is especially important to keep the cards in alignment, but the tray is recommended for all needling. It keeps the cards from falling in all directions on the table. The other difficulty with sorting is the failure of some cards to fall. This can result from pressure at some point, from surface friction which makes cards adhere to each other, or from the interlocking of the notched edges. It takes proper equipment, well-notched cards, patience, and a little skill to get a 100 percent drop at each needling. The success of the needling also depends on the number of cards. Because of their bulk, efficiency decreases in direct proportion to the number of cards, the cutoff point being somewhere around 2000.

The holes along the edge of the card represent the *coding field*. The Bambara card has three fields: a semantic one, a phonological one (subdivided into a section for segmental phonemes and a section for suprasegmentals), and one for a syntactic device (that is, reduplication). The simplest system is to assign each hole a *descriptor,* as is done on the Bambara card, because a single needling will select out all of those cards containing the item, the phoneme /m/, for instance. But where many categories are required, a combinatory system should be adopted. For example, by assigning numbers 1, 2, 4, and 7 to a single field one gets 14 possible descriptors, almost enough to accommodate the semantic categories needed for the Bambara ideophones. In order to get the other numbers, one simply makes arithmetical combinations of 1, 2, 4, and 7: by notching 2 and 4 one produces 6. This system has the disadvantage of requiring needling even for the simple numbers. For example, when 1 is needled all the other cards which have been notched for N + 1 (3, 5, 10, and so on.) will also fall out. A well-planned system can eliminate some of this multiple needling but not all of it. One can, for example, have a zero notched for each simple number: 0 + 1 for 1.

It is most convenient if the code is printed on the card itself. The cost of letterpress need not prevent this being done, for if the holes are spaced widely enough and one uses elite type, one can use a mimeographing machine to duplicate the cards. The alternative is to use blank cards on which one superimposes a master card already fully notched. With the two cards firmly in hand one can notch the unused one. Because of the danger of damaging the master card one can use it simply to mark off with a pencil each slot to be notched.

For *direct sorting* the cards do not have to be stored systematically, but since the cards will be frequently examined for particular kinds of information, they should be groupd according to some major headings. (Ancillary coding is helpful if one uses felt-tipped markers to make lines over the top edges of the cards.) For this purpose the general fields can be used, but in more complicated systems there will have to be a special "ordering field" which guides in *sequence sorting*. It consists of needling the distinguishers in the sequence of increasing magnitude and keeping the numbers in the proper order. If one has a field with the numbers 1, 2, 4, 7, he first needles out all the ones. Keeping them in the order in which they occurred, he places them *behind* the other cards. Then he needles for the twos and puts these behind the others. In this way he needles for the fours and the sevens. The steps are illustrated below; the first column of numbers represents the order in which the cards first occurred. After step IV has been executed, the cards will be in order from 1 to 14—on the condition that no operation has been omitted, that the cards were always placed in the correct order, and that none was omitted or fell out of place!

		I	II	III	IV
(2, 7)	= 9	(1)	(2, 7)	(4, 7)	(7)
(2, 4)	= 6	(1, 4, 7)	(2, 4)	(4)	(1, 7)
(4, 7)	= 11	(1, 2, 4, 7)	(2, 4, 7)	(1, 4, 7)	(2, 7)
(1)	= 1	(1, 7)	(2)	(1, 4)	(1, 2, 7)
(1, 4, 7)	= 12	(1, 2)	(1, 2, 4, 7)	(2, 4)	(4, 7)
(2, 4, 7)	= 13	(1, 2, 7)	(1, 2)	(2, 4, 7)	(1, 4, 7)
(4)	= 4	(1, 4)	(1, 2, 7)	(1, 2, 4, 7)	(2, 4, 7)
(7)	= 7				(1, 2, 4, 7)
(1, 2, 4, 7)	= 14				
(1, 7)	= 8				
(2)	= 2				
(1, 2)	= 3				
(1, 2, 7)	= 10				
(1, 4)	= 5				

There are two advantages of edge-card filing. The principal one is that a single entry can be coded in a number of different ways, eliminating the necessity of having to make duplicate cards. Thus on the single Bambara card 48 discrete bits of information are retrievable. (How much time is actually saved is difficult to determine; in the calculation one must include the time devoted to notching the cards and to needling.) There is also the advantage of interrelating several discrete categories of information, such as in the Bambara project. One field worker used punch cards to determine the extremely complex interrelationships between length, stress, and tone in Huichol (Grimes 1959).[4] The ease with which the cards can be maneuvered permits examination from many different points of view. A hypothesis can be quickly checked out by sorting through the prepared cards.

If the code is not too complex, edge cards can be processed in part by unskilled assistants. Since error will be committed, however, one must decide where there will be the greatest toleration of error. It is probably in the needling rather than in the notching, for with the former spotchecks can sometimes be made, but with the latter omitted notchings cannot be systematically discovered—or only recovered at a great cost in time. Even after careful checking, the original notching error on the Bambara card discussed above was not discovered: /n/ and /y/ were notched instead of /ny/.

The simplicity of this data-retrieving technique is disarming. Its efficiency is dependent, in fact, on a number of considerations. The first one is the number of cards. Processing 10,000 or so cards requires more than ten times the work that 1000 cards would require. On the other hand, a few cards with a limited field of information might possibly be examined with far less trouble by the simple process of inspection. The second requirement is that one has previously determined the categories of information which are to be coded. For example, one cannot use edge cards in morphological analysis before morphemic cuts and morphophonemic relations have been determined. Modifications of the coding system very quickly reduce the efficiency and usefulness of the technique. (But expanding the existing code is possible if undesignated holes have been left for this purpose. It is, in fact, always wise to do so.) In the third place, the most efficient use of the holes results from a thorough familiarity with the innumerable ways that wanted information is retrieved and unwanted information ignored. Careful planning is required to determine, for example, that at some particular point hand sorting will be more efficient than an additional needling step.

---

[4] For another linguist's use of edge cards see Pence 1962. For a general but thorough discussion of the subject of edge cards see Casey *et al.*, 1958.

There is a different punch-card system which deserves mentioning, even though it has not yet to my knowledge been used by linguistic field workers. But anthropologists, archeologists, and sociologists, among others, have found it more efficient for their purposes than the system just described (Garbett 1965). It is familiarly called the "light filing system" for a reason which soon becomes clear; it is also known as the inverted data system. Its distinguishing feature is that the cards—such as those supplied by Carter-Parrat, Ltd. (London), Jonker Business Machines (Gaithersberg, Maryland), and Royal McBee Corp. (New York) —are made for each attribute instead of each unit or form. If, for example, we were attempting to correlate the use of Sango with the age, sex, marital status, ethnic background, religion, literacy, and amount of education, of Central African speakers, we would make out one card for each of these attributes. If 1000 people were interviewed, there would not be that many cards, but only as many attributes as we were studying; the unit system, on the other hand, would require 1000 cards, one for each individual, each one punched appropriately. One can add attributes almost at will without inconveniencing the file. By placing the cards on top of each other in systematic ways, one determines not only the frequencies of units per attribute (how many women know Sango) but also correlations between attributes (how many married women who know Sango also speak French). This system does not require needle filing, for one simply counts up the coincident holes through which light shines.

Computerized data processing is fundamentally the same as edge-card processing: it sorts precoded material on the yes/no principle. Here too one starts with cards which are inserted in a special "typewriter" (a card-puncher) which, rather than producing a copy of the original text, makes a translation of it. The script of this language is in the form of holes punched in the cards by the "typewriter." This is a script which is read by an electronic computer, not by the researcher. But the language that governs the computer is a mathematical system devised by the researcher and by which he communicates with the computer, telling it what to do with the data it receives. There are several kinds of computer languages or "software", all of which are best known by their abbreviations: MAD (Michigan Algorithm Decoder), FORTRAN (Formula Translation), ALGOL, JOVIAL, IT, NELIAC, GAT, and FLOWMATIC. The "hardware" is the computer itself. It consists of the following components: a place to store data and instructions (the wired program); a means of controlling the over-all action of the system; devices for obtaining the needed results; a way of getting information into the computer; and a way of getting results out of the computer. Each computer has its appropriate language to which each project must be adapted. Some computer-language combinations are more suitable for some projects than they are for others.

The linguistic use of electronic computers already has a relatively long history.[5] Evidence for the place of this hardware in linguistic research is seen in the establishment of the Association for Machine Translation and Computational Linguistics which publishes a journal in this field. The use of computers in machine translation is well known; literary scholars have to some extent utilized computers to study such things as style and questions of authorship. Long-range plans are also projected for the study of English syntax and semantics with the storage of over one million words at Brown University (Providence, Rhode Island),[6] at the University of Texas (Austin), and in London.

Only one extensive computer project designed especially for field workers is known to me at this time. This is the one supervised by Joseph E. Grimes and Archie M. Kahan under a joint arrangement between the Summer Institute of Linguistics and the University of Oklahoma Research Institute.[7] It is partially supported by the National Science Foundation. Members of the Summer Institute of Linguistics are eligible to submit text collections for processing. At last report concordances had been made in over 40 languages and about 100 more were to be processed. The concordances are being used mainly in grammatical analysis, but also in semantic research, preparation of materials for fundamental education, and checking of word usage in translations. The programs that make up the system are available to any linguist, although the cost of using them must be met independently of the S.I.L. grant. Arrangements can be made directly with the University of Oklahoma Computer Laboratory. The University of Oklahoma also maintains a file of input texts in machine-readable form which are available for use (by permission of the person who collected the texts) by arrangement with the Computer Laboratory. This text archive is said to be one of the largest of its kind for non-Indo-European languages.

Texts are submitted for processing in an orthography compatible

---

[5] The reader is referred to Jacker's *Man, Memory, and Machines* for a helpful general introduction to the use of computers.

[6] At Brown University there is a corpus of "edited" English (English prepared for publication) chosen at random (using a table of random numbers) from preselected categories of literature. See Francis 1965.

[7] Description of this project is based on correspondence from the S.I.L. member Dr. Grimes. For a general discussion of concordances see Lamb and Gould 1964, Lamb 1965, and the review by Grimes 1965. There are several projects where computers are being devised for the analysis of various aspects of linguistic structure. Pierce has used an IBM 1620 "to sort out random inconsistencies, determine which of several transcriptions of a given word is the phonemic sequence which probably represents the citation form of that word, and collect variant phones, either free or positionally determined, into phonemes" (1965a:128). For an exemplification of how a computer was used in the study of dialects see Atwood 1962.

with the computer typed in a manuscript format such that one line of manuscript is punched as one input card. Below are shown the first two sentences of text TA of the Chipaya concordance project. Line A is in a phonemic notation, Line B in a popular orthography, Line C in the computer-compatible orthography, and Line D is the literal morpheme-by-morpheme translation.[8] From this manuscript, cards are punched with text, a two-letter text identification code, and a three-digit card sequence number. The cards are verified and corrected, then run through a data check program (figure a on pp. 172–3) which finds any format errors

1

A	chi·	kintu	šehl-ča		ķit-štan	škar-štan.
B	tsjii	quintu	žejl-čha		kit-žtan	žkar-žtan.
C	TSJII	QUINTU	ZHEJL-TCHA		KIT-ZHTAN	ZHKAR-ZHTAN.
D	one	story	exist	indicative	fox with	hawk with

2

A	chi	noŋx	ašnu	šerwi	waht-či-ki-ča.			
B	tsjii	nongjj	aznu	zerwi	wajt-chi-qui-čha.			
C	TSJII	NONGJJ	AZNU	ZERWI	WAJT - CHI -	QUI -		TCHA.
D	one	day	burrow	carcass	find	completed aspect	noneyewitness	indicativɛ

that might cause difficulty in the main program. After those errors are corrected, the cards are read and processed into concordance lines. At the same time a printout of the entire input is made in which each sentence is numbered automatically (figure b). In the concordancing operation all the words of the text are printed out in alphabetic order, each in the center of a full line of context (figure c). If desired, a second concordance can be prepared in which all items having hyphens on one or both sides are printed out alphabetically (figure d). A rarely used option permits generation of another set of concordance lines with punctuation marks at the extreme left (figure e). This last output can help in the analysis of certain kinds of syntactic configuration. The printouts in each instance come in the form of sheets of lined paper 11 by 15 inches in size which are folded in alternation but are perforated for tearing apart and assembling into a book.

There is no contesting the value that such a concordance project has in linguistic analysis. The computer does quickly and accurately what the investigator would have to spend long hours at: typing up frequencies

[8] The phonemes are described in R. D. Olson's Mayan affinities with Chipaya of Bolivia I: Correspondences, *International Journal of American Linguistics,* Vol. 30 (1964), 313–324.

(a)

000001

UNIVERSITY OF OKLAHOMA COMPUTER LABORATORY

PROJECT CODE RS-00307A PROGRAMMER NO   NAME/COMMENT   DATA CHECK RUN ON INPUT TEXT

EXECUTE   RUN   DATACHECK

THE FOLLOWING RUN WAS MADE ON 07/28/65 AT 17.60 BY KD   JULY 28, 1965

TSJII QUINTU ZHEJL-TCHA KIT-ZHTAN ZHKAR-ZHTAN. TSJII NONGJJ AZNU ZERWI WAJTTA001
-CHI-QUI-TCHA. ANCHA TCHJERI EEC-ZI-TA-QUI-TCHA NII KIT-ZHTAN ZHKAR-ZHTAN-ATA002
QUI. KITI-KAZ ZINA LUJL-Z PEC-QUI-ZH. ANA JAK-SIL-TA KALL-I AT-QUI-TCHA. NETA003

(b)

CHIPAYA, BOLIVIA-RONALD D. OLSON - SUMMER INSTITUTE OF LINGUISTICS-JULY 14, 1965
SENTENCE 001, TEXT TA   TSJII QUINTU ZHEJL-TCHA KIT-ZHTAN ZHKAR-ZHTAN.
SENTENCE 002, TEXT TA   TSJII NONGJJ AZNU ZERWI WAJT-CHI-QUI-TCHA.
SENTENCE 003, TEXT TA   ANCHA TCHJERI EEC-ZI-TA-QUI-TCHA NII KIT-ZHTAN ZHKAR-ZHTAN-AQUI.
SENTENCE 004, TEXT TA   KITI-KAZ ZINA LUJL-Z PEC-QUI-ZH.
SENTENCE 005, TEXT TA   ANA JAK-SIL-TA KALL-I AT-QUI-TCHA.
SENTENCE 006, TEXT TA   NEKZ-TAN ANCHA KICHJ-AS-QUI-TCHA ASTA AZHKA OT-CHAN-TJEPI.
SENTENCE 007, TEXT TA   ANCHA OT-CHI-QUI-TCHA.
SENTENCE 008, TEXT TA   JJUS NI-NAC-PQRA CON-AS-SI-QUI-ZH KICHJ-AS-CU.
SENTENCE 009, TEXT TA   KITI-QUI LAS ANCHA JJOO-QUI-TCHA.
SENTENCE 010, TEXT TA   ANCHA OT-CHI-QUI-TCHA.
SENTENCE 011, TEXT TA   AJR-KJI-QUI-TCHA.
SENTENCE 012, TEXT TA   ZHKARA-MI NI-ZHA-ZA.
SENTENCE 013, TEXT TA   ANCHA ATA WAA-CHI-QUI-TCHA.
SENTENCE 014, TEXT TA   ANA JAK-SIL-TA NII ZERWI LUL-I AT-QUI-TCHA.
SENTENCE 015, TEXT TA   NEKZ-TAN-AQUI CUNTURI-QUI TJON-CHI-QUI-TCHA.
SENTENCE 016, TEXT TA   NI-NACA CHER-ZH-QUI-ZH.
SENTENCE 017, TEXT TA   ANA-QUI-ZH LUL-I AT-A-TA NII ZERWI.
SENTENCE 018, TEXT TA   WAAA CUNTURI-QUI NUZH-QUIZ NII ZERWI K*ALA CHJIT-CHI-QUI-TCHA.
SENTENCE 019, TEXT TA   KUZH-C CURU OJK-CHI-QUI-TCHA.
SENTENCE 020, TEXT TA   WAAA KIT-ZHTAN ZHKAR-ZHTAN AMUL-AZ-ZI-QUI-ZH NII ZERWI-QUIZTAN.
SENTENCE 021, TEXT TA   NUZH-QUIZ KJONYI IS-SI-QUI-ZH.
SENTENCE 022, TEXT TA   NII QUINTU-QUI ZHER-ZH-TA-TCHA.
SENTENCE 023, TEXT TA   NUZHU-KAZ-ZA.

(c)

ZHEL-AT-QUI-TCHA ANCHA ANCHA CHACHA ANA WIRA ACHUCU TAN-I AT-NYI. ACHUC-ZH-QUIZ ATIP-S-KAT-NYI-PAN-KAZ-ZA. NII CHAWC MIZI-QUI QH003.001
UI-TCHA. TCHJER KAJJ-A OJK-LAY-QUI-ZH ZHONY-QUIZTAN ZHONYI. ACHUC-ZH-QUIZ TJON-ZI-QUI-TCHA, TCHJERI KAJJ-ZH-NA, CJI-CAN. QD009.001
ZHEL-AI-QUI-TCHA. ANA WAC-JAT-A-QUI-TCHA, CJICHIQUIZH PARTI ACHUC-ZH-QUIZ. NII MIZI-QUI ANA MAC-JAI-A-QUI-TCHA. ANA-MI-Z QH015.005

3

TSJII PAJK KJUY-QUIZ TSJII PAWC-ZH-TAN TSJII MIZ-TAN TSJII ACHUC-ZH-TAN TSJII CUCH-ZH-TAN TSJAA WALLPA-TAN TUNCA OZMACH QL002.009
TSJII QUINTU ZA-KAZ ZHEJL-TCHA YACA-YAC-ZH-TAN ACHUC-ZH-TAN. TUQUI IIMPU PARLI-CHI-QUI-TCHA. ACHUCU-QUI CUJ QD001.006

2

(d)

WEJR-QUI ASTA T*AKJIRA ZHELJ-CHINY-*A T*AKJIRA CHJIT-ZH-TA-*A CJICAN MAZ-QUI-ZH. NEKZIAN ASTA MAA EJP-QUI NUZH-QUIZ TUR TT046.010
C-ZA-*A, CJIQUIZH. AAAA TII JUR-QUIZ LAYCU WEJR KUZH-A-ZA-*A CJIQUIZH. OJALA-M KUZH-CAA-JJ CJIQUIZH TURQUI. KUZH-ZIN-Q TT033.006
N OJK-ZH-CU-QUIASTA NUZH WEJR-QUI ASTA T*AKJIRA ZHELJ-CHINY-*A T*AKJIRA CHJIT-ZH-TA-*A CJICAN MAZ-QUI-ZH. NEKZTAN ASTA M TT046.008
ACHJA JOR-QUIZ-ALL-CHIZ-QUI-TCHA. TII JOR-QUIZA-LL PAC-A-ZA-*A, CJIQUIZH. AAAA TII JOR-QUIZ LAYCU WEJR KUZH-A-ZA-*A CJIQ TT032.003

4

ACHA KJAR-CHIZ. JAZIC OJK-CHINY-ZH JAZIC PJAZILA JAZI JAKZI--QUIN WAJT-QUINA-MI TRABAJ-A-QUI-MA AM-QUI, CJI-T-KAL-ZH NII MA039.006

1

(e)

. ANCHA LLAQUI-TA PUJ AT-QUIZ JUL-ZI ZHEL-AT-QUI-TCHA NII ZHONYI-QUI. JALLA NEKZ-TANA-QUI SIRINU-QUI TJON-ZI-QUI-TCHA NII ZHO QF015
. ANCHA LUJL-CHUCA. NEKZTANAC NAA LJOC WALLPIQUI NII ZHONYINACA WILTA ZAKAZ PEWC-ZINY-QUI-TCHA. JEQUI-T WERJ T*ANTA LUL-I YAN QL040
. ANCHA OT-CHI-QUI-TCHA. AJR-KJI-QUI-TCHA. ZHKARA-MI NI-ZHA-ZA. ANCHA ATA WAA-CHI-QUI-TCHA. ANA JAK-SIL-TA NII ZERWI LUL-I AT TA010
. ANCHA OT-CHI-QUI-TCHA. JJOS NI-NAC-PORA CON-AS-SI-QUI-ZH KICHJ-AS-CU. KITI-QUI LAS ANCHA JJOO-QUI-TCHA. ANCHA OT-CHI-QUI-TC TA007
. ANCHA PEC-CHUCA. ANCHA LUJL-CHUCA. NEKZIANAC NAA LJOC WALLPIQUI NII ZHONYINACA WILTA ZAKAZ PEWC-ZINY-QUI-TCHA. JEQUI-T WERJ QL039

Excerpts from print-outs for Chipaya concordance project.

of occurrence and arranging data in specified ways. The material is accurate too, that is, as accurate as the original text is. Another advantage is that it presents the data in a way which makes comparison extremely easy. On the other hand, it is certainly much more expensive than, say, the complete filing system described above. The Summer Institute of Linguistics project, for example, is not recommended for a corpus exceeding 200 double-spaced pages of text, although the Yale University concordance program might be more economical for larger projects. One must also reckon with other difficulties: the preparation of the texts for the card-making typist, the delay in finding a computer center with free time for one's project, the difficulties and risks involved in mailing the texts to the computer center and in having the printouts shipped. (The printouts are bulky and heavy.) If the investigator has returned from the field and is located at a university with a center, these last risks are of no concern to him. The loss of a set of printouts is fortunately not irretrievable since one always has the original punch cards, and a carbon printout can be made at the same time as the original. The preparation of the text which was just mentioned is no simple task, and, as was earlier pointed out in connection with manually processed punch cards, the more that one requires the retrieving system to accomplish, the more work one needs to do on the text. Some of this will be low-level mechanical work, like putting hyphens between morphemes. But where class labels, such as N for noun and so on, are added to the text, the possibility of error is severalfold. It is in fact admitted by Grimes (1963) that one probably cannot consistently class-label throughout 20,000 words of text.

This is where we are today in the processing of linguistic data. One cannot avoid writing down material in notebooks which will be used in that raw form as one looks for significant information or which will be copied and filed away for future use. Greater efficiency can be introduced if one is able to transcribe onto spirit-duplicator masters for complete filing. And punch cards, whether hand-sorted or computerized, have decided advantages which, however, must be frankly weighed against their disadvantages.

PROCEDURES IN FIELD ANALYSIS

9

A collector of language material is not necessarily a linguistic field worker. What distinguishes the amateur from the scientist is that the latter expects to find structure revealed by his data and organizes his investigation to discover it most easily. He does not just amass a large sampling of what people have said in a language. He knows, by and large, what he has to do to achieve his goal of a description—complete or partial —of the language under study. The further he gets in the study, the more explicit his immediate goals become. What this means is that he begins to have a clearer and more thorough knowledge of the interrelationships between elements at each level of the language and between levels. In field work he cannot possibly have the whole picture; that will appear only at the end of the investigation. Rather, the investigator asks himself the question: "What is the significance of this apparent pattern?"

Patterns become apparent in limitations of distribution. Restrictions occur everywhere in language. Whether a person's vocal chords vibrate or not is determined by rules in the language. Take also the use of *any* and *some*. We can say *he didn't buy any ice cream, did he buy any ice cream? I don't think he bought any ice cream,* but not *he bought any ice cream.*

Only *he bought some ice cream* would be appropriate. In other words, *any* is used where doubt or negation is implied and *some* is used elsewhere. A field worker having come this far would want to determine in what other ways these two kinds of sentences would reveal differences, for it is obvious that the difference between *any* and *some* is not simply a lexical one. A lexical difference is one such as *bouteille* "bottle" and *flacon* "flask" in French. But even here the field worker's concern with discovering significant (that is distinctive) traits is illustrated. What makes one word different from the other? With what features is the difference between *bouteille* and *flacon* correlated? As a language learner seeks to answer these questions, so does the field worker, but in more comprehensive and sophisticated ways.

Phonology, grammar, and lexicon were just mentioned in connection with the goals of linguistic field work. They will now be taken up separately in the remainder of this chapter, but it should not be assumed that field research can be compartmentalized in this way. At no time, for example, is the competent linguist investigating only the phonology of the language. Even if phonology is his principal concern at a particular moment, he is probably using clues derived from grammatical observations. It would therefore be wrong to affirm that there are independent steps in language analysis.[1] There are rather several aspects interrelated in different ways at different times to different degrees. It is impossible for anyone to tell the person venturing into linguistic field work for the first time, "Here is the way; walk ye in it!" It is convenient, nonetheless, to follow a certain sequence in acquiring linguistic data for analysis, it being understood that one will prize every bit of speech that may accidentally fall his way.

This chapter on linguistic analysis is only an introduction to procedures which in some instances are quite complex. The purpose of the following pages is to discuss various kinds of matters which are important in field work. This material should be used along with works which deal more thoroughly with language analysis (for example, Gleason 1961, Hockett 1958, Martinet 1964, Robins 1964).

It is always possible to find some minimal but natural utterance, a kind of predication. It may be a noun in isolation, in response, for example, to the question "What is that?" In any case, one can collect several hundred citation forms with relatively little difficulty; they will help the investi-

---

[1] It is therefore surprising to find a linguist who was engaged in considerable field work in the thirties and forties implying that some of his colleagues felt otherwise: "One of us was conducting a LI [Linguistic Institute, sponsored during the summer by the Linguistic Society of America] seminar which was being visited by colleagues . . . ; the seminar was provided with a Delaware informant and devoted to eliciting. Before all problems in phonemics were finalized, it was proposed that the following session should begin eliciting in morphology. But great objection was made to this suggestion by the more rigorous linguists, as though a violation of levels were being proposed" (C. F. and F. M. Voegelin 1963:19).

gator to become familiar with the sounds of the language and will constitute the basis of the next stage. The danger is not in being unable to
elicit words but in getting too many of the wrong kind. At this initial
stage it is not necessary, for example, to get the names of all the body
parts, all the numerals from 1 to 1000, or a full set of kinship terms.
What one wants is a good variety of currency with which to negotiate the
business which comes next.

One should not have too much difficulty in getting verblike words, although it is not always easy to say what the simplest form of the verb will
be. In one language it may be that which is used in a command; in another, it may be what is said in answer to the question "What are you
doing?" Getting "simple" forms of words, however, is not procedurally
necessary, just convenient.

Having obtained utterances containing verblike words, one proceeds to
nominal and verbal modifiers, pronominals, and so on. Starting with these
same lexical items, one elicits brief sentences in which the elements are
found in different positions. For example:

She cooked rice.
The cooked rice is here.
She took some cooked rice.
The cost of rice is high.
They planted rice.
They are rice-planters.
This is not the time for planting rice.
Did they plant much rice?
Their rice fields are over there.
This beer is made of rice.
They planted rice and yams.
They planted rice but I planted yams.
I saw them planting rice.

These sentences illustrate how much one can do with a few basic lexical
items to elicit different categories and constructions. More will be said
below about the procedures which might be followed in grammatical
analysis.

Very soon in field work these sketchy directions become useless. Without map or compass the investigator finds himself wandering in space,
motivated by his own insight and enthusiasm. If at a particular session,
the investigator finds it of some value—and interest—to make a brief ex-
cursion in the study of riddles, he should by all means do so. The work
session will probably benefit from it.

Phonology[2]

TRANSCRIPTION.   Linguistic work begins with writing down specimens of speech. Because no electronic hardware has yet been perfected
which will take a spoken text and prepare it for analysis, the scribal role
of the investigator is indispensable. This transcription of speech is crucial;
a linguistic description in some measure stands or falls on this foundation.
But quarrying the stones and putting them solidly in line for some languages is no easy task.

The analysis of a stream of speech into its component features and segments is difficult when the field worker is unfamiliar with certain articulatory habits. This is why phonetic training is so important to the field
worker.[3] But the difficulties of accurately interpreting an utterance are
increased several-fold by other factors, some of them inherent in the language and others due to the habits of the speaker or to the circumstances
surrounding the speech act. The first are illustrated by what happens under the influence of emphatic sentence stress in Polar Eskimo (spoken in
Thule, Greenland). "As a rule a final stopped consonant is weakened so
much that it can hardly be distinguished, or is simply lost. Only in very
distinct speech the correct stops q, k, t, p will be heard. If the pace gets a
little accelerated q will change into r, or sometimes into the corresponding
ɯ (often further weakened into ŋ), the other stops becoming nasalized to
ŋ, n, m, which, when loosely articulated, can hardly be kept apart. If the
ending [i.e. inflection] contains a long vowel, ɑ· or ɔ·, just this vowel may
turn out to dominate the word. It may furthermore influence whole passages which in this way are characterized by the vowel in question" (Holtved 1952:21). Kenneth L. Pike reports features of higher phonology in
some South American Indian languages extremely different from those
characteristic of European languages. For example, one Arabela "abdominal type is a ballistic start with a controlled but rapid decrescendo through

---

[2] After one has become familiar with the general principles of phonemic analysis, he is advised
to read essays in which authors describe the problems they had to face and the procedures they
followed in coming to their conclusions. These are more common in the *International Journal of
American Linguistics* than in other journals. The following is a random sample: Grimes 1959
(section 4); Haugen 1958; Healey 1964*b*; Hockett 1953; E. V. Pike 1948; K. L. Pike and W.
Kindberg 1956; G. Turner 1958. K. L. Pike (1948) is still important for the analysis of pitch
phenomena. Gleason (1961) devotes one chapter to phonemic field work. A challenge to "traditional" phonemics is to be found in Halle (1954).

[3] There is an abundance of material on phonetic transcription. For example: Bloch and
Trager 1942; Boas *et al.,* 1916; Heffner 1949; International Phonetic Association 1949;
Ladefoged 1964; K. L. Pike 1947; Smalley 1963; Westermann and Ward 1933; C. F. and F. M.
Voegelin 1959.

the rest of the pulse" (1957:31). Since such features will be interpreted according to the connotative values of the investigator's own language, he will often find it difficult to focus his attention on the lower level of phonology which carries lexical meaning.

The second kind of difficulty includes the tendency of the informant to mumble or talk "in his teeth"; the effect of fatigue, illness, or psychological state on articulation; and the influence of poor acoustics and noise on one's perception. The effects may be so subtle that the investigator is aware of nothing but an infuriating inability to take accurate transcription. At other times the source of the trouble is easily isolated, as when an investigator's study of a difficult tonal problem in a Mexican Indian language was made impossible by the behavior of an informant with a bad head-cold. Auditory acuity was driven away by the informant's rhythmic snuffling, her substitute for a handkerchief.

It also happens that field workers sometimes cannot get their informants to reduce their output to a size that can be recorded with a modicum of accuracy. In such situations the tape recorder may prove effective. After recording a text of some kind, the investigator plays it back to the informant in small bits, asking him to repeat what he had just heard himself say on the tape. In this way the informant can be trained to say short phrases and words in isolation.

An informant might also provide useful information if asked to explain how he thinks a particular sound is pronounced. Beach was not averse to using this procedure when he worked on Hottentot: ". . . in inquiring of Salomon Witbooi how the click in [a certain syllable] was formed, I did not ask him, 'Does the air come in at the side?' but rather 'Where does the air come in?' His answer was to click thoughtfully a few times and then to reply, 'At the side,' feeling with his forefingers at the same time fairly far back in his mouth between the *right* molars" (1938:11). This statement also illustrates how careful Beach was in observing even the slightest bit of the informant's behavior.

Field workers seem to disagree on how thoroughly one needs to transcribe phonetic features in the early stages of language work. For example, does one indicate fine vocalic distinctions? What about prosodic features like juncture, stress, and pitch (that is, intonation)? "In the first quarter of this century, Sapir's *Sound Patterns* had the immediate effect of tempting field workers to transcribe texts of preliterate languages phonemically. In reaction, Boas wrote to some of his former students who were then actively engaged in field work . . . to warn them that if they transcribed phonemically, phonetic detail of the languages which they were recording would be lost to posterity" (C. F. and F. M. Voegelin 1963:30). But Morris Swadesh and C. F. Voegelin hold views different from Boas'. The former maintains that "we can realistically expect a linguistic field worker to have some notion of a phonemic system within fifteen minutes of beginning work, and the main essentials within an hour or so. Any problems discovered and still unsolved probably can be better studied later when the researcher has better hold of the material, say towards the end of his first field trip. Even unexpected subtle points, missed or falsely analyzed at first, can be better handled later on. This permits the use of a simplified phonemic alphabet from the first, the teaching of the system to intelligent informants, and mechanical ease in copying and handling notes" (Swadesh 1965:149).[4] Voegelin says that "Time and a variety of voices are worth more for field work than initial phonetic virtuosity" (1942:70). The only demand that Voegelin would make of a field notation is "that upon reading [a text] back to the informant, the informant could translate the text which he dictated into a language known by himself and the investigator. To this notation the field worker would then add phonetic detail gained by listening to the informant repeat parts of the text during the process of translation" (1949:80).

The most prudent procedure would seem to be that of recording as much as one heard—within reason. That is, one should not spend an excessive amount of time making certain that all phonetic features, both segmental and suprasegmental, have been somehow represented. But one should record whatever is heard, even if the transcription is not consistent. This procedure will tend to prevent the investigator from becoming too quickly adjusted to the phonetic differences between his own and the language being studied. An option for phonetic underdifferentiation poses the danger of lowering the general threshold of phonetic perception; one soon believes what he has written. The result may be a failure to identify variations which will turn out to be of allophonic or allomorphic significance.[5] In fact, if the data that one collects in the first 100 or so hours are uniform in transcription, one can be fairly certain that he has normalized the transcription too soon.

It should go without saying that one ought to transcribe neatly and legibly. It is bad enough trying to decode what one has written in one's own language; it is exceedingly more difficult to do it in a foreign language in exotic symbols! One's symbols should also be used consistently, but this does not mean that changes will not have to be made for one

---

[4] An earlier statement appears to be more cautious: "The procedure may take from a couple of days to a week or so, depending on the difficulty of the language and the ability of the student" (1937:728). Compare section entitled "Time Required for Field Work" in Chapter 4 of this book.

[5] Consider the testimony of Hans Vogt about his own field work: "Later on, when I was analyzing my material, many problems arose for which my material did not always allow definite conclusions. Undoubtedly an unconscious selection of phonetic facts takes place, according to the ideas concerning the phonemic structure of the language which are formed during the first few weeks" (1940:7).

reason or another. Exactly what symbols are adopted is partly a matter of personal choice, since field notes are for private use. One may find it convenient to write *zh, ny,* and *ng* instead of [ž], [ñ], and [ŋ]. One wants to make certain, however, that a phonetic distinction is not being concealed —for instance, a language may have [ña], [nia], and [nya].

Below are set forth consonantal and vocalic grids to help the field worker orient himself with respect to the phonology of the language under investigation. The variety of sounds is much greater than these charts indicate; other sounds can be accommodated by inserting them between these, either on a horizontal or vertical axis. (In fact, the consonant chart was made compact by collapsing the alveopalatal and palatal series.) The consonant chart also omits the gliding sounds: [y], [w], [r], and [H]. It should also be noticed that a chart such as this is not restricted to one system of classification: "labial" is opposed to "alveolar" as a point of articulation; in "alveolar" the articulator is implied and in "labiodental" it is made explicit.

As is evident from these charts, sounds are symbolized by their traditional Roman characters, by characters from other orthographies (as with epsilon for the lower-mid vocoid), by the modification of existing characters (as with [š]), and by the creation of new symbols. There is universal agreement for the phonetic representation of some sounds ([p] and [b] for some kinds of bilabial stop), but other sounds are variously represented. For example:

$$p = \Phi = f$$
$$ɓ = \beta = v$$
$$đ = \delta$$
$$š = \int$$

There have been partisans of orthographies consisting of old-symbols-plus-diacritics opposed to partisans of orthographies consisting of new symbols, seen in two representations of retroflexed consonants (ṭ ḍ ṇ = t ɖ ɳ) and the various ways that the click sounds have been represented. The first set was adopted for use in the International Phonetic Alphabet, the second by R. Lepsius for Hottentot, and the third for Nguni languages (e.g. Zulu) by C. M. Doke and others:

Dental	ʇ	/	c
Lateral	ʖ	//	x

Below is a list of some of the ways that phonetic symbols can be modified, mostly with the aid of diacritics.

What is neatly and economically symbolized in type might not have a good equivalent in transcription. Some special symbols seem to defy adaptation in a cursive script (in handwriting). A person who letters is more fortunate, for he can often imitate the type symbols. In marking pitch, it

PHONETIC GRIDS
Consonants

	Bilabial	Labiodental	Alveolar	Palatal	Velar	Glottal
Stops						
Voiceless	p		t	c	k	ʔ
Voiced	b		d	j	g	
Fricatives						
Voiceless	ᵽ	f	s	š	x	h
Voiced	ƀ	v	z	ž	g̲	ħ
Resonants						
Nasals, voiced	m	ɱ	n	ñ	ŋ	
Laterals, voiced			l	ʎ		
Flaps, voiced	ρ	vᵇ	ř			

Vowels

	Front unrounded	Central unrounded	Back rounded
High	i	ɨ	u
Lower-high	ɪ	ɫ	ʊ
Higher-mid	e		o
Mean-mid	ɛ	ə	ʌ
Lower-mid	ɛ	ɘ	ɔ
Higher-low	æ		
Low	a	ɑ	ɒ

Some Phonetic Diacritics

Aspiration	(ʰ)	[pʰ]
Backing of consonant	(.)	[ķ]
Backing of vowel	(ˈ)	[aˈ]
Breathiness; voiceless	(₊)	[a̟]
Breathiness; voiced	(ɦ)	[bɦ]
Click	(˦)	[p˦]
Coarticulation	(ˆ)	[k͡p]
Devoicing, voicelessness	(₀) or capitalization	[m̥], [ḁ]; [M], [A]
Flap articulation	(ˇ)	[d̆], [ĭ]
Fortis	(‖)	[t‖]
Fronting of consonant	(ʌ)	[k̭]
Fronting of vowel	(‹)	[aᶜ]
Glottalization	(ˀ)	[pˀ]
Implosion	hook	[ɓ]
Labialization	(w), (‿), (ʷ)	[ķ͜w], [ḳ], [a̫], [kʷ]
Laryngealization	(ˀ)	[m̰], [a̰]
Length	(·)	[b·], [a·]
Lenis	(ɛ)	[b̢]
Lowering	(˅)	[i˅]
Nasalization	(˜), (.)	[ã], [a̰]
Palatalization	(˙)	[ṗ]
Pharyngealization	(˷)	[m̰], [a̰]
Prenasalization	(ᴺ)	[ᴺp]
Raising	(ˆ)	[aˆ]
Retroflexion	(.)	[ţ], [a̢]
Spreading, lip-	(˒)	[m̩], [a̰]
Syllabification	(ˌ)	[m̩]
Trilling	(˜)	[r̃]
Unrounding	(˝)	[ï], [ë]
Unreleased	(⁻)	[p⁻]
Velarization	(ˠ)	[tˠ]

is not advisable to use the diacritics (ˊ ˋ ˆ ˇ) until one has completed the phonemic analysis, for one needs to indicate the relative heights and glides of pitch from syllable to syllable. Numbering the levels, with a super-script (¹), say, for the lowest level, will solve only part of the problem. The most efficient system seems to be the use of a line which runs through the utterance, as shown below:

"I speak (it) a little, sir." (Nyanja)
The dotted lines indicate uncertainty concerning the level of pitch.

One of the values of indicating prosodic features, about which a question was raised above, is that one can thereby more accurately reproduce the informant's utterances. Even in a nontonal language features of pause, length, stress, and pitch make up a total utterance. The consonants and vowels recorded in the notebook bear as much resemblance to the real thing as does a skeleton to a man! The informant will more easily recognize his speech if it is properly clothed. One can also obtain clues concerning morphological breaks by paying attention to the places where pauses and pitch changes occur. For example, when a Gbeya informant was providing the forms

[amdǔŋnu]	I am sitting down
[mɛdǔŋnu]	you are sitting down
[ǎdǔŋnu]	he is sitting down
[ɛrɛdǔŋnu]	we are sitting down

he must have observed the paradigmatic nature of the expressions, because he put a rising glide on the second vowel of [ɛrɛ] and introduced a pause after it which did not occur before [dǔŋ] in the preceding expressions. As it turns out, [ɛrɛ] is a free form, a separate word, and so is [nu] "ground."

ORGANIZING THE PHONETIC DATA.   Very early in the work of transcription (at the end of the first hour would not be too soon), the researcher should make an inventory of the phonetic elements he has recorded. This is done with the use of tables or diagrams, any means which best organizes the data instructively. The patterned clusters of sounds, such as [ᵐb, ⁿd], can be included with the unit phones, or they can be studied separately. Below, for example, are listed the vocoids recorded during the first eight hours of work on Marathi; the data were mostly nouns in isolation. Phones contained within parentheses constitute the only environment for the preceding phone, and *C* and *V* indicate that several different consonants or vowels occur in the given position. With the aid of this chart one begins to seek the answers to several questions, among which are the following: (a) What phones were possibly recorded because of a hearing error? For example, is there really a difference between [e] and [eⁱ]? (b) What phones are found in free variation? That is, is the same morph heard once with one phone and elsewhere with another phonetically similar phone? (c) What sounds have the greatest limitation of occurrence (in frequency, in being limited to certain morphs, in phonological environment)? (d) Can any of the phones be explained by phonological conditioning? For example, does the voiceless [ɛ] occur only after voiceless consonants in utterance final position? (Since these questions can be answered only by reference to the data, examples of each of the phones should be right at hand. The best procedure is to have them on separate slips in a file.) Notice, for example, how restricted are [ɪ] and [ï]

Short	Long	Nasalized	Retroflexed	Nonsyllabic	Followed by nonsyllabic	Voiceless
i	i·	ĩ		ɨ(a)		
				Vɨ		
ɪ						
ɨ(a)						
e	e·	ẽ	ę	Vɛ ɛɑ	eɨ	E
ɛ	ɛ·					
æ						
ï						
ə		ɜ̃	ə̨	Cə	əɨ	
ɑ	ɑ·	ɑ̃			ɑɤ	
u	u·					
ʊ					aʊ	
o	o·	õ			oɤ	
ɔ						

in comparison with [ə] with which they can easily be confused. The data also reveal that [ɨ] and [ɔ] occur only once, the latter in what appears to be a borrowing from English.

CHECKING AND TESTING. Knowledge gained from the preceding step can be used either as a control on further transcription or as a guide to the checking of what has already been recorded. In any case, sooner or later the investigator will need to determine the accuracy of some of his transcription and may have to identify some sounds as same or different. Checking is needed most wherever there is a great deal of asymmetry, that is, where sounds do not occur in neat sets in points or manners of articulation, or whenever several phones cluster around a particular point in the articulatory chart. For example, if one found that he had recorded [s̺ s š ş], which include fronted, alveolar, alveopalatal, and retroflexed forms, he would certainly suspect that he had not yet identified the informant's sound.

Checking serves another purpose. By going over the sounds that seem to offer no problems one's confidence grows, and the line between certainty and uncertainty sharpens; transcription improves remarkably when

one is sure of what he knows. At some point, therefore, it will prove helpful to make a list of words which contain these unproblematic sounds in
various environments. In this way one can assemble a list of words to provide check sounds when doubts arise. Thus, although the Kikuyu vowel
between [i] and [ɛ] is very high and often difficult to distinguish from [i],
the word [kéréré] "mattress, bed" as used by one informant had vowels
which were clearly distinct from [i] and [ɛ]. Some informants can be
trained to answer a question like "Is that sound like the sound in
[kéréré]?"

In preparing material for checking, one must be careful and systematic.
The important rule to follow is to compare elements in environments
which are as similar as possible. It serves no good purpose to compare an
[e] surrounded by consonants in the first syllable of one word with an [ɛ]
in an open syllable at the end of another word. One may not have a minimal pair like [pe] and [pɛ], but he may have something like [peko] and
[pɛtamara]; and the latter would be better than [pɛɽ̃ã] where [ɽ̃] is a nasalized retroflexed flap.

Words should never be checked in isolation. That is, one does not
simply ask for particular words when there is uncertainty about their
vowels. The proper procedure is rather to run through a list of forms, first
those which contain the sound in question (say, List A), then those which
contain a similar sound (List B). In the process, some solid corrections
will be made, but new problems may arise. Then one proceeds to compare
one word from A with one from B, in various combinations: A_1–B_1,
A_2–B_4, and so on.

A somewhat similar procedure is the one which uses countermodels.
By this term I designate a form deliberately produced by the researcher
with which to compare the one uttered by the informant. The principal
characteristic of a countermodel is that it varies in only one specific way
from the form that the linguist thinks the informant has given. If it seems
that the Sango-speaking informant has said [kɔ́lī], with high-mid pitch
levels, the investigator says [kɔ́lí]. This procedure can be followed with the
segmental phones too. The goal is to present the informant with several
different options, some of which are incorrect, with the assumption that he
will identify the correct one. Obviously, this procedure demands considerable phonetic virtuosity. There are also several ways to carry it out. If
the informant is trained, the investigator can simply tell him, "I'm going
to say the word in different ways. Tell me which one is the best way."[6]
There should not be more than two or three options at a time. Here as
elsewhere one does not take the informant's responses at 100 percent
face value.

[6] Compare "corrective elicitation" in Chapter 6.

Repetition is not the only way to check forms, however. Equally useful is the changing of phonological environments. If, for example, one should hear something at the end of *want* (as in one American dialect where the word is, at least in some environments, pronounced [wãʔ]) which did not seem to be [t], he should elicit such sentences as: *I want a sandwich. What do you want? He wants a sandwich. He wants just a sandwich. He got what he wanted.* If the original environment somehow affected the investigator's perception of the sound, these new environments might help him to identify the phone in question.

In this discussion checking has naturally overlapped with testing, for at this stage of field work the investigator is still trying to determine what is what. There is one more discrimination test which must be mentioned. It is useful after all other study has failed to identify the distinguishing features in pairs of words. That is, one is left with words whose meanings are different but which either sound alike to the investigator because they are homonyms, or seem to vary in unsystematic ways. Very briefly it takes the following form. One selects the words to be compared and arranges with an informant to record them, in random order, with a tape recorder. The list could contain just one pair of words, although two pairs might be used. Since one is not certain to begin with that the words in question are not homophonous, it is important that each member of a pair be uttered the same number of times, for the discrimination test is based on the assumption that a phonemically distinct pair will be distinguished nearly 100 percent of the time by the informant, but if they are homophonous, the figure will be around 50 percent; that is, the informant can only guess at the meanings from the sounds.[7] The list should not contain too many forms, for fear of fatiguing those who will take the test. The recording must contain nothing but the informant's words; the cues as to which words—carefully noted in writing by the investigator—he must give are nonoral. If, for example, one were going to record the Gbeya words [tuwa] "house" and [duwa] "goat," drawings of these objects could be shown to him. After this one plays the recording to various subjects, recording their responses. They can point to an object or provide the appropriate translation. If the response of the subject is somewhere between 50 and 100 percent, one should examine the responses to see which forms were most often identified accurately. For example, it may be that where the score was 70 percent, the word [duwa] accounts for 20 percent of the

[7] It has been discovered while working with Spanish, however, that some known phonemic contrasts were identified only 90 percent correctly, and the range was from 100 to 30 percent (Saporta and Contreras 1962:261). The test here described seems to have first been suggested by Z. Harris who called it the "paired utterance test" (1951:32ff). A more complete description is in Healey (1964*a*:911). Attention here and elsewhere given to this test illustrates the need for more published statements of what procedures field workers have found to be useful in their own work.

error. This figure might indicate that although [t] and [d] were phonemically distinct, there was some free variation. This hypothesis should be tested with other words which have a [t : d] contrast, for the variation might have a lexical restriction. In any case, it would be prudent to use more than one pair of words to test any set of sounds, such as [teá] "came," [dɛá] "did"; [kɔ̃] "hole," [gɔ̃] "leopard."

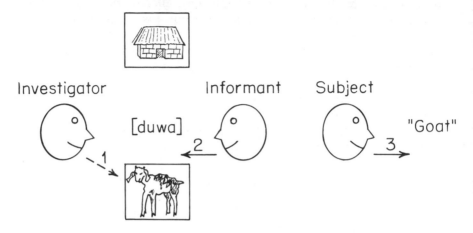

This test can be administered without the use of a tape recorder, but one will need the trained speaker every time the test is administered. The subject in the test, the hearer, must face in another direction to make certain that he gets no clues from the other participants in the test. These can be seated as illustrated in the drawing above. The broken line represents a nonverbal stimulus, the solid line 2 the verbal stimulus, and 3 the verbal response in translation.

No matter what procedure the field worker uses in testing pairs of words, he must always avoid inducing the informant to insist on a difference when none exists. I have seen informants do just this.

There are not many mechanical aids for phonological research in the field. In analyzing sounds which are produced by the tongue coming in contact with the palate, one can, however, use a particular linguagraphic and palatographic examination. This is accomplished by spraying the alveolar ridge and palate with a powder consisting of equal parts of powdered medicinal charcoal (obtained from a pharmacist) and "sweetened drinking chocolate," using a spray (which can also be obtained from a pharmacist). The informant is then asked to articulate the problematic word two or three times to assure the identification of a pattern. By examining the area of the roof of the mouth which has been discolored (or "wiped off") and the part of the tongue which has picked up the powder, one can draw some conclusions about the distinguishing articulatory features. It can be illustrated by Peter Ladefoged's study of the sounds in Ewe and some of the Central Togo languages (West Africa) which have been represented by *d* and *ḍ*. His conclusion is stated as follows: ". . . in all these languages the principal difference between these two sounds is in the part of the tongue that is used. Orthographic *d* is articulated with the blade of the tongue against the teeth and alveolar ridge, whereas *ḍ* is articulated with the tip of the tongue against the alveolar ridge (usually, but not always, the posterior part). [The accompanying figure] shows palatograms of an Ewe (Kpandu) speaker saying the words *é dà* 'he throws' and *é ḍà* 'he cooks.' It will be seen that the area of contact between the tongue and the roof of the mouth is smaller in the second phrase than in the first. Examination of the subject's tongue after the pronunciation of each phrase also made it clear that in the case of *é dà* the black medium had been wiped off by the tip and blade, but in *é ḍà* only a small part of the tip about 5 mm across had touched the roof of the mouth; since the area of contact on the roof of the mouth is wider than 5 mm the tip of the tongue must have moved as it made contact" (1964:20).[8]

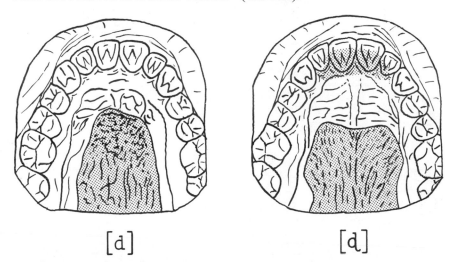

[d]   [ḍ]

Palatograms illustrating the difference between a voiced (laminal) denti-alveolar [d] and a voiced (apical postalveolar) [ḍ] in Ewe. (*Adapted from Ladefoged 1964 by permission of the author and the Cambridge University Press.*)

A photographic record can be made of the palatographic impressions by rigging up a camera with flash attachment as devised by Ralph L. Vanderslice. Figure A shows the apparatus fully extended. The mirror, at the extreme left, is inserted in the mouth. When the palate is appropriately

[8] For a more thorough discussion see Firth 1947/1948.

A

B

Camera and attachments
for direct photopalatogra-
phy. (*Photographs by permission of Ralph L. Vanderslice.*)

C

D

E

reflected on it, a photograph is taken. Without the mirror, the articulating part of the tongue is also photographed. Figures B–E show the apparatus being collapsed.

Another technique that the field worker can use is reverse playback. This is done with a one-track tape recording by turning over the reel, and playing the tape in the reverse order in which it was first recorded. One advantage of this technique is being able to listen to a stretch of speech from a different point of view. This procedure sometimes helps in the perception of certain segments or sequences of segments. More important is the way in which one can verify some of his statements about the phonetic make-up of a form. If a person claims, for example, that the syllabic nucleus of the English word *maim* in his own pronunciation is a long vowel, something like [e·], how can he—without spectrographic analysis— verify the fact? It is not certain that he will come to any different conclusion by listening to others who supposedly speak the same dialect. He may make the error of interpreting their pronunciation in terms of his own. Getting competent outsiders would introduce the necessary objectivity, but people have been known to reject this kind of evidence on the claim that as speakers of their own language they themselves were the ultimate judges. Verification is in fact rather simple with reverse playback. All that one needs to do is state what he would expect to hear. He might insist that since there is only one syllabic bordered by undifferentiated consonants, he will hear [me·m] forwards and [me·m] backwards. The person who claims, on the other hand, that there is a vocalic glide should hear something like [mʸem]. Both of them may be surprised in hearing features other than those they expected: the [m]'s might be different in articulation, the glide might be accompanied with some lip rounding, and so on. But such a procedure should provide strong, if not conclusive, evidence for one or the other interpretation.[9] One must realize, however, that this device and others like it cannot assure one of objectivity. The viewpoint is changed; one set of prejudices is replaced by another. The change may be a good thing, but it is still nothing more than a change. Ultimately, a decision must be based on carefully weighed evidence of various sorts.

If one decides to submit his data for spectrographic analysis—equipment for which appears to be still rather uncommon at universities where linguistics is taught—he should record the problematic words on tape. Every effort must be made to achieve a high fidelity recording: strong, steady electrical current; recorder in good condition; tape speed at 7½

---

[9] The use of reverse playback is reported by Martin Joos in the discussion of Haugen 1959 (p. 66). Haugen contests the value of this technique, pointing out that the phonemic sequence /yiy/ in his speech sounded in reverse playback like the word *he* (p. 67).

i.p.s. or even higher. It is also extremely important to have very dead acoustics in the recording room; echo and background noise must be reduced to as close to zero as possible, otherwise the spectrogram will include this noise in its readings. The words should also be repeated, in a monotone, several times in succession. The recording must be accompanied by a careful discussion of the problem and a transcription of the words with translation.

All of these mechanical techniques are helpful, but the field worker must not pin his hopes on them. It is good to remember what phoneticians have long known, namely, that "even the most extensive array of instruments can never be a substitute for the linguist's accurate observation and imitation of an informant" (Ladefoged 1964:xviii).

The goal of all of this phonological investigation is plainly the determination of the structurally significant units of speech and the description of their interrelationships: phonemics (including allophonics) and morphophonemics. But this final analysis does not come at the end of the project, after the phonetic questions have all been settled. One begins very early to draw some conclusions about the phonemics of the language; in fact, except for a few knotty problems, a fairly valid phonemicization can be arrived at in a surprisingly short time. While it is taking shape—this is important—it contributes to a realistic perception of the language's sounds. The sounds are heard, not as isolated and exotic entities, but as pieces in an integrated, rational system. Therefore, of all the techniques which have been treated in connection with phonological analysis, the indispensable one is the phonemic approach.

As in all linguistic analysis, the investigator can be both helped and hindered by translations as he works on phonology. On the one hand, translations which do not appear to have anything in common can be used as clues for the existence of phonologic contrasts, and, on the other hand, these same differences might be unconsciously used as proof that forms which were transcribed differently were in fact different words. The one is a problem of underdifferentiation and the other of overdifferentiation.

UNDERDIFFERENTIATION.   Since it is the function of phonologic features to "distinguish" morphemes, one expects phonologic differences when he finds similar forms with different meanings. Therefore a set of words tentatively classed as homonymous is valuable, because it may provide evidence for minimal or near-minimal contrasts. For example, if one finds two separate slips in one's Sango file with the form glossed in the one instance as "beer" and in the other as "co-wife in a polygamous household," he supposes an error in transcription. Further checking reveals that there are two words distinguished by tones (low-low and low-high respectively): *samba* "beer" and *sambá* "co-wife."

After one has checked a set of words and found that there is no phonologic difference, he concludes that they are homonyms. But if the glosses for a single word are numerous, one's problem may be semantic instead of phonologic. That is, he may be failing to see the semantic range of each member of the homonymous set. The error is one which is easily committed by a person not fully acquainted with a particular foreign culture. This point can be illustrated by the entries in one dictionary of the Bambara language. For example:

> *ba:* mother, goat, river, big, thousand
> *gwa:* porch, verandah, family, kitchen, hearthstones

For the word *ba* one suspects that there are different words for mother, goat, and river, distinguished by tone, vowel quality, or vowel length. If no contrast were found between the forms associated with these concepts, one would have to accept them as homonymous—or admit that a phonologic difference still eluded him. Between "big" and "thousand," on the other hand, he might not find any contrast at all, because it is possible for these two meanings to be related; "big" and "thousand," after all, both refer to large quantities. One might therefore conclude with the following lexical differentiation: ba_1 "mother," ba_2 "goat," ba_3 "river," ba_4 "big, thousand."

The second entry, *gwa,* more clearly illustrates the sometimes unexpected meanings that words may have. We start with "hearthstones," the place where the family meals are prepared. From the Western, especially American, point of view, the place where meals are prepared is called a kitchen, and if this place happens to be in some type of enclosure, the equivalence is all the more appropriate. If the meal is regularly prepared at the side of the house, under the eaves of the overhanging thatched roof, one can imagine that this area can be called by extension porch or verandah, although it is quite different in form from the part of a house so called in Western society. Finally, since those who normally sit around the hearthstones to keep warm are members of a family, it is easy to see how *gwa* would come to be applied to this group. (In Gbeya, for example, a kin group is called *nú-wey* "edge of the fire.")

It is therefore only as the investigator becomes acquainted with a culture that he begins to see why so many apparently different meanings can be associated with a particular word. Sometimes, however, knowledge of the contemporary scene is not enough; one will understand better if he knows something of the history of the culture or of the words being examined. For example, *butter* in many American homes refers both to dairy butter and to oleomargarine (and in fact it would be insulting to one's host to ask for *margarine* to be passed at the table!), and nowadays *blackboards* in many schools are green.

OVERDIFFERENTIATION.   In the early stages of field work one can
easily overdifferentiate, but the overdifferentiation discussed here is not
simply the hearing of unstructured phonetic differences. This latter kind
of over-hearing will to some degree always occur until an investigator has
become more familiar with the sounds of the language he is studying.
What is called overdifferentiation in this context is the premature fixation
of a particular transcription because of a supposed difference in meaning.
For example, one might transcribe [lé] for Sango "eye" and [lɛ́] for "face"
and believe that he had a minimal pair which proved the phonemic contrast between /e/ and /ɛ/. The error here is failing to see the semantic
relationship between "face" and "eye." In this language, as in some other
African languages, a single word refers to all of the human being's visage
as well as to that part of it we call "eyes." (And as we can speak in English
of the *face of the water,* one says in Sango *lé tí ngú* "face of water.")

Morphology and Syntax

The bulk of linguistic field work is taken up with grammatical analysis. The results will constitute the grammar proper: the description of
all the meaningful units with statements about their form, function, distribution, and—in the case of some classes—inventory. Semantics has
until now been excluded from this domain, because techniques had not
been developed to approach it structurally. The picture today is considerably different. Semantics is being studied from different points of view by
numerous investigators. We restrict ourselves to some practical suggestions on field lexicography later in this chapter.

There has been considerable discussion concerning the organization of
grammatical analysis. For a long time morphology was rigorously distinguished from syntax, if not in theory then certainly in practice.[10] For over
a decade now concerted efforts have been made to comprehend all of
grammar within a single conceptual framework. While linguistic theory
will always have a bearing on the discovery procedures utilized in field
work, the researcher can proceed with whatever linguistic tools he has in
hand. For him the question "Is syntax different from morphology?" is not
a crucial one. It will be convenient, in any case, to distinguish them in this
treatment of procedure.

Two important steps in grammatical analysis are *determining the mean-*

---

[10] For example, in Eugene A. Nida's *Morphology: the Descriptive Analysis of Words* (1949,
2d ed.), where morphology is defined (p. 1) as "the study of morphemes and their arrangements
in forming words [used in the traditional sense]," and morphemes as "the minimal meaningful
units which may constitute words or parts of words."

ing and *editing the data*. In the case of material obtained by reverse translation, the meaning will already be in the notes. (This is not to imply, of course, that changes may not have to be made.) But where recorded texts are to be used, these must be carefully gone over with the informant. The researcher can test his understanding of the text by the extent to which he can render it in a readable and intelligible form in his own language.[11] It is a step which should not be omitted, even when the linguist has a fairly good grasp of the language. He will certainly find later, as he works with pieces from the text, that analysis is slowed down or rendered impossible (or dubious) because of not understanding what was meant. Is this to say that meaning is necessary in linguistic analysis? Although the answer might appear to be an obvious yes, the suggestion has been made that distributional criteria alone are theoretically sufficient for structural analysis, but the view has not gone uncontested among linguists. The field worker need not take sides, however, for it is generally recognized (i) that a great deal of analysis can be accomplished (recurrent partials identified) by comparing utterances of the same language or paired utterances of two languages, both of which are unintelligible to the researcher;[12] and (ii) that although meaning is not a prior known factor available as a criterion in analysis, it certainly constitutes a heuristic tool in analysis. It should also be pointed out that without a proper grasp of the meaning of forms, one may fail to identify all the structure which exists in a language. In any case, it is legitimate for the analyst to use every possible evidence to arrive at linguistic patterns as long as he is not led by the nose. The criteria for linguistic analysis must be rigorously established, and they must be consistent within some theoretical framework.

By editing a text we mean preparing it for analysis. This will involve (i) adopting a consistent symbolization which will render the data amenable to analysis and (ii) identifying those stretches of speech which seem to resist description. Choosing one way to represent a particular morph is a form of editing. It involves not only deciding what sounds (or phonemes) must represent it but also where, in fact, it begins and ends. The determination of sentencelike stretches is also one of the concerns of editing. The problem is illustrated by two ways of handling the supposedly "cryptic reply" of President Eisenhower to a reporter's "I wonder if you could tell us how you feel and how you enjoyed returning to what has been reported one of your favorite sports?" *Time* magazine (July 26, 1963, p. 17) edited the reply in the form under A:

---

[11] For several articles which deal with translation in field work see the *International Journal of American Linguistics,* Vol. 20, No. 4 (1954).

[12] H. A. Gleason, Jr., has experimented with these procedures with students, using material from the Kâte language.

A	B
I like it. I was—didn't think I was going to play golf again until my trip— I don't want to get into a discussion of back difficulties—but my trip to Europe, I think, helped—getting out of that office did something. So I enjoy it.	I like it. I was . . . didn't think I was going to play golf again until my trip. I don't want to get into a discussion of back difficulties, but my trip to Europe, I think, helped. Getting out of that office did something. So I enjoy it.

Although we do not have a tape recording of the reply, where intonational clues would be very helpful, it would seem that there was only one "false start," indicated in B with (. . .). Otherwise, *Time*'s long second "sentence" is a sequence of three "sentences." The "sentence" in A would probably defy description as a single unit, except on an *ad hoc* basis, but each of the sentences of B is entirely normal.

There will be errors in almost any text, but especially if it is spoken and extemporaneous, a matter which we have already looked into. At this point we need only to be reminded that anomalous constructions, when edited out, must not be thrown out. What appears to be an "incorrect" form may, after a larger collection is obtained, prove to illustrate a valid, although rare, pattern. The second thing to remember is that editing must be done judiciously. The investigator applies his own knowledge and the informant's feelings to each text. Although the language is the informant's he is not automatically an infallible judge as to what is admissible. Notice what happened to a field worker investigating Colorado, a language spoken in Ecuador. In this language "the particle *titi* is the most common indicator of historical past tense in folk tales. When tape-recorded folk tales have been transcribed for analysis, however, every informant has unconditionally rejected *titi* as 'bad' and has substituted for it the suffix *-manti*, even though the tape may be of his own speech" (Moore 1964:85). No explanation is given for this rejection, presumably because the investigator had not yet discovered one. We can assume that there is one; if it is not grammatical, then it is stylistic. The point in any case is that the informants had a double standard for "correctness" of speech: what is rejected at one level of consciousness is permitted at another level.

Whether it be a part of editing or not, *segmentation* is a definite step in analysis. What is bound and what is free? Where does the stem end and the suffix begin? These are the kinds of questions which one asks himself in breaking up the stream of speech into its fundamental units. The most common procedure is the assembling of utterances in such a way that recurrent partials will stand out in contrast with the rest of a paradigmatic set. As we have already seen one of the functions of eliciting is to collect material for such comparisons. In languages where there is a great deal of vocalic elision, such as Yala and Kikuyu, eliciting is also necessary for breaking up long utterances and reconstructing the "basic" forms of the constituent parts.

When a literate and intelligent informant is available, a text can be segmented and forms identified on the basis of recurrence of forms. The procedure, called "operational pre-syntax," as suggested by D. L. Olmsted, is designed to come after phonology but before syntax; and while independent of morphemic analysis, it would prepare some of its raw material.[13] Its purpose is to increase replicability at this stage of analysis: devising a way for different field workers to prepare similar (if not identical) bodies of data based on the same language. For Olmsted the identification of "potential pauses," as distinct from real pauses, does not have this power, because it depends so heavily on the efficiency of the instructions given to discriminate between the two kinds of pauses. It is also claimed that it avoids the weaknesses inherent in the use of substitution (which is the technique implied in the preceding paragraph) as a criterion for identifying units. The operations, somewhat modified by myself, would involve the following directions to the informant-transcriber:

1. Use spaces for separation:
    a. When a pause actually occurs between the items in the texts.
    b. When the items on each side of the space can occur elsewhere by themselves in exactly the form in which they occur here.
2. Use hyphens for separation: When only one of the items on each side of the hyphen occurs elsewhere by itself either in the same form, or in a slightly changed form.
3. Use equals sign: When neither of the items on each side of the sign occurs elsewhere by itself.

Applied to an English sentence (in orthography), there would result the following notation: *The boy-s re = ceive-d two dollar-s.* It must be pointed out, however, that this procedure must be subjected to further testing, for it has been used by only one linguist on one language with the aid of a single informant. But it is precisely this kind of experimentation with field techniques which is so much needed in linguistics.

The next steps are *collation* and *comparison*. In collation (treated already in Chapter 8) one brings together all the occurrences of different kinds of units, and in comparison one brings together different but similar sets for the purpose of identifying contrastive features. In other words, one prepares various arrays of data in order to discover the structure revealed in them. How one arranges his data seems to contribute substantially to the ease with which one accomplishes an analysis. Putting forms in columns, for example, is much more instructive than putting them in rows. It is useful, moreover, to look at the same set of data from different

---

[13] The procedure is described in *Korean Folklore Reader* (1963). The theoretical justification for it is found in the *Reader* and in Olmsted 1961.

points of view. In other words, the configuration of a battery of forms can be drastically changed, now emphasizing one part, now another. In the terminology of K. L. Pike and his colleagues this is "matrix analysis":

> A matrix is first set up with rows and columns determined by some arbitrary arrangement of semantic categories, or units, or components of various types. Then one column is moved to right or left so as to bring together—or closer together—similar formatives (phonological intersects in the cells); this operation is repeated as often as is desired. Similarly—or alternately, with a column change—a row can be moved up or down to bring formatives together. The goal: (a) to get the most compact blocks of formatives together, and then (b) to study semantic or formal characteristics of these blocks (Pike and Erickson 1964:201).

Further explication is to be found in K. L. Pike 1962 and 1963.

One of the values of any two-dimensional cellular array of data is to reveal what is permitted in the language or what theoretically possible constructions need verification. Notice the limitation on the use of the verb *ought* in English:

eats	*eating*	*ate*	*eaten*
hits	*hitting*	*hit*	*hit*
beats	*beating*	*beat*	*beaten*
meets	*meeting*	*met*	*met*
ought	———	———	———

As has already been pointed out in Chapter 4, gaps such as these are checked with an informant by elicitation. Not every single form needs to be checked out during preliminary analysis, however; as soon as the field worker is able to predict the form that will go into any cell, he can assume that he has ascertained the relevant bit of structure. Where precisely the cut-off point is in elicitation is hard to say, but the following array of forms is not the kind that the researcher can have confidence in:

eats	———	*ate*	*eaten*
hits	*hitting*	———	*hit*
———	*beating*	*beat*	———
meets	*meeting*	*met*	*met*
ought	———	———	———

No one has a patent on particular ways of arranging forms for comparison. All that the field worker needs to do is use his imagination. When he finally comes up with a particularly ingenious manner of identifying the morphs, it may not be due so much to the arrangement but the thought which went into its creation. A reverse alphabetical arrangement, for example, has nothing about it which is distinctive, but for a language which has a considerable amount of suffixation, it might reveal a great deal.

Looking at data in the ways which have just been suggested is part of the next aspect of the investigator's task, *analysis* itself. More than once we have said that it begins very early in field work. When it comes to looking at one's data in a systematic way, one should always start with those sections of one's file where documentation is more abundant. The reason is that in general the ease with which grammatical structure is discovered is in proportion to the diversity of the environments in which a linguistic element occurs. In other words, one is probably going to learn more—and be more certain about what he learns—with 25 slips than with 8 or 12. With the lower number no pattern at all might emerge, and all that one would have accomplished by an examination of the slips is to become more familiar with the data. When faced with one section of 150 slips and another with 63, there will frequently be the temptation to start with the smaller batch—man being the lazy creature that he is. In the long run this is the less productive alternative.

Beyond this there is not much that one can say about preliminary analysis. One must, of course, have prior understanding of the nature of grammatical structure. This knowledge is gained either from going profoundly into one or two languages or from problem-solving of an eclectic nature. E. A. Nida's *Morphology* (1949) is of the latter type. A. A. Hill's *Introduction to Linguistic Structures: From Sound to Sentence in English* (1958) is an example of the former type.

Researchers going to the field for the first time will always be prepared in different degrees and in different linguistic traditions. But none of them can apply his theory and his techniques to the data with the assurance that a description will automatically appear. Analytical procedure is for everyone a trial and error—or as one linguist put it, guess-and-check-process.[14] One must expect to make errors in the application of any method (although it is certainly the job of linguistics to discover those procedures which lead to the least errors). In linguistic field work, as in so many other areas of life, the proverb "Nothing ventured, nothing gained" applies. The linguist must take risks, intelligent ones of course, but they are still risks. Deciding not to indicate vowel length in transcribing language material may prove to be harmless, but if it was the wrong decision, the researcher will have to recheck as much material as he has already collected.

In any analysis many things can go wrong. The most common error is simply failing to see the better way of describing the same data. The causes for this failure are psychological, and there is nothing that one can prescribe against it. But there are other errors which one can do something about. The first is being satisfied with *ad hoc* explanations, that is, those

---

[14] For a particularly interesting discussion of the procedures which were followed in the analysis of Huichol see Grimes 1959.

which account only for a very restricted amount of data. A discussion of English noun plurals which related *children* to *child* without incorporating *brother* : *brethren* and *ox* : *oxen* in the statement would be such an explanation. To avoid *ad hoc* descriptions one must be certain that he has examined every bit of data which could possibly be covered by the tentative statement. Most of all, one must be suspicious of any phenomenon which seems to demand its own justification.

The other error which must be avoided is underanalysis. This is the failure to identify all the linguistically relevant units. Its cause is quite often the premature identification of forms in the language being studied with those in the contact language. The inexperienced linguist will stop analyzing when something is equated with a word in his own language. Thus, if a person heard the Gbeya forms [áɔánu] "he's asleep" and [wáɔánu] "they're asleep," he might think that [ɔánu] meant "be asleep." It actually consists of ɔ "be, sleep" + -á "perfective suffix" + *nu* "ground." Another example of underanalysis is the treatment of the so-called set of 14 Cherokee verbs for washing which have been bandied about since 1823 (Hill 1964:86) and which have been alleged to prove that "primitive tongues have a multiplicity of forms, fail to generalize, and are almost exclusively concrete." Below, on the left we have a few of the original forms—which were interpreted as single words in spite of the disjunctive writing—and on the right A. A. Hill's tentative analysis:

I am washing myself, as in a river	*Cŭ tŭ wō*	*k-ata-wo*	I-*reflexive*-bathe (in a stream)
I am washing my head	*Cŭ lē stū lā*	*k-ali-sdul-e*	I-*reflexive*-head-wash
I am washing my hands	*Tā cà sā lā*	*de-k-asul-e*	*plural object*-I-extremely-wash
I am washing my face	*Cŭ cŭ squō*	*k-a-gəsk-wo*	I-him (or it)-face-wash
I am washing my clothes	*Tā cŭng kē lâ*	*de-g-egil-e*	*plural object*-I-him-clothing-wash
I am washing dishes	*Tā cŭ tē yā*	*de-k-atiy-e*	*plural object*-I-dish (or spoon)-wash

One problem that gives considerable difficulty to inexperienced people is the determination of the larger classes of linguistic forms. They may know how to go about working out the morphology of the verb with all of its inflectional complexities, but they stumble at distinguishing, for example, a verb from a noun, especially if some forms function both as nouns and verbs. But perhaps it is not just inexperience which accounts for this difficulty. It may be nothing more than the inability of the linguist to completely detach himself from the part-of-speech categories of his own language.

The linguist's task is to identify all those forms which have a similar behavior. The "sameness" does not have to be identical for every form, for if we chose all criteria we could think of, almost every linguistic form in a language would be unique. All we need do is set up increasingly more comprehensive criteria. The procedure can be illustrated by the following outline:

A.
    1.
    2.
B.
C.
    1.
      a.
      b.

Such an outline can be read as follows: There are three classes of forms, all of which have in common features 1. . .$_n$, and each of which is distinguished by its peculiar features. Thus, A1 and A2—as members of class A—both contrast with and share features with classes B and C, but neither A1 nor A2 can be compared with any other sub-class, such as C1 and C1b. Therefore in devising linguistic classes the analyst must ask himself questions such as these: With what other class is this one coordinate? What features distinguish the two?

In languages where there is extensive inflection, the part-of-speech problem may not be as acute as it is where there is no inflection whatsoever. (But even for English one must decide if *running* is the same in *he's running* and in *running water*: in the second expression is *running* an adjective?) In a language with no inflection, however, one has a different task. In Vietnamese, for example, whose grammar must be presented in syntactical statements, every word must be examined in as many constructions as possible. Chinese also has been described as being without parts of speech, but even here selection limits the range of variation, and every form, as a rule, has a limited range of functions, which have to be learned in connection with it.

At some point during his project the investigator will have to concern himself with linguistic units larger than morphemes and words, for words enter into constructions. The sentence is one such construction, which in turn is built of smaller classes of constructions, but sentences also enter into even larger constructions.[15] It is this whole area of investigation

[15] The word "built" implies a certain metaphor. It is not the only one. Each approach to syntactic analysis has its own repertoire of metaphors for explaining the models which are used.

which has been called syntax. Up until very recently most grammars which resulted from field work devoted very little space to this part of linguistic structure. Grammar writers could have handled it with the techniques at their disposal. Their failure to be more concerned about the subject is probably due to preoccupation with other matters and to the very practical desire of wanting to publish their grammars without delay. The linguistic scene is considerably different now, since stratificationalists and transformationalists have brought stimulating questions to bear on the subject. How all of this recent ferment is going to affect field techniques is not yet clear, but we can certainly expect some change.

Traditionally the study of syntax has been just as inductive as the study of morphology. That is, the investigator collected samples of independent utterances which were presumed to be normal and complete as well as samples of connected discourse. Then by an examination of the distribution of the words contained in these sentences and experimentation with permitted replacements, he arrived at interword and interphrase or interclause specifications.[16] Informants were used in selecting the data which would be submitted to analysis and in experimenting with them. In the latter case the informant would in effect be making up new sentences with the material with which the investigator provided him. The informant was therefore very important in the study, but his practical knowledge of his language could never be fully utilized by these procedures.

Transformationalists, who believe that a grammar should somehow reflect the speaker's intuition about his language, want to make up the deficiencies in the traditional approach.[17] Kenneth Hale, for example,

[16] The explication of this procedure for students was attempted by E. A. Nida in two different experimental publications: *Syntax. A Descriptive Analysis* (1946) and *Outline of Descriptive Syntax* (1951), both published by the Summer Institute of Linguistics, Glendale [now Santa Ana], Calif. A more theoretical approach is to be found in Garvin 1964.

[17] In general, however, their interests have been in areas other than discovery procedures. At times some seem almost to disclaim any interest at all in improving techniques for linguistic analysis (Halle 1959). But Chomsky does not want to be criticized for rejecting discovery procedures: "We are not . . . denying the usefulness of even partially adequate discovery procedures. They may provide valuable hints to the practicing linguist or they may lead to a small set of grammars that can then be evaluated. Our main point is that a linguistic theory should not be identified with a manual of useful procedures, nor should it be expected to provide mechanical procedures for the discovery of grammars" (1957:55 fn.). See also 1964 where three "levels of success for grammatical description" are ranked, with *observational adequacy,* when "the grammar presents the observed primary data correctly" (62), at the lowest level. The highest level is held by *explanatory adequacy:* "In this case we can say that the linguistic theory in question suggests an explanation for the linguistic intuition of the native speaker" (63).

It should be very clearly understood that native reaction, which is what we are concerned with here, has been and should be used at every stage and in every possible area of language study. This has been implied throughout this book. For a general discussion of native reaction see Hoijer 1958 and K. L. Pike 1954. For its place in phonological analysis see Gudschinsky 1958, K. L. Pike 1947, and Sapir 1933; for semantics see Bendix 1966.

writes that "[transformational rules] succeed in reflecting a native speaker's knowledge that certain grammatical constructions in his language which have superficially different structures are related in some sense additional to the obvious one that they belong to the same language. And it is this intuition which . . . can be directly used in field-work with intelligent informants of any language" (1965:109). In his work with a Papago-speaking informant (in the context of a university course in field methods) he used a three-phase procedure. In phase 1 he asked the informant to replace elements in a sentence which had been deleted and to adjust the sentence wherever necessary. (For example, if English were being analyzed and *men* were replaced in *They saw the men* by *man,* the informant would have to say *They saw the man* or some other grammatical form. This procedure is familiar to those who in language classes were told to change the masculine gender to feminine or change all the appropriate future forms into the conditional.) These sentences had nothing unusual about them; they were available from the earlier work on the language. In phase 2 the informant was given two sentences and asked to make up a single sentence which would contain them both. Finally, the informant was given complex sentences and was asked for the simple sentences which underlay them. The claim is made that the procedure worked so well that the informant was able to suggest a relationship between nominal agentives such as *cípkandam cíoj* "working man" and future duratives: *hígai cíoj mat wo cípkanad* "any man who works" (literally, "the man who will [or, should] be working"). He had thought that transformations would derive these nominals from a sentence like *cíoj ʔo cípkan* "The man is working" via nominals with embedded clauses, *hígai cíoj mo cípkan* "the man who is working."

It will be interesting to see how successful others are with this or similar procedures. It is not without its difficulties. First, one will have to establish a transformational metalanguage which is comprehensible to the informant. One is already available in English (and presumably in French and German), but the informant's understanding of it certainly cannot be taken for granted. In a preliterate language, where a linguistic metalanguage is rudimentary indeed, the investigator must expect to have considerable difficulty in finding equivalents for such terms as permutation, subject, underlie (as in "What are the simple sentences which underlie X?") which Hale found convenient to use. It is certain, moreover, that only an intelligent and interested informant can be expected to draw upon his internalized linguistic resources in the way a transformationalist would like him to. This kind of informant would be a good one for any kind of field worker. But the transformationalist may want to argue that when such an informant is available, it is he who can use him best. This would be an interesting claim. It may even be true, although its proof would not come easily.

At the moment, it is difficult to say exactly how a transformationalist's field techniques differ fundamentally from anyone else's. Nor has it been demonstrated that with any set of procedures the investigator can indeed discover the speaker's intuition.[18] One has the impression that most of the techniques were used by others, by Franz Boas, for example. The important thing, in any case, is getting the data. The use of free substitutions (Hale's phase 1) will certainly produce interesting and valuable data. A modified version of this technique requires the informant to provide left-hand and right-hand expansions to sentences. If we took *the bottle fell down* and asked our informant to put something before it, we might get something like *I was talking to the clerk when the bottle fell down*. A right-hand expansion, on the other hand, might result in *The bottle fell down and broke into a thousand pieces*. In this way we have obtained with the minimum of stimulus on our part one sentence which illustrates subordination and the other coordination. (There is no reason to expect that all of the informant's responses will be of these types. He might just as easily have said *The green bottle fell down*, moving the word *the*, or *The bottle fell down off the table*.) By varying the content and structure of the stimulus clause, one should try to get data on categories such as condition, sequence, obligation, result, comparison, direct and indirect discourse, and desire.

It should be noted that tagmemicists do not consider themselves any more bound to their corpora than do transformationalists. They would claim, in fact, that when the use of matrices (referred to above) is added to the discovery procedures characteristic of tagmemic analysis, they have an efficient tool for laying bare a language's grammatical structure. In other ways these two approaches to the study of language are extremely different. This is to be expected, since they differ considerably in goals and assumptions. But the question here is only that of the relative merits of a particular linguistic model in field analysis.[19]

---

[18] This view is shared by Bright (1965:260–261). A statement by Matthews, the author of a transformational grammar of Hidatsa syntax, seems to suggest that the personal element is as important in linguistic field work as one's analytical model: "Concerning . . . the inherent ability of discovering the grammar of a language not one's own . . . I feel that the accuracy of this grammar of Hidatsa has increased with my knowledge of the language. This fact, as well as both my own work and the work of others on English leads me to expect that only one who speaks the language 'as a native' can ever hope to give an exhaustive account of the structure of that language" (1965:6). Paul Postal also is not sanguine about the possibility of developing field techniques to get the data necessary for "deep linguistic research"; this may not come until native speakers are trained linguistically (1966:93).

[19] Two pedagogically oriented introductions to tagmemic analysis are those of Elson and Pickett 1962 and Longacre 1964. Although Longacre's work is subtitled "A Field Manual," its use in the field would seem to presuppose some prior knowledge of the terminology and methodology of tagmemics. It does, however, give explicit instructions step by step, in grammatical analysis at various levels. Stevick 1963 is not based on tagmemics, but it too is pedagogical in nature. Pages 97–124 ("Talking about grammar") are especially recommended. Garvin's collected papers (1964) deal to some extent with discovery procedures.

Lexicon[20]

A field linguist begins a lexical file early in his investigation. He needs it as a finder device for the material which he collects and analyzes. The definitions he gives the target language forms are tags (ordinarily called glosses) which distinguish them from each other and which facilitate handling them in work with the informant ("Would you say the word for 'goat' once again?"). When the words are grouped by grammatical classes (nounlike, verblike), or by semantic domains (food products, gardening tools, weapons), the field worker can quickly find the kinds of words or morphemes he needs for one thing or another. The source-to-target language section, on the other hand, helps the investigator to find the forms he has forgotten.

If this were all that a lexical file is good for, there would be relatively little need for precision in determining the meanings of the entries: Gbeya verbs *yɔ̃ŋ* and *ri* would be adequately distinguished by the glosses "eat (something which has to be chewed)" and "eat (something in liquid form)." But even with this minimum objective one cannot be certain that he has identified the contrasting semantic features with the initial gloss. If he defines *ko* as "give birth (to a child)," how is it different from *hɔ* and *gbay* which can also be used of bearing children? Not until he learns that *hɔ* means "appear" (of one person) or "go away" and *gbay* means "appear" (of many people or liquid) can he claim to have tagged *ko* correctly. This means that every bit of deviation from the norm increases the possibility of error, much out of proportion to the amount of deviation; a person can hardly overestimate the significance of lexical errors in field work. For example, having glossed *ko* as "to give birth," a person might want to use it of goats, but neither *ko* nor *hɔ* apply to them. One must rather say *pĩ nu*, literally "throw ground," or, because kids are usually born two at a time, *gbay* "make appear." If a particular verb on the other hand, were used only of animals, it might be shockingly insulting to use it of humans. From all of this we see that precision is necessary even for the minimal use of a lexical file.

How is meaning determined?[21] For objects and events within the sight of both the informant and the field worker the easiest way is to point.

[20] Householder and Saporta (Eds., 1962) contains 17 papers on lexicography. Although none of them deals specifically with the problems faced by a field linguist, there is much of value in this volume.

[21] The subject is treated from different points of view by Garvin (1964:98–143), Nida (1958), and Weinreich (1962). Garvin actually suggests a procedure for the processing of semantic field data. Weinreich evaluates the metalanguage of definitions and suggests, among other things, how synonyms can be distinguished. (He also affirms that "There is no known discovery procedure for correct semantic descriptions" [26].)

But this technique does not always guarantee accuracy. Even if the investigator and the informant are looking at the same thing, they may be seeing different aspects or parts of it. The investigator may consequently include too much or too little in his definition: the smoke-hole of a dwelling may be identified as just a "hole."

The gloss "hole" may be all that the investigator can provide at the moment, but in order to improve the definition later on, he needs to include more information. In this case it might be in the words "opening in the roof of a house, apparently made intentionally." The principle here is that of recording information about as much of the linguistic and physical context as might account for or explain a term. The clearest case is when one describes the appearance or construction of a basket instead of simply recording "a certain basket." This is why source books of an encyclopedic nature are so important to have on a field trip. A book on basketry would identify certain patterns by name and describe how they were made; guides to the flora and fauna of the area would permit more accurate identification of objects outside of the experience of the field worker.

There is a point, of course, where the linguist—as a linguist—stops recording contextual information. He cannot, after all, do the work of an ethnographer, or a philosopher, or a psychologist. If he were an ethnographer, for example, he would have to describe in considerable detail the activities which go under the Gbeya word *gaza* "circumcision," for circumcision played an important part in the life of the society. On the other hand, he cannot be excused for giving a one-word gloss of this term; as a scholar, he is obliged to give some indication of its cultural significance.

Malinowski had decidedly different ideas about the linguistic part of ethnography. In fact, he would not separate semantics—of his type—from ethnography. For him words had to be studied within three kinds of contexts: the context of culture, the context of situation (what is done at the time when speech is uttered), and the context of language (the actual speech in which a word is embedded). In some respects he is certainly right, but his view leads to the conclusion that a word cannot be understood (and defined) without understanding (and explicating) the life and universe of the relevant speech community. For example:

> . . . for an exact appreciation of the shades and details of meaning a full knowledge of the native customs and psychology, as well as of the general structure of their language, is indispensable (1923:305).

> In order to reconstruct the meaning of sounds [by which he apparently means words] it is necessary to describe the bodily behaviour of men, to know the purpose of their concerted action, as well as their sociology (1935, II:8).

> To arrive . . . at an understanding of meaning, we have to study the dynamic
> rather than the purely intellectual function of words (1935, II:52).

As applied to a particular word, we have the following suggestions:

> What do we achieve in the rendering: *dayma* = "digging-stick"? A digging-
> stick is not an implement familiar to an English curate or clerk, even if he
> happens to be an amateur gardener; he has never seen one, never heard of
> one, certainly never used one; and even if he knows that peoples exist who
> break their soil and plant their seed by means of a pointed stick, he still
> does not understand the term unless he also realizes that the use, the type and
> the institutional setting of a digging-stick are not the same in every primitive
> culture. But to the reader [of his account] the meaning of *dayma* has become
> real in that he knows something about its material, shape and size; the techni-
> cal uses and economic associations, even the values and sentiments which the
> digging-stick derives from its daily employment and from the part it plays in
> magic and ceremonial. He is able to place it within the gardening scheme of
> the Trobriands (1935, II:17–18).

It is necessary to point, out, however, that Malinowski did not suggest
that all words in a language need this kind of attention. There are also
"generic words," those which "are used in all speech" and "have no place
in any part of this ethnographic study" (1935, II:29). In this way he has
sliced language in two, and some words are given the least of attention.
A linguist can hardly afford to approach language with this kind of bias,
nor can an ethnographer.

Linguistic context is no less important than situational. It is, in fact, on
the basis of collated excerpts from spoken and written language that
modern dictionaries are produced. Here is where field lexicography fails
miserably. There is remarkably little attestation in a field linguist's lexical
file. He has entered words because they were new to him; he was interested in words as words, as elements that he would have to manipulate in
his structural analysis. The glosses represent emasculated definitions, because the field worker has simply not set about to systematically collect
a large corpus of material. And a plurality of slips for particular words
often reveals only extended uses of a word which struck the field worker
as novel or striking, so-called idiomatic constructions.

Such sampling of a language's semantics—to use the word broadly—
is fortuitous and deplorably lopsided. It implies that all other words have
a "literal" or transparent meaning which is adequate for understanding
language in actual use. The falsity of this assumption is illustrated by a
very simple Sango sentence: *ngú akánga yángá tí í.* When we use a typical
field dictionary, we translate the sentence as follows: "water shuts mouth
of us." But *ngú* can also mean "river" or "rain" or in fact almost any
liquid. The word *kánga* does mean "shut, lock, close," but it is precisely in
a sentence such as this one that it gets its meaning "prevent." Likewise
yángá here means not "mouth" but rather "eating." The whole sentence

means "The rain prevented us from eating." (It does this by making it impossible to go out to the gardens to get food.) In short, the chief failing of a field dictionary is that it indicates not so much the meanings of words but the fact that they exist. They do not define; they document. It is as if the dictionary were saying, "If you want proof that the word *yángá* occurs in the language, elicit for the concept 'mouth.' "

Another failing of a typical field dictionary is that it sheds too little information about the common words. Their very frequency may conceal extremely diverse and complex uses. The word *to* in English should be adequate to illustrate this point. Anybody learning English has to be able to distinguish it from the other prepositions and to know in what locutions it is necessary.

There is only one means of correcting the weaknesses just described: systematic and thorough collation of words.[22] To start with, everything in the field worker's notes should be filed. Then a certain number of well-varied texts should be completely processed. This means that a concordance is made of the texts. After that one can listen to other tape recordings for new words or what appear to be new uses of already recorded words. (If the texts have been transcribed, it is faster to read through them for this purpose.) Then one goes through the whole file, making a list of those words for which there is insufficient attestation. Further attestation must be elicited from informants; the use of informants in field lexicography is treated below.

Only by the careful study of an abundance of examples and comparison with other forms can meaning be determined. But there will always be areas of the language where problems are more intractable than elsewhere. It may be a long time, for example, before a person would discover that a certain Cherokee plural affix is used only for animals which are born in a litter (Nida 1950*a*:227). A particularly difficult problem is illustrated by the obviative in Kutenai which "has no equivalent, either distributionally or semantically, in any one Indo-European grammatical category. There is no immediately apparent correlation between obviation and any feature of external reality or of Kutenai nonlinguistic culture, and direct translations of obviative as opposed to absolute forms are extremely difficult to obtain" (Garvin 1964:99). Garvin uses the Kutenai obviative to demonstrate an empirical procedure for processing semantic data collected by a field worker. The following statement in his own words best summarizes the procedure:

> ... the morphological distribution of the obviative suffix provides no clue to its semantic content. It is impossible to elicit usable translations of isolated

[22] For a description of some basic lexicographic procedures and an exemplification of the kind of work which can be produced, surpassing by only a small margin what can be expected of "normal" field work, see Taber 1965.

obviative forms—the usual response is that it "means the same" as the corresponding absolute form, but "is used a little differently"; it is furthermore quite difficult to elicit obviative forms separately, although they regularly appear in context. The analysis must then be based entirely on an extensive examination of syntactic usage—that is, the distribution, not of the obviative suffix within the word, but of words containing the obviative suffix (obviative forms) within larger syntactic frame units, by contrast with the distribution of absolute forms within comparable units. It will be found that there are significant and consistent differences in the translation of syntactic units containing forms of these two kinds, and that sets of units containing both obviative and absolute forms in comparable distributions exhibit consistent similarities in the structure of the translations. Finally, it will be found that the translation of the contexts of the units under consideration contains information supplementing and confirming these consistencies, even where the translations of the units themselves are not sufficiently informative to allow inductive differences. These consistent translation differences and similarities will be considered contextual variants of meaning, comparable to allophones or allomorphs, and an attempt will be made to abstract from them a system-derived general meaning for the category of obviation, in a manner similar to that in which the multitude of directly observable sounds and forms are included in the ranges of abstractive units such as phonemes and morphemes (1964:108–109).

Comparison in the determination of meaning must include sets of different words as well as different occurrences of the same words. Words, after all, acquire their meaning by being in opposition to other words in similar contexts. Thus, in defining the Sango verb *mé* which has something to do with the preparation of food, one needs to compare it with several other verbs. It turns out that the whole set is roughly categorized into four classes:

1. General terms
   lɛkɛ *kóbe*   to fix food
   sára kóbe   to make food
2. Preparing ingredients
   píka   to pound (especially in a mortar)
   pɛtɛ   to pound (more specific than *píka*)
   nɛka   to crush by rolling an oval object over a flat surface
   ri   to be thoroughly crushed
3. Mixing the ingredients
   fúru   to mix or work in water with the hands so as to produce a
                  homogeneous mass or liquid
   mé   to mix ingredients with an implement
4. Cooking the food
   tó   to boil
   yɔ́rɔ   to fry or roast in a pan without a lid
   zɔ́   to roast by direct exposure to a flame

It is clear from this classification that to define *mé* as "to prepare food" is far from correct, but one would not see this until he had gathered all the other related words. If the linguistic context did not provide clues as to its precise meaning, as here defined, the investigator would have to ask a native speaker to describe the process and contrast it with *fúru kóbe*.

While it is true that the determination of meaning depends on studying the use of words in context, a corpus of texts collected by the field worker will always be inadequate for the task. There are two reasons: first, there will be far too little exemplification of many words contained in it; second, the translation of the texts (or the field worker's understanding of them, if he happens to speak the language)—which is a first approximation of the meaning of the words—will determine the accuracy of the definitions. What the investigator must expect in any bilingual's translation is inconsistency. A given form or construction will be translated now one way, now another. Taken separately, each rendering may be inadequate for determining the meaning of the forms involved, but the inconsistency might point up a problem which should be looked into. In such a case the informant's difficulty may be due to the incongruity of the two linguistic (or semantic) structures, unless it is due to nothing more than the informant's poor knowledge of the contact language. For these reasons it is necessary to use the informant in studying certain words or sets of words. He can serve, with some limitations, in several ways. Some of these have already been mentioned in other contexts; here they are examined from a different point of view.

An informant can attempt a definition either in the contact language or, by preference, in his own language. He contributes most if he can provide synonymous words or equivalent expressions while making explicit those features which distinguish the word in question from other semantically similar ones. Definitions of this type cannot generally be expected from informants. All that one can hope for is various degrees of success, fairly high for some words but very low for others. Since dictionary-type definitions of the kind we are now speaking of depend on conceptualized hypostasis (extracting from a large number of contexts the semantic contribution of a particular word), the informant's success will depend on his knowledge of the language and on his ability to conceptualize. Clearly, then, the fact that the informant is a native speaker of the language does not make him a better lexicographer than the field worker. More specifically the informant's limitations can be stated in the words of K. L. Pike:

> . . . the native speaker is less likely to understand the significance of the defining contexts in general, or to preserve an awareness of the particular defining contexts relevant to a particular word—and, to the extent that he does operate theoretically in the same hypostasic or conceptualized-hypostasic manner, does so less systematically (1955:139–140).

Besides, as we have already seen, talking *about* language is a peculiar response to language. The principal target of language is not itself but outside itself, the conceptual and objective universe of man.

The difficulties that informants have in explaining or translating, which implies an explanation, are not alike for all parts of the language. One of the areas most impervious to informant analysis seems to be affixation. Amuesha Indian informants, for example, were unable to explain the difference between the use of the verb suffixes *–os* and *–apy* as in *nentós ma'nóz* and *nentápy ma'nóz* both of which mean "I see a deer." It was not until two years after the discovery of this opposition that the analyst learned that *–os* indicates that an object is not in motion whereas *–apy* indicates that it is in motion (Fast 1950:79). The difference is important to an Amuesha hunter, but the sentences were the "same" when talking with the investigator!

That an informant can be in some respects inexperienced in his language should be obvious, but the fact needs to be clearly understood. So dependent can the field worker become on his informant, especially in a hostile situation, that he may forget that the informant is, like himself, an imperfect human being; he is not linguistically omniscient. H. L. Landar (1960), for example, reports that one male Navaho informant, married and in his twenties, did not know what *čooɣin* meant, although he knew that because his uncle's wife was *čooɣin* he had taken her sister; the word means "menstrual flux." Another informant, a girl, gave "my male clan relatives" as the meaning of *sizáanii,* but a man said it used to mean "my *female* clan relatives" but now is coming more and more to be used for "my wife." But the differing competence of individuals can be seen just as easily in our own society.

No study so clearly documents the inability of naive informants to define terms as does the one by F. C. Redlich (1949). In an attempt to learn what understanding people had of medical terms, some of them among the most common, he interviewed a variety of patients. The results—startling because of the amount of education in the United States—are illustrated by the following definitions of *nerve*:

> a tiny thread all over your body
> a telephone line from body to brain
> nerves is something in the system; if they get irritated you can't find peace and
>   you worry
> feels like strings and gives sharp sensation all over the body
> a nerve would be what shakes; you have nervous headaches, a nervous stomach
> you have to have them, they keep you excited

Redlich's impressions of the inadequacies of the definitions are those of a layman in linguistics, but they are accurate enough: "The amount of circular definitions in our material . . . is amazing. Few patients observed the fundamental rule of definition to establish a familiar starting point and to define outside the speech situation, i.e., to denote" (158). He also points out one more reason for poor informant-definitions, namely, inability to verbalize: "Many definitions are unsatisfactory because people who are not accustomed to expressing themselves in such a manner are unable to verbalize sufficiently for linguistic reasons or because consciously or unconsciously they do not wish to verbalize" (156).

As Redlich implies here, there are psychological reasons why some people are worse at defining—or defining certain words—than others. "It is quite evident," he writes, "that, in addition to general intelligence and general vocabulary of the patient, other factors determine the test scores. Interest in the disease, the degree of anxiety, hypochondriacal tendencies, curiosity, as well as the age of the patient, cultural and ecological background, duration of the disease and reward or punishment of previous explorations seem to play a role" (156). The experience of a linguist, P. Alexandre, working with an African informant educated in Africa but in European schools also illustrates the psychological barriers an informant may have. He had asked her to explain the use of a particular word which, he later learned, referred to the smell of pus. It was apparent that the girl knew the word but felt restrained in talking about it. Her only explanation was "Je suis une jeune fille convenable" ("I'm a *proper* girl.").

Having outlined the limitations of an informant in lexicographic work, we must defend him. Every failure on his part may not be his fault exclusively. When an anthropologist writes that "all informants [of the named Indian tribe] find it virtually impossible to help the investigator with the etymology of words," we may suspect that either his methods were wrong or he was asking them to perform analytical tasks which only a linguistically sophisticated person could handle.[23] We cannot, as in the case of these Indians, expect them to relate verbal and nominal stems surrounded by affixes and modified in the process of affixation. The investigator may consider it very important to know if the stems of two words are the same, but the discovery is his responsibility, and there are techniques to assist him.

The informant can also be used in obtaining additional uses of words being studied. If the investigator has no idea what a word may mean, he

---

[23] It can be said of the Aucas also that they can not etymologize—at least when it comes to their names. Although almost every personal name is that of some plant, animal, or bird, they do not equate, nor will they allow another to equate, the personal name with the object. If one were to ask the meaning of *Comë*, the answer would be "Nothing. That's his name." Only in another context would one learn that *comë* meant "cotton thread or string" (*Translation* [Summer Institute of Linguistics], Summer/Fall 1964, p. 15). Therefore if one wanted to acquire these names for his lexical file, he would have to use some other technique for obtaining their meanings. He could, for example, ask "Is *comë* an animal?" ("No") "Is it something humans eat?" ("No").

can only ask for another sentence with the word in question. (As we saw in Chapter 7, however, this kind of request may not be expressed easily in some languages.) The more the investigator knows about the word, the more guidance he can give the informant. Instead of sentences, the informant may produce a short text—in Malinowski's terms a "definition text"—by which he describes a situation where the word would properly be used. These texts should be recorded in their entirety and reference to them made in the lexical file.

Paraphrasing is another technique where the informant's help is important. He is presented with a sentence which contains the word whose meaning is still uncertain and is asked to say the same thing in other words. This technique can be applied to individual words, but it would probably produce greater results if done with sets of words within specific semantic domains or with words which appear to be synonymous. The value of this technique is that it tends to make explicit some of the semantic features implicit in the term. Instructions to the informant will depend on the degree to which he comprehends the purpose of the paraphrasing. The investigator wants to give the informant as much liberty as possible, but he does not want him to give a supplementary sentence or to go off on some tangent.

Because the informant cannot possibly think of all the different uses to which a word can be put, the investigator can learn much by testing its collocability with a list of words chosen to represent various semantic domains. If we were studying a certain word which we had glossed as "soft," we could ask "Is a pillow X?" and proceed in this way with a piece of cotton, a half-pumped basketball, or the flesh of one's thigh. In this way Landar (1960) discovered that the Navaho word *dic'id,* glossed "it is tough, sinewy" and which "usually refers to rope-like objects, stringy, strong, resistant to breaking, strain, or pulling, and to tough meat," can be used with a word glossed "bird" (in speaking of the meat), "his older brother" (in a metaphor), "his hair, his head" (in speaking of "vigorous hair, as opposed to the brittle hair of an old person or to dead hair"), "saliva" ("of the drool of a cow exhausted from running about five miles, and thirsty; the saliva hangs in several gooey, sticky, clear strings that break off halfway down to the ground"), and "snake." It will be found, as with the word *dic'id,* that some words would not co-occur in certain constructions. This negative information, as much as the positive information, will contribute to the determination of a word's meaning. Thus, the definition of the verb *drink* in my own speech would have to include the specification "of taking a liquid without the use of a spoon." I do not think that I would ever *drink soup;* some other expression would always be sought to circumvent this one.

Lists of words, arranged in different ways, can be simply examined for clues about contrastive semantic features, but C. O. Frake recommends a more sophisticated technique. He takes both the lists of words and the queries which elicited them as an interrelated set of data to work with. The technique is described as follows:

> . . . knowing the queries that can be appropriately posed about a given topic reveals the features of that topic that are relevant to the inquirer. Furthermore, the topic of a given query will be a response to some other query, making it possible to produce lists of utterances *interlinked* as topics and responses of specified queries. . . .

> If "meaning" has to do with (extra-grammatical) rules of use, then to the extent to which the conditions for the use of an utterance are verbally constrained or verbally specifiable, the interlinking of queries and responses says something about the meaning of utterances even if we cannot as yet identify the nonverbal objects and events (if any) to which these utterances apply. For example, even if we cannot identify an instance of a "tree," if we learn the verbal response *tree* is interlinked with *plant* by one pair of queries, to *elm, oak, pine,* etc. by another, to *leaf, stem, branch, trunk, root,* etc. by another, to *lumber, firewood,* etc. by another, then we have discovered some of the kinds of relationships that can exist among categories of things in a culture (1964:134).

The application of this technique requires the use of the language being studied, for the questions are as important as their responses. They must be explicit (leading to unambiguous responses) and of the widest possible variety. Some of those used by Frake in his study of the ingredients used in making *gasi,* a fermented beverage of the Eastern Subanun, are these: "What is X used for?" "What kind of X is it?" "What is that ingredient of X?" What are you using there for making X?" "What is X (a kind of)?" "What does this come from?" For difficulties one may encounter in the use of this technique see Bright and Bright 1965.

In this section on field lexicography we have been primarily concerned with the determination of meaning regardless of the use to which this knowledge might be put. The preparation of a dictionary is an entirely different matter. It requires a taste for layout and format in addition to skill in the art of defining. It is reported that the G. and C. Merriam Company assigns each new definer to an experienced one for six months of full-time training under close supervision, and it takes sometimes as long as one year or more before a person is fully at ease in this job. Defining is an extremely demanding task, one which calls upon a person's knowledge of the language the definitions are being written in and ability in expressing himself explicitly and succinctly.

Rare is the field worker whose lexical studies will result in a commercially published dictionary, but because they will in some form continue to be published—as indeed they ought to be—a few more words need to be added to what has already been said.

All the entries in the dictionary (or word list, if the linguist is more modest about his creation) should first be checked for accuracy and consistency in representation. Because some words are rarely looked at once they have been entered in the file (as would be true of technical terms poorly suited for grammatical analysis) and because symbolization and phonemicization may undergo changes during the long investigation, it is easy to overlook changes which need to be brought up to date. While thus going through all the words, one should also be on the lookout for overdifferentiated words (discussed above). Failing to do so in work on Sango led to two pairs of words which should not have been distinguished: *ngbagba* "lower mandible, lower jaw, chin" and *mbángbá* "cheek"; *gindí* "bow" (used with arrow in hunting) and *ngindí* "a rat snare made of a cord noose stretched by a spring made of a flexible stick." The spelling differences (including tone) are due either to inaccurate hearing or to legitimate variations in pronunciation; but because Sango is a lingua franca, some speakers may in fact differentiate these words.

After the meanings of the words have been determined to suit one's needs, the next step is to experiment with defining. The experimental nature of these first attempts is important. It would be foolish to start with the *A*'s before one is sure that he has confronted—and solved—the major problems which his task presents. He must adopt symbols which are economical and explicit and a style which is clear and consistent. Any time spent at this stage will save untold hours of editing later on.

Distinguishing between the various uses of words will always be a headache (as will the need for distinguishing between two or more divergent uses of a single word and one word with several divergent uses). Hitherto all such distinctions have been made pragmatically, and until semantic theory is much more refined—and techniques for using them economically are provided—practical considerations will continue to exert the greatest influence.

The definitions themselves should be neither too wordy nor too brief. Single-word translations must be carefully chosen to reflect the native range of meaning; a plethora of synonymous renditions must be avoided. Of the list "foreign, alien, strange, exotic, undesirable; guest, visitor," for example, it might be possible to eliminate "alien," "exotic," and "guest." On the other hand, artificial limits should not be imposed on the length of the definition since one cannot expect similar concepts to be expressed with equivalent lengths of utterances in two languages. If a one-syllable word refers to a particular form of greeting whereby a person places his left hand on the forearm of the right hand which grasps the other person's right hand at the same time leaning forward from the hips—then all of this information must be included in some way. Indeed, in a society such as the Javanese, where postural and gestural accompaniments of speech are reported to play an important role in communication and etiquette, it is important to furnish all this information. Each entry should also be followed by at least one translated, preferably unelicited, example, carefully selected to be maximally revealing of meaning and use. A sentence in Sango like *ála kánga awe* "They have shut it" tells us very little about *kánga,* whereas the following sentences illustrate the transitive and intransitive uses of the verb with the meanings "to fasten, shut, imprison":

ála kánga kámba na gɔ́ tí lo	They tied a rope around his neck
kánga yángá tí dú ní	Close up the opening of the hole
lége ní akánga awe	The way is closed
kánga lo na yá ní	Shut him up in it
lungúla na kángángɔ́ ní	Take it out still tied up

It would also help to list related words, such as synonyms, antonyms, hyponyms, hypernyms, characteristic collocations, and names of parts (of a trap, tool). In connection with *kánga,* for example, information should be given about the following: *du* "to tie," *tíngbi* "to join up, meet," *bóngbi* "to meet, mix together"; *gbánzi* "to prevent"; *kpíngba* "to harden", *kɔlée (<* French *coller)* "to congeal"; *lungúla* "to open," *zi* "to untie, release"; *kánga bέ* "to persevere" (literally "to tie up liver").

If three words were to characterize a one-way bilingual dictionary they would be *replicable, authentic,* and *usable.*[24] It would be replicable because another person would be fairly successful, if not entirely so, in reeliciting the word from the meanings and conversely the meanings from the word. That nonreplicability can be high in dictionaries of non-Western languages is illustrated by the fact that O. Werner (1965) found only 47 instances, out of 110 items, where Navaho informants were in complete agreement with the designations of medical terms in existent dictionaries. There was disagreement with 35 and complete rejection of 28 of the terms. The dictionary would be authentic if it represented the conceptual and cultural categories of the language being studied instead of the language of the investigator. Finally, it would be usable if the information it contained could be found without the necessity of reading through it as one does a book. Usability depends heavily on types and amount of cross-referencing.

The field linguist generally ends up with a one-way lexical file; that is, from the language being studied into the contact language, for he is primarily concerned with one-way translation. He sees no need for, say, an English-Banda file; or if he does have one, it is much smaller than the other. A published dictionary is another matter: a Banda-English dictionary will have only a restricted use without some back-translating index. The least that should be provided by a field worker, therefore, is an alpha-

---

[24] Mager's *Gedaged-English Dictionary* can serve as a starting point for a field linguist planning a dictionary. For a very favorable review see Gleason 1955.

betical list of words and expressions in the contact language which are
to be found in the other section. In the case of our hypothetical word
mentioned above we would list "foreign," "strange," "undesirable," and
"visitor" with the appropriate native language word. Alternately, one
could enter each word with the notation "see *foreign*" where the complete
list is given, followed by the native language word.

To make the dictionary even more useful the linguist should check his
contact language entries with some reliable word frequency dictionary.
H. S. Eaton's *Word Frequency Dictionary* (1940) will serve well. In this
way he will be more successful in covering both the important semantic
categories and actual words which the dictionary user might employ.
Thus, although *narrow* is among the first thousand most frequently referred to concepts in English, it might be missing from one's dictionary.
If he decides to enter it, he must find a natural equivalent for it. It will
often turn out that a concept is easily covered by some native language
word or expression and its omission in the first part of the dictionary is
just an oversight. The additional value of such checking is therefore that
of verifying the range of meaning of each native language entry.

APPENDIX

LEXICOSTATISTICAL WORD LIST

Provided below is a list of words which has been widely used in the comparative study of languages and dialects, particularly by those who have used the glottochronological method of Morris Swadesh. It is assumed (a) that there is a basic core vocabulary which is much less subject to change than general vocabulary, (b) that the rate of retention for this basic core is relatively stable through time, and (c) that the rate of loss of this vocabulary is constant for all languages. (For a discussion of glottochronology see Swadesh 1950, 1951a, 1955; Gudschinsky 1956; Hymes 1960; in these and in Hymes 1964 other references are listed.) The selection of this basic vocabulary is critical to the technique; after considerable experimentation the words listed below were chosen. Hence, it has been dubbed the Swadesh list. There are several redactions of it, depending on what list was available to a particular worker at a particular time and what adaptations had to be made to fit the local situation ("ice" would not be appropriate in the Central African Republic). The practice has been to start with the largest list and reduce it whenever problems arose.

The lexicostatistical word list has come in two forms: a 200-word list and a 100-word list. These are given below, with the qualification that the longer list here contains 218 items, because it is a conflation of

Swadesh 1955 (where the words are listed both by semantic groups and alphabetically) and Gudschinsky 1956. Words missing in Gudschinsky are marked by (*); she also adds "heavy" which is not in Swadesh. The 100-word list was supplied by Swadesh (and used by permission), although I am responsible for its present from.

These lists are recommended to the field worker, not because of the validity of the claims for glottochronology (about which I prefer to be neutral here), but because they are the most widely known. Moreover, in comparative studies it is desirable to have as much uniformity as possible. Future work will be greatly facilitated if field workers would make certain that their lexical collections contained these words. For other purposes —for example, in the determination of dialect differences—one will certainly want to add other words, because one's goal is as much to measure change in cultural vocabulary as it is to measure retention of the basic vocabulary.

Because these words can be used for different purposes, they must be elicited in different ways. For glottochronological purposes it is the most common conversational equivalent that is desired. (On the problems involved in getting these equivalents see the works cited above and Taylor 1959.) The most common equivalent for "animal" in Gbeya is *sad'e,* a word which does not reveal the language's membership in the Niger-Congo family. Further elicitation, however, would reveal the word *nám,* which is used of feline animals in the expression *nám-wéey* (literally, "animal of male"). A collection of vocabulary will be richer and useful for more purposes if the field worker will take the time to ask for other ways that an object can be designated; after the words are collected, he is advised to get other ways in which they can be used. For example, Gbeya *nú* is "mouth," but it is also used for "edge" and "tip."

It is generally easier to collect words in phrases or sentences than in isolation; for some words, such as "at," "because," it is absolutely necessary to do so. Paradigmatic frames are useful for certain kinds of words: in the Gbaya-Ngbaka-Manza languages it was easier to get body parts in the phrase "an animal's ——— (back, eye, leg, etc.)" than in "my ———." One can include several items in a sentence: "The dog bit my child." An instrument for the elicitation of lexical data must be compiled with great care and experimentation. For further suggestions see the recommended reading on dialectology; Swadesh 1954 is extremely valuable for its detailed description of an intensive project for vocabulary collection.

I: 200-Word List

all	eight*	if	rightside	————
and	eye	in	river	tail
animal	————	————	road	ten*
ashes	fall	kill	root	that
at	far	knee*	rope	there
————	fat/grease	know	rotten	they
back	father	————	rub	thick
bad	fear	lake	————	thin
bark	feather	laugh	salt	think
because	few	leaf	sand	this
belly	fight	leftside	say	thou
big	fire	leg	scratch	three
bird	fish	lie	sea	throw
bite	five	live	see	tie
black	float	liver	seed	tongue
blood	flow	long	seven*	tooth
blow	flower	louse	sew	tree
bone	fog	————	sharp	turn
breast*	foot	man/male	shoot*	twenty*
breathe	four	many	short	two
brother*	freeze	meat/flesh	sing	————
burn	fruit	moon*	sister*	vomit
————	full*	mother	sit	
child	————	mountain	skin	walk
clothing*	give	mouth	sky	warm
cloud	good	————	sleep	wash
claw*	grass	name	small	water
cold	green	narrow	smell	we
come	guts	near	smoke	wet
cook*	————	neck	smooth	what?
count	hair	new	snake	when?
cut	hand	night	snow	where?
————	he	nose	some	white
dance*	head	not	spear*	who?
day	hear	————	spit	wide
die	heart	old	split	wife
dig	heavy	one	squeeze	wind
dirty	here	other	stab/	wing
dog	hit	————	pierce	wipe
drink	hold/take	person	stand	with
dry	horn*	play	star	woman
dull	how	pull	stick	woods
dust	hundred*	push	stone	work*
————	hunt	————	straight	worm
ear	husband	rain	suck	————
earth	————	red	sun	ye
eat	I	right/	swell	year
egg	ice	correct	swim	yellow

* This word is not in the Gudschinsky list.

II: 100-Word List

English	Spanish	French	German	
I	yo	je	ich	
thou	tú	tu	du	
we	nosotros	nous	wir	
this	este	celui-ci	dieser	
that	aquel	celui-là	jener	(5)
who?	quién?	qui?	wer?	
what?	qué?	quoi?	was?	
not	no	ne ... pas	nicht	
all	todos	tous	alle	
many	muchos	beaucoup	viele	(10)
one	uno	un	eins	
two	dos	deux	zwei	
big	grande	grand	gross	
long	largo	long	lang	
small	chico	petit	klein	(15)
woman	mujer	femme	Weib/Frau	
man	hombre	homme	Mann	
person	gente	personne	Mensch	
fish	pez	poisson	Fisch	
bird	pájaro	oiseau	Vogel	(20)
dog	perro	chien	Hund	
louse	piojo	pou	Laus	
tree	árbol	arbre	Baum	
seed	semilla	semence	Samen	
leaf	hoja	feuille	Blatt	(25)
root	raíz	racine	Wurzel	
bark	corteza	écorce	Rinde	
skin	piel	peau	Haut	
flesh	carne	viande	Fleisch	
blood	sangre	sang	Blut	(30)
bone	hueso	os	Knochen	
grease	grasa	graisse	Fett	
egg	huevo	oeuf	Ei	
horn	cuerno	corne	Horn	
tail	cola/rabo	queue	Schwanz	(35)

English	Spanish	French	German
feather	pluma	plume	Feder
hair	cabello	cheveu	(Kopf-) Haare
head	cabeza	tête	Kopf
ear	oreja	oreille	Ohr
eye	ojo	oeil	Auge (40)
nose	nariz	nez	Nase
mouth	boca	bouche	Mund
tooth	diente	dent	Zahn
tongue	lengúa	langue	Zunge
fingernail	garra/uña	griffe	Nagel (45)
foot	pie	pied	Fuss
knee	rodilla	genou	Knie
hand	mano	main	Hand
belly	barriga	ventre	Bauch
neck	cuello	cou	Nacken (50)
breasts	senos	sein	weibliche Brust
heart	corazón	coeur	Herz
liver	hígado	foie	Leber
drink	beber	boire	trinken
eat	comer	manger	essen (55)
bite	morder	mordre	beissen
see	ver	voir	sehen
hear	oír	entendre	hören
know	saber	savoir	wissen
sleep	dormir	dormir	schlafen (60)
die	morir	mourir	sterben
kill	matar	tuer	töten
swim	nadar	nager	schwimmen
fly	volar	voler	fliegen
walk	andar	marcher	gehen (65)
come	venir	venir	kommen
lie	acostado	être couché	liegen
sit	sentado	être assis	sitzen
stand	parado	être debout	stehen
give	dar	donner	geben (70)
say	decir	dire	sagen
sun	sol	soleil	Sonne
moon	luna	lune	Mond
star	estrella	étoile	Stern
water	agua	eau	Wasser (75)

English	Spanish	French	German
rain	lluvia	pluie	Regen
stone	piedra	pierre	Stein
sand	arena	sable	Sand
earth	tierra	terre	Erde
cloud	nube	nuage	Wolken (80)
smoke	humo	fumée	Rauch
fire	fuego	feu	Feuer
ash	ceniza	cendres	Asche
burn	arder	brûler	brennen
path	camino	chemin	Weg (85)
mountain	cerro	montagne	Berg
red	rojo	rouge	rot
green	verde	vert	grün
yellow	amarillo	jaune	gelb
white	blanco	blanc	weiss (90)
black	negro	noir	schwarz
night	noche	nuit	Nacht
hot	caliente	chaud	heiss
cold	frío	froid	kalt
full	lleno	plein	voll (95)
new	nuevo	nouveau	neu
good	bueno	bon	gut
round	redondo	rond	rund
dry	seco	sec	trocken
name	nombre	nom	Name (100)

REFERENCES

The following bibliography serves two purposes: to provide full documentation for sources of information used in this book and to indicate further reading on subjects mentioned in the text. Many other titles could have been added, but their inclusion in this list would have been merely academic; one can consult Conklin 1960c and Hymes 1959. For two early general discussions see Lounsbury 1953 and Nida 1947.

The references indicate that some of the subjects taken up in this book are of concern also to anthropologists and sociologists. The literature on the field problems of these disciplines is extensive, as is evident in Conklin and Hymes (above). *Human Organization,* the journal of the Society for Applied Anthropology (Cornell University, Ithaca, New York), has had a "Field Methods and Techniques" department. Linguistic field problems are frequently discussed in *The Bible Translator* (published by the United Bible Societies, 101 Queen Victoria Street, London E.C. 4), which is concerned primarily with translation going on in non-Indo-European languages. Dialectology, while not treated explicitly in this book, is comprehended by it. Dialectologists have made important contributions to the description of effective field techniques: for example, Brook 1963, Cassidy 1953, McIntosh 1952, Pop 1950, and Smalley 1957, of which the most important are McIntosh and Pop. For techniques used in the study of social dialects see the works by Labov.

General research guides are being prepared under the auspices of the Committee on International Anthropology, established by the Division of Anthropology and Psychology of the National Academy of Sciences— National Research Council (Washington, D.C.), from whom they are purchased. To date, four have been published: Beals and Hitchcock 1960 for India, Beardsley 1959 for Japan, Keesing 1957 for Oceania, and Wolfe 1959 for West and Central Africa. Although they are not all of equal quality, they cover the same general ground. For example, the one on Japan has the following chapters: Introduction, The Region, Preparations for Field Research, American and Other Agencies and Interests in Japan, European Research Institutions and Societies, Relations with Japan National Agencies, Relations with Informants, plus an appendix listing leading Japanese journals in anthropological fields and three maps.

The abbreviation *IJAL* stands for the *International Journal of American Linguistics*. In a few cases the names of authors are more complete here than in the works cited.

ADAMS, RICHARD N., and JACK J. PREIS (Eds.), 1960, *Human Organization Research: Field Relations and Techniques*. Homewood, Ill.: The Dorsey Press, Inc. 456 pp.

AITKEN, BARBARA, 1955, A note on eliciting. *IJAL* 21:83.

ALBERT, ETHEL M., 1964, 'Rhetoric,' 'logic,' and 'poetics' in Burundi: Culture patterning of speech behavior. In Gumperz and Hymes 1964:35–54.

ALTSHULER, NATHAN, 1956, Linguistic forms as symbols of people. *IJAL* 22:106–112.

ARMSTRONG, ROBERT G., 1963, The subjunctive in Idoma. *Journal of African Languages* 2:155–159.

ATWOOD, ELMER BAGBY, 1962, *The Regional Vocabulary of Texas*. Austin: University of Texas Press. 273 pp.

BARKER, M. A. R., 1963, *Klamath Dictionary*. Berkeley and Los Angeles: University of California Press (University of California Publications in Linguistics, Vol. 31). 550 pp.

BARNES, J. A., 1963, Some ethical problems in modern fieldwork. *British Journal of Sociology* 14:118–134.

BASSET, ANDRÉ, 1951, L'enquête linguistique. *Conférences de l'Institut de Linguistique de l'Université de Paris. X. Années 1950–1951*. Paris: Librairie C. Klincksieck. Pp. 7–22.

BEACH, D. M., 1938, *The Phonetics of the Hottentot Language*. Cambridge, England: W. Heffer & Sons, Ltd. xv, 329 pp.

BEALS, ALAN R., and JOHN T. HITCHCOCK, 1960, *Field Guide to India* (with a section on Pakistan by Mary Jean Kennedy). Washington, D.C.: National Academy of Sciences–National Research Council (Field Guide Series Number 4, Committee on International Anthropology of the Division of Anthropology and Psychology). ix, 61 pp.

BEALS, RALPH L., 1957, Native terms and anthropological methods. *American Anthropologist* 59:716–717.

BEARDSLEY, RICHARD K., 1959, *Field Guide to Japan*. Washington, D.C.: National Academy of Sciences–National Research Council (Field Guide Series Number 3, Committee on International Anthropology of the Division of Anthropology and Psychology). 55 pp.

BEE, DARLENE, and ALAN PENCE, 1962, Toward standardization of a survey word list for Papua and New Guinea. In Summer Institute of Linguistics New Guinea Branch, *Studies in New Guinea Linguistics*. Sydney: *Oceania Linguistic Monographs*, No. 6. Pp. 64–75.

BEIDELMAN, T. O., 1965, Some Baraguyu cattle songs. *Journal of African Languages* 4:1–18.

BENDIX, EDWARD HERMAN, 1966, *Componential Analysis of General Vocabulary: The Semantic Structure of a Set of Verbs in English, Hindi, and Japanese*. Bloomington: Indiana University Research Center in Anthropology, Folklore, and Linguistics (*IJAL*, Vol. 32, Publication 41). 190 pp.

BERREMAN, GERALD D., 1962, *Behind Many Masks: Ethnography and Impression Management in a Himalayan Village*. Ithaca, N.Y.: Society for Applied Anthropology. 24 pp.

BLOCH, BERNARD, 1935, Interviewing for the Linguistic Atlas. *American Speech* 10:3–9.

BLOCH, BERNARD, and GEORGE L. TRAGER, 1942, *Outline of Linguistic Analysis*. Baltimore, Md.: Linguistic Society of America. 82 pp.

BLOOMFIELD, LEONARD, 1925, Why a linguistic society? *Language* 1:1–5.

———, 1927, Literate and illiterate speech. *American Speech* 2:432–439.

———, 1942, *Outline Guide for the Practical Study of Foreign Languages*. Baltimore, Md.: Linguistic Society of America. 16 pp.

BOAS, FRANZ, 1911, Introduction. In *Handbook of American Indian Languages*. Washington, D.C.: Government Printing Office (Smithsonian Institution. Bureau of American Ethnology. Bulletin 40). Vol. 1, pp. 1–83. Reprinted with a foreword by C. I. J. M. Stuart. Washington, D.C.: Georgetown University Press. xiv, 70 pp.

———, 1917, Introduction. *IJAL* 1.1–8. Reprinted in F. Boas, *Race, Language, and Culture*. New York: The Macmillan Company. 1940. Pp. 199–210.

BOAS, FRANZ, P. E. GODDARD, E. SAPIR, and A. L. KROEBER, 1916, *Phonetic Transcription of Indian Languages*. Washington, D.C.: Smithsonian Institution (Smithsonian Miscellaneous Collections, Vol. 66, No. 6).

BOHANNAN, PAUL, 1958*a*, On anthropologists' use of language. *American Anthropologist* 60:161–162.

———, 1958*b*, Rejoinder to Taylor. *American Anthropologist* 60:941–942.

BORGMAN, DONALD, and SANDRA L. CUE, 1963, Sentence and clause types in Central Waica (Shiriana). *IJAL* 29:222–229.

BOWEN, ELENORE SMITH [pseudonym for LAURA BOHANNAN], 1954, *Return to Laughter*. New York: Harper & Row, Publishers. 276 pp.

———, 1964, *Return to Laughter* (with a foreword by David Riesman). New York: Doubleday & Company, Inc. xviii, 297 pp., paper.

BOWMAN, ELIZABETH, 1959, An attempt at an analysis of Modern Yucatec from a small corpus of recorded speech. *Anthropological Linguistics* 1(4):43–86.

————, 1963, The classification of imperative sentences in English. *Studies in Linguistics* 17:23–28.

BRIDGEMAN, LORAINE I., 1961, Kaiwa (Guaraní) phonology. *IJAL* 27:329–334.

BRIGHT, JANE O., and WILLIAM BRIGHT, 1965, Semantic structures in northwestern California and the Sapir-Whorf hypothesis. In E. A. Hammel (Ed.), *Formal Semantic Analysis.* Menasha, Wisconsin: American Anthropological Association (*American Anthropologist,* Special Publication, Vol. 67, No. 5, Part 2). Pp. 249–258.

BRIGHT, WILLIAM, 1965, Review of Horace G. Lunt (Ed.), *Proceedings of the Ninth International Congress of Linguistics.* The Hague: Mouton & Co. *IJAL* 31:259–263.

BROKENSHA, DAVID, 1963 Problems in fieldwork. *Current Anthropology* 4:533–534.

BROOK, G. L., 1963, *English Dialects.* New York: Oxford University Press. 232 pp.

BROWN, ROGER, and DAVID MCNEILL, in press, The "tip of the tongue" phenomenon. *Journal of Verbal Learning and Verbal Behavior.*

CALAME-GRIAULE, GENEVIÈVE, in press, *Ethnologie et langage. La parole chez les Dogon.* Paris: Gallimard.

CAPELL, ARTHUR, 1945, *Methods and Materials for Recording Australian Languages.* Sydney, Australia: University of Sydney. 67 pp. Reprinted from *Oceania* 16(2): 144–176 (1945).

————, 1952, *Methods and Materials for Recording Papuan and New Guinea Languages.* Port Moresby, New Guinea: Department of Education (Official Research Publication Number 2).

————, 1962, *Some Linguistic Types in Australia.* Sydney, Australia: University of Sydney (Handbook of Australian Languages, Part 2. *Oceania Linguistic Monographs,* Number 7). 183 pp.

CASAGRANDE, JOSEPH B. (Ed.), 1960, *In the Company of Man. Twenty Portraits by Anthropologists.* New York: Harper & Row, Publishers. 540 pp.

CASEY, ROBERT S., JAMES W. PERRY, ALLEN KENT, and MADELINE BERRY (Eds.), 1958, *Punched Cards: Their Applications to Science and Industry,* 2d ed. New York: Reinhold. 697 pp.

CASSIDY, FREDERIC G., 1953, *A Method for Collecting Dialect.* Gainesville, Fla.: American Dialect Society (Publication 20). 96 pp.

CHAFE, WALLACE L., 1962, Estimates regarding the present speakers of North American Indian languages. *IJAL* 28:162–171.

————, 1965, Corrected estimates regarding speakers of Indian languages. *IJAL* 31:345–346.

CHOMSKY, NOAM, 1957, *Syntactic Structures.* The Hague: Mouton & Co. 116 pp.

————, 1964, Current issues in linguistic theory. In Jerry A. Fodor and Jerrold J. Katz (Eds.), *The Structure of Language. Readings in the Philosophy of Language.* Englewood Cliffs, N.J.: Prentice-Hall. Pp. 50–118.

CHURCH, CATARINA MASS DE, 1962, Algunas observaciones de la elaboración de cartillas en lengua Jacalteca. *Guatemala Indígena* 2(1):29–34. See abstract in *IJAL* 30:399 (1964).

CHURCHWARD, C. M., 1963, Honorific language in Tongan. *The Bible Translator* 14:192–196.

COHEN, MARCEL S., 1950–1951, *Questionnaire Linguistique.* Nimègue, Netherlands:

Comité International Permanent de Linguistes, Commission d'Enquête Linguistique.

CONKLIN, HAROLD C., in manuscript, The collection of linguistic data. 1950. Written for a manual of ethnographic field method then projected under the editorship of John H. Rowe. Typescript, 15 pp.

——, 1951, *Lexical Check List for Philippine Languages*. New Haven, Conn.: Human Relations Area Files. Duplicated.

——, 1960*a*, Maling, a Hanunóo girl from the Philippines. In Casagrande 1960: 101–118.

——, 1960*b*, A day in Parina. In Casagrande 1960:119–125.

——, 1960*c*, *Bibliography on Ethnographic Research (Theory, Methods, Techniques)*. "Prepared with the help of the members of the seminar and with the generous assistance of the Institute for Intercultural Studies. Columbia University, Seminar in Ethnography." 102 pp., duplicated. *Bibliographic Supplement*, 5 pp. (1962).

CONWELL, MARILYN, and ALPHONSE JUILLAND, 1963, *Louisiana French Grammar. 1: Phonology, Morphology, and Syntax*. The Hague: Mouton & Co. 207 pp.

COVNER, BERNARD J., 1944*a*, Studies in phonographic recordings of verbal material: III. The completeness and accuracy of counseling interview reports. *Journal of General Psychology* 30(2):181–203.

——, 1944*b*, Studies in phonographic recordings of verbal material: IV. Written reports of interviews. *Journal of Applied Psychology* 28(2):89–98.

DECAMP, DAVID, 1959, Review of Stanley M. Sapon, *A Pictorial Linguistic Interview Manual*. *Language* 35:394–402.

DEVEREUX, GEORGE, 1949, Mohave voice and speech mannerisms. *Word* 5:268–272.

DOCKSTADER, FREDERICK J., 1955, Spanish loanwords in Hopi; a preliminary checklist. *IJAL* 21:157–159.

DOKE, CLEMENT M., 1943, *Outline Grammar of Bantu*. Johannesburg. 65 pp., duplicated.

DOZIER, EDWARD P., 1951, Resistance to acculturation and assimilation in an Indian Pueblo. *American Anthropologist* 53:56–66.

DYAR, T. GERALD, 1959, Techniques and devices: tape. *Ethnomusicology* 3:124–128.

——, 1960*a*, Techniques and devices: pitch control. *Ethnomusicology* 4:19–21.

——, 1960*b*, Techniques and devices: miscellaneous. *Ethnomusicology* 4:82–83.

——, 1960*c*, Techniques and devices: microphones. *Ethnomusicology* 4:137–141.

——, 1961*a*, Techniques and devices: microphone placement. *Ethnomusicology* 5:49–51.

——, 1961*b*, Techniques and devices: standardization. *Ethnomusicology* 5:130–132.

——, 1962*a*, Techniques and devices: processing tape recordings in the laboratory. *Ethnomusicology* 6:25–29.

——, 1962*b*, Techniques and devices: miscellaneous II. *Ethnomusicology* 6:188–190.

DYEN, ISIDORE, 1962, The lexicostatistical classification of the Malayo-Polynesian languages. *Language* 38:38–46.

DYK, WALTER, and DELL H. HYMES, 1956, Stress accent in Wishram Chinook. *IJAL* 22:238–241.

EATON, HELEN S., 1961, *An English-French-German-Spanish Word Frequency Dictionary*. New York: Dover Publications. xix, 441 pp.

ELKINS, RICHARD, 1964, The anit taboo: a Manobo cultural unit. *Practical Anthropology* 11:185–188.

ELSON, BENJAMIN, and VELMA PICKETT, 1962, *An Introduction to Morphology and Syntax*. Santa Ana, Calif.: Summer Institute of Linguistics. 167 pp.

EMENEAU, MURRAY B., 1940, Review of Lt. Col. D. L. R. Lorimer, *The Burushaski Language* and E. O. Lorimer, *Language Hunting in the Karakoram*. *Language* 16:351–357.

————, 1958, Oral poets of South India—the Todas. *Journal of American Folklore* 71:312–324.

EVANS-PRITCHARD, EDWARD E., 1940, *The Nuer*. Oxford, England: The Clarendon Press. 271 pp.

FAST, P. W., 1952, Problems of basic vocabulary in a culturally restricted area. *The Bible Translator* 3:79–80.

FEIGENBAUM, IRWIN, 1961, *Translation as a Criterion for Grammaticalness*. Indiana University, M.A. thesis, unpublished.

FERGUSON, CHARLES A., 1963, Assumptions about nasals; a sample study in phonological universals. In Joseph H. Greenberg (Ed.), *Universals of Language*. Cambridge, Mass.: M.I.T. Press. Pp. 42–47.

————, 1964, On linguistic information (a luncheon address). In C. I. J. M. Stuart (Ed.), *Georgetown University Monograph Series on Languages and Linguistics, Number 17* (Report of the 15th Annual Round Table Meeting on Linguistics and Language Studies). Washington, D.C.: Georgetown University. Pp. 201–208.

FIRTH, J. R., 1947–1948, Word-palatograms and articulation. *Bulletin of the School of Oriental and African Studies* 12:847–864.

FOSTER, GEORGE M., 1964, Speech forms and perception of social distance in a Spanish-speaking Mexican village. *Southwestern Journal of Anthropology* 20: 107–122.

FOSTER, MARY L., and GEORGE M. FOSTER, 1948, *Sierra Popoluca Speech*. Washington, D.C.: U.S. Government Printing Office (Smithsonian Institution, Institute of Social Anthropology, Publication Number 8). 45 pp.

FRAKE, CHARLES O., 1964, Notes on queries in ethnography. In A. Kimball Romney and Roy Goodwin D'Andrade (Eds.), *Transcultural Studies in Cognition (American Anthropologist,* Special Publication. Vol. 66, No. 3, Part 2). Pp. 132–145.

FRANCIS, W. NELSON, 1965, A standard corpus of edited present-day American English. *College English* 26:267–273.

FRENCH, DAVID, 1958, Cultural matrices of Chinookan non-casual language. *IJAL* 24:258–263.

FRIEDRICH, PAUL, 1964, Review of Aert Kuipers, *Phoneme and Morpheme in Kabardian (Eastern Adyghe)*. The Hague: Mouton & Co. *American Anthropologist* 66:205–209.

GARBETT, G. KINGSLEY, 1965, A note on a recently introduced card system for processing numerical data. *Man,* July–August, No. 106. Pp. 120–121.

GARVIN, PAUL L., 1953, Short Kutenai texts. *IJAL* 19:305–311.

————, 1958, A descriptive technique for the treatment of meaning. *Language* 34: 1–32. Reprinted in Garvin 1964: 98–143.

————, 1964, *On Linguistic Method. Selected Papers.* The Hague: Mouton & Co. 164 pp.

GLEASON, H. ALLAN, JR., n.d., *Hints on Gathering a Corpus.* 4 pp., duplicated.

————, 1955, Review of Mager 1952. *Language* 31:163–165.

————, 1959, Bantu classes 1a and 2a. In Richard S. Harell (Ed.), *Georgetown University Monograph Series on Languages and Linguistics, Number 12* (Report of the 10th Annual Round Table Meeting on Linguistics and Language Studies). Washington, D.C.: Georgetown University. Pp. 25–35.

————, 1961, *An Introduction to Descriptive Linguistics,* rev. ed. New York: Holt, Rinehart and Winston, Inc. 503 pp.

GOLDSTEIN, KENNETH S., 1964, *A Guide for Field Workers in Folklore,* Hatboro, Pa.: Folklore Associates (Memoirs of the American Folklore Society, Vol. 52). xviii, 199 pp.

GRAY, LOUIS H., 1939, *Foundations of Language.* New York: The Macmillan Company. 520 pp.

GREENBERG, JOSEPH H. (Ed.), 1963, *Universals of Language.* Cambridge, Mass.: M.I.T. Press. 269 pp.

GRIERSON, SIR GEORGE ABRAHAM, 1903–1928. *Linguistic Survey of India* ("principally compiled and edited by G. A. Grierson"). Calcutta, India: Superintendent Government Printing Office. Eleven volumes. (Sometimes listed under: India. Linguistic Survey.)

————, 1919, *TheLinguistic Survey of India and the Census of 1911.* Calcutta: Superintendent Government Printing Office. 73 pp.

GRIMES, JOSEPH E., 1959, Huichol tone and intonation. *IJAL* 25:221–232.

————, 1963, *Automatic Data Processing for You. A Guide to the Concordance Project.* Norman, Okla.: Summer Institute of Linguistics and the University of Oklahoma Research Institute. 22 pp.

————, 1965, Review of Lamb and Gould 1964. *IJAL* 31:178–181.

GUDSCHINSKY, SARAH C., 1956, The ABC's of lexicostatistics (glottochronology). *Word* 12:175–210. In abridged form in Hymes (Ed.) 1964:612–622.

————, 1957, *Handbook of Literacy,* rev. ed. Santa Ana, Calif.: Summer Institute of Linguistics. 47 pp.

————, 1958, Native reactions to tones and words in Mazatec. *Word* 14:338–345.

GUMPERZ, JOHN J., and DELL HYMES (Eds.), 1964, *The Ethnography of Communication.* Menasha, Wis.: American Anthropological Association (*American Anthropologist,* Special Publication, Vol. 66, No. 6, Part 2). 186 pp.

GURSKY, KARL-HEINZ, 1963, Einige Perspektiven und Probleme der nordamerikanischen Sprachwissenschaft. *Abhandlungen der Völkerkundlichen Arbeitsgemeinschaft,* Vol. 2. 33 pp. See abstract by Peter T. Furst in *IJAL* 30:393–394.

GUSFIELD JOSEPH R., 1955, Field work reciprocities in studying a social movement. *Human Organization* 14(3):29–33. Reprinted in Adams and Preis 1960:99–108.

HAAS, MARY R., 1941, *Tunica,* New York: J. J. Augustin, Inc. (Extract from *Handbook of American Indian Languages,* Vol. IV). 143 pp.

————, 1944, Men's and women's speech in Koasati. *Language* 20:142–149. Reprinted in Hymes (Ed.) 1964:228–233.

————, 1957, Thai word games. *Journal of American Folklore* 70:173–175. Reprinted in Hymes (Ed.) 1964:301–304.

HALE, KENNETH, 1965, On the use of informants in field-work. *The Canadian Journal of Linguistics* (Journal of the Canadian Linguistic Association) 10(2, 3):108–119.

HALLE, MORRIS, 1954, The strategy of phonemics. *Word* 10:197–209.

———, 1959, *The Sound Pattern of Russian: A Linguistic and Acoustical Investigation.* With an excursus on the contextual variants of the Russian vowels by Lawrence G. Jones. (Description and analysis of Contemporary Standard Russian, Vol. I). The Hague: Mouton & Co. 206 pp.

HANNA, WILLIAM J., 1965, Image-making in field research: Some tactical and ethical problems arising from research in tropical Africa. *American Behavioral Scientist* 8(5):15–20.

HARRIS, ZELLIG S., 1951, *Methods in Structural Linguistics,* Chicago: University of Chicago Press. 384 pp.

———, and CARL F. VOEGELIN, 1953, Eliciting. *Southwestern Journal of Anthropology* 9:59–75.

HAUGEN, EINAR I., 1958, The phonemes of Modern Icelandic. *Language* 34:55–88.

———, 1959, From idiolect to language. In Richard S. Harrell (Ed.) *Georgetown University Monograph Series on Languages and Linguistics, Number 12* (Report of the 10th Annual Round Table Meeting on Linguistics and Language Studies). Washington, D.C.: Georgetown University. Pp. 57–64.

HAYES, ALFRED S., 1954, Field procedures while working with Digueño. *IJAL* 20:185–194.

HEALEY, ALAN, 1964a, *Handling Unsophisticated Linguistic Informants.* Canberra: Australian National University (Linguistic Circle of Canberra Publications, Series A: Occasional Papers, No. 2). 30 pp.

———, 1964b, *Telefol Phonology.* Canberra: Australian National University (Linguistic Circle of Canberra Publications, Series B: Monographs, No. 3). 53 pp.

HEFFNER, ROE-MERRILL SECRIST, 1949, *General Phonetics.* Madison: University of Wisconsin Press. 253 pp.

HENRY, JULES, 1940, A method for learning to talk primitive languages. *American Anthropologist* 42:635–641.

HICKERSON, HAROLD, GLEN D. TURNER, and NANCY P. HICKERSON, 1952, Testing procedures for estimating transfer of information among Iroquois dialects and languages. *IJAL* 18:1–8.

HILL, ARCHIBALD A., 1964, A note on primitive languages. In Hymes (Ed.) 1964: 86–89. Originally in *IJAL* 18:172–177 (1952).

HOCKETT, CHARLES F., 1948, Implications of Bloomfield's Algonquian studies. *Language* 24:117–131.

———, 1953, Short and long syllable nuclei. *IJAL* 19:165–171.

———, 1955, *A Manual of Phonology.* Bloomington: Indiana University Publications in Anthropology and Linguistics (*IJAL,* Memoir 11, Vol. 21). v, 246 pp.

———, 1957, How to learn Martian. In Martin Greenberg (Ed.), *Coming Attractions.* New York: Gnome Press, Inc. Pp. 38–51.

———, 1958, *A Course in Modern Linguistics.* New York: The Macmillan Company. 621 pp.

HOIJER, HARRY (Ed.), 1954, *Language in Culture* (Conference on the Interrelations of Language and other Aspects of Culture). Chicago: University of Chicago Press. 286 pp.

HOIJER, HARRY, 1958, Native reaction as a criterion in linguistic analysis. In Eva Sivertsen (Ed.), *Proceedings of the Eighth International Congress of Linguists.* Oslo: Oslo University Press. Pp. 573–583.

———, 1961, Anthropological linguistics. In Christine Mohrmann, Alf Sommerfelt, and Joshua Whatmough (Eds.), *Trends in European and American Linguistics 1930–1960.* Utrecht and Antwerp: Spectrum Publishers. Pp. 110–125.

HOLTVED, ERIK, 1952, Remarks on the Polar Eskimo dialect. *IJAL* 18:20–24.

HOLLINGSHEAD, AUGUST DE BELMONT, 1949, *Elmtown's Youth: The Impact of Social Classes on Adolescents.* New York: John Wiley and Sons, Inc. 480 pp.

HOUSEHOLDER, FRED W., and SOL SAPORTA (Eds.), 1962, *Problems in Lexicography* (Report of the Conference on Lexicography, Indiana University, November 11–12, 1960). Bloomington: Indiana University Research Center in Anthropology, Folklore, and Linguistics [*IJAL*, Vol. 28, Part IV]. 286 pp.

HYMES, DELL H., 1958, Linguistic features peculiar to Chinookan myths. *IJAL* 24: 253–257.

———, 1959, Bibliography: field work in linguistics and anthropology. *Studies in Linguistics* 14(3–4):82–91.

———, 1960, Lexicostatistics so far. *Current Anthropology* 1:3–44.

HYMES, DELL (Ed.), 1964, *Language in Culture and Society.* New York: Harper & Row, Publishers. xxxv, 764 pp.

———, 1965, *The Use of Computers in Anthropology.* The Hague: Mouton and Co. 558 pp.

———, 1966, On 'anthropological linguistics' and congeners. *American Anthropologist* 68:143–153.

INTERNATIONAL PHONETIC ASSOCIATION, 1949, *The Principles of the International Phonetic Association.* London: University College. 53 pp.

JACKER, CORINNE, 1964, *Man, Memory, and Machines. An Introduction to Cybernetics.* New York: The Macmillan Company, 126 pp.

JACOBSON, ROMAN, 1958, Discussion [on Hoijer 1958]. In Eva Sivertsen (Ed.), *Proceedings of the Eighth International Congress of Linguists.* Oslo: Oslo University Press. Pp. 589–590.

KABERRY, PHYLLIS M., 1957, Malinowski's contribution to field-work methods and the writing of ethnography. In Raymond W. Firth (Ed.), *Man and Culture; an evaluation of the work of Bronislaw Malinowski.* London: Routledge & Keegan Paul, Ltd. Pp. 71–92.

KARPELES, MAUD (Ed.), 1958, *The Collecting of Folk Music and Other Ethnomusicological Material: A Manual for Field Workers.* London: International Folk Music Council and the Royal Anthropological Institute of Great Britain and Ireland. 40 pp.

KEESING, FELIX M., 1957, *Field Guide to Oceania.* Washington, D.C.: National Academy of Sciences—National Research Council (Field Guide Series Number 1, Committee on International Anthropology of the Division of Anthropology and Psychology). 51 pp.

KRONES, ROBERT, JESSE O. SAWYER, and GLEN M. GROSJEAN, 1964, On the marking of low-frequency tones for marking language laboratory tapes. *Language Learning* 14:51–54.

KURATH, HANS, 1939, *Handbook of the Linguistic Geography of New England.* Providence, R.I.: Brown University. xii, 240 pp.

LABOV, WILLIAM, 1964*a*. *The Social Stratification of English in New York City*. New York. Columbia University, Ph.D. Dissertation.

——, 1964*b*, Phonological correlates of social stratification. In Gumperz and Hymes 1964:164–176.

——, 1964*c*, Stages in the acquisition of Standard English. In Roger W. Shuy (Ed.), *Social Dialects and Language Learning*. Pp. 77–103

LADEFOGED, PETER, 1964, *A Phonetic Study of West African Languages*. Cambridge, England: Cambridge University Press (West African Language Monographs I). 74 pp.

LAMB, SIDNEY M., 1965, Linguistic data processing. In Hymes (Ed.) 1965:159–188.

——, and LAURA GOULD, 1964, *Concordances from Computers*. Berkeley and Los Angeles: Mechanolinguistics Project, University of California. 90 pp.

LANDAR, HERBERT J., 1960, A note on accepted and rejected arrangements of Navaho words. *IJAL* 26:351–354.

LAWTON, DENIS, 1963, Social class differences in language development: A study of some samples of written work. *Language and Speech* 6:120–143.

——, 1964, Social class language differences in group discussions. *Language and Speech* 7:183–204.

LEHISTE, ILSE, 1963, Review of Kerstin Hadding-Koch, *Acousticophonetic Studies in the Intonation of Southern Swedish*. *Language* 39:352–360.

LE PAGE, ROBERT B., 1964, *The National Language Question*. London: Oxford University Press. 82 pp.

LOEWEN, JACOB A., 1964, Culture, meaning and translation. *The Bible Translator* 15:189–194.

LONGACRE, ROBERT E., 1964, *Grammar Discovery Procedures: A Field Manual*. The Hague: Mouton & Co. 162 pp.

LORIMER, EMILY OVEREND, 1939, *Language Hunting in the Karakoram*. London: George Allen & Unwin, Ltd. 310 pp. *Cf.* Emeneau 1940.

LOUNSBURY, FLOYD G., 1953, Field methods and techniques in linguistics. In A. L. Kroeber (Ed.), *Anthropology Today. An Encyclopedic Inventory*. Chicago: University of Chicago Press. Pp. 401–416.

LOWIE, ROBERT H., 1940, Native languages as ethnographic tools. *American Anthropologist* 42:81–89.

——, 1959, *Robert H. Lowie, Ethnologist. A Personal Record*. Berkeley and Los Angeles: University of California Press. 198 pp.

LYONS, JOHN, 1962, Phonemic and non-phonemic phonology: Some typological reflections. *IJAL* 28:127–134.

LUGG, H C., 1952, A method for reproducing Zulu words. *African Studies* 11:35–36.

MCDAVID, RAVEN I., JR., 1954, Review of E. Bagby Atwood, *A Survey of Verb Forms in Eastern United States*. *IJAL* 20:74–78.

MCEWEN, WILLIAM J., 1959, Native language and field problems. *American Anthropologist* 61:681–682.

MCINTOSH, ANGUS, 1952, *An Introduction to a Survey of Scottish Dialects*. Edinburgh: Thomas Nelson & Sons. xii, 122 pp.

MACLAY, HOWARD, and MARY D. SLEATOR, 1960, Responses to language: Judgments of grammaticalness. *IJAL* 26:275–282.

MAGER, JOHN, 1952, *Gedaged-English Dictionary* (with a foreword by A. Capell). Columbus, Ohio: Board of Foreign Missions of the American Lutheran Church. xiv, 353 pp.

MALINOWSKI, BRONISLAW, 1923, The problem of meaning in primitive languages. In Charles K. Ogden and I. A. Richards, *The Meaning of Meaning.* New York: Harcourt, Brace & World, Inc. See 5th. ed. 1938, pp. 296–336.

———, 1935, *Coral Gardens and their Magic. A Study of the Methods of Tilling the Soil and of Agricultural Rites in the Trobriand Islands.* Volume I: *The Description of Gardening;* Volume II: *The Language of Magic and Gardening.* New York: American Book Company. xxxv, 500 pp.; xxxii, 350 pp. Reprinted as *Soil Tilling and Agricultural Rites in the Trobriand Islands: Coral Gardens and their Magic,* Vol. I (with an introduction by Edmund Leach); *The Language of Magic and Gardening: Coral Gardens and their Magic,* Vol. II (with an introduction by Jack Berry). Bloomington: Indiana University Press.

MARTIN, SAMUEL E., 1956, *Essential Japanese. An Introduction to the Standard Colloquial Language,* rev. ed. Rutland, Vt.: Charles E. Tuttle Co. xvi, 461 pp.

MARTINET, ANDRE, 1964, *Elements of General Linguistics.* With a Foreword by L. R. Palmer. Translated from the French (1960) by Elisabeth Palmer. Chicago: University of Chicago Press. 205 pp.

MATTHEWS, G. HUBERT, 1955, A phonemic analysis of a Dakota dialect. *IJAL* 21:56–59.

———, 1965, *Hidatsa Syntax.* The Hague: Mouton & Co. (Papers on Formal Linguistics, Department of Linguistics, University of Pennsylvania). 299 pp.

MEAD, MARGARET, 1939, Native languages as field-work tools. *American Anthropologist* 41:189–205.

MEEUSSEN, A. E., 1962, L'informateur en linguistique africaine. *Aequatoria* 25(3): 92–94.

MOORE, BRUCE R., 1964, Second thoughts on measuring 'naturalness.' *The Bible Translator* 15:83–87.

MURDOCK, GEORGE P., et. al, 1950, *Outline of Cultural Materials,* 3d rev. ed. New Haven, Conn.: Human Relations Area Files, Inc. xxiii, 162 pp. (4th rev. ed., 1961).

NIDA, EUGENE A., 1946, *Syntax: A Descriptive Analysis.* Glendale [Santa Ana], Calif.: Summer Institute of Linguistics. 114 pp., duplicated.

———, 1947, Field techniques in descriptive linguistics. *IJAL* 13:138–146.

———, 1949, *Morphology: The Descriptive Analysis of Words,* new ed. Ann Arbor: University of Michigan Press. xvi, 342 pp.

———, 1950a, *Learning a Foreign Language: A Handbook for Missionaries.* New York: Committee on Missionary Personnel of the Foreign Missions Conference of North America. ix, 237 pp.

———, 1950b, Training the translation helper. *The Bible Translator* 1:56–62.

———, 1952–1953, Selective listening. *Language Learning* 4:92–101.

———, 1958, Analysis of meaning and dictionary making. *IJAL* 24:279–292.

OLMSTED, DAVID L., 1961, Substitution and frequency-estimation in linguistic analysis. *IJAL* 27:308–319.

———, with the collaboration of PETER PARK and DO-SIK KIM, 1963, *Korean Folklore Reader (Texts with Presyntactic Analysis).* Bloomington: Indiana University Publications (Uralic and Altaic Series, Vol. 16). vii, 97 pp.

OSGOOD, CORNELIUS, 1940, *Ingalik Material Culture*. New Haven, Conn.: Yale University Press (Yale University Publications in Anthropology, No. 22). 500 pp.

PAUL, BENJAMIN D. 1953, Interview techniques and field relationships. In A. L. Kroeber (Ed.), *Anthropology Today. An Encyclopedic Inventory*. Chicago: University of Chicago Press. Pp. 430–451.

PENCE, ALAN, 1962, Punched card filing for linguists. In Summer Institute of Linguistics New Guinea Branch, *Studies in New Guinea Linguistics*. Sydney, Australia: *Oceania Linguistic Monographs,* No. 6. Pp. 76–89.

PICKETT, ANDREW G., and M. M. LEMCOE, 1959, *Preservation and Storage of Sound Recordings*. Washington, D.C.: U.S. Government Printing Office. 74 pp.

PICKFORD, GLENNA R., 1956, American linguistic geography: A sociological appraisal. *Word* 12:211–233.

PIERCE, JOE E., 1952, Dialect distance testing in Algonquian. *IJAL* 18:203–210.

———, 1965a, Computer analysis of Alsea. *IJAL* 31:128–131.

———, 1965b, The field situation in Oregon: 1964. *Canadian Journal of Linguistics* 10(2,3):120–128.

PIKE, EUNICE V., 1948, Problems in Zapotec tone analysis. *IJAL* 14:16–170.

———, 1956, *Not Alone*. Chicago: Moody Press. 127 pp.

———, 1958, *Words Wanted*. Chicago: Moody Press. 159 pp.

PIKE, KENNETH L., 1947, *Phonemics. A Technique for Reducing Languages to Writing*. Ann Arbor: University of Michigan Press. xvi, 254 pp.

———, 1948, *Tone Languages. A Technique for Determining the Number and Type of Pitch Contrasts in a Language, with Studies in Tonemic Substitution and Fusion*. Ann Arbor: University of Michigan Press. 187 pp.

———, 1954, *Language, in Relation to a Unified Theory of Structure of Human Behavior*. Preliminary edition, Part I. Glendale [Santa Ana], California: Summer Institute of Linguistics. 165 pp.

———, 1955, Meaning and hypostasis. In Ruth H. Weinstein (Ed.), *Georgetown University Monograph Series on Languages and Linguistics, Number 8* (Report of the 6th Annual Round Table Meeting on Linguistics and Language Teaching). Washington, D.C.: Georgetown University. Pp. 134 141.

———, 1957, Abdominal pulse types in some Peruvian languages. *Language* 33:30–35.

———, 1962, Dimensions of grammatical constructions. *Language* 38:221–244.

———, 1963, Theoretical implications of matrix permutation in Fore (New Guinea). *Anthropological Linguistics* 5(8):1–23.

———, and BARBARA ERICKSON, 1964, Conflated field structures in Potawatomi and in Arabic. *IJAL* 30:201-212.

———, and WILLARD KINDBERG, 1956, A problem in multiple stresses. *Word* 12:415–428.

PITTMAN, DEAN, 1948, *Practical Linguistics: A Textbook and Field Manual for Missionary Linguistics*. Cleveland, Ohio: Mid-Missions. xiii, 229 pp.

POLUNIN, IVAN, 1965, Stereophonic magnetic tape recorders and the collection of ethnographic field data. *Current Anthropology* 6:227–230.

POP, SEVER, 1950, *La Dialectologie: Aperçu Historique et Méthodes d'Enquêtes Linguistiques*. Louvain: l'Auteur. 2 volumes.

POSTAL, PAUL M., 1966, A note on 'understood transitively'. *IJAL* 32:90–93.

PRESTON, W. D., 1946, Problems of text attestation in ethnography and linguistics. *IJAL* 12:173–177.

RADIN, PAUL, 1949, *The Culture of the Winnebago: As Described by Themselves.* Bloomington: Indiana University Publications in Anthropology and Linguistics (*IJAL* Vol. 15, Memoir 2). 119 pp.

REDLICH, FREDERICK C., 1949, The patient's language. In Irving J. Lee (Ed.), *The Language of Wisdom and Folly. Background Readings in Semantics.* New York: Harper. Pp. 151–159. Original and more complete version appeared in the *Yale Journal of Biology and Medicine* 17(3):427–453 (1945).

ROBINS, R. H., 1964, *General Linguistics: An Introductory Survey.* London: Longmans, Green Co., Ltd. 390 pp.

ROBINSON, DOW F., 1963, *Field Notes on Coatlán Zapotec.* Hartford, Conn.: Hartford Seminary Foundation (Hartford Studies in Linguistics, No. 7). v, 53 pp.

ROBINSON, W. P., 1965, The elaborated code in working class language. *Language and Speech* 8:243–252.

ROSING, OTTO, 1951, Kleinschmidt Centennial II: Samuel Petrus Kleinschmidt. *IJAL* 17:63–65.

ROYAL ANTHROPOLOGICAL INSTITUTE OF GREAT BRITAIN AND IRELAND, 1951, *Notes and Queries on Anthropology,* 6th ed. London: Routledge and Kegan Paul, Ltd. 403 pp.

RYCHLAK, JOSEPH, PAUL H. MUSSEN, and JOHN W. BENNETT, 1957, An example of the use of the incomplete sentence test in applied anthropological research. *Human Organization* 16(1):25–29.

SAINT, RACHEL, and KENNETH L. PIKE, 1962, Auca phonemics. In Benjamin Elson (Ed.), *Studies in Ecuadorian Indian Languages: I.* Norman, Okla.: Summer Institute of Linguistics of the University of Oklahoma. Pp. 2–30.

SAMARIN, WILLIAM J., 1964, Review of Jan Voorhoeve, *Sranan Syntax. IJAL* 30:430–434.

———, 1965a, The attitudinal and autobiographic in Gbeya dog names. *Journal of African Languages* 4:57–72.

———, 1965b, Controlling elicitation of equivalents. *Bible Translator* 16:36–38.

———, in press, *The Gbeya Language.* Berkeley and Los Angeles: University of California Press (University of California Publications in Linguistics.

———, in press. *A Grammar of Sango.* The Hague: Mouton & Co.

SAPIR, EDWARD, 1929, Male and female forms of speech in Yana. In St. W. J. Teeuwen (Ed.), *Donum Natalicum Schrijnen.* Nijmegen-Utrecht: Dekker and Van de Vegt. Pp. 79–85. Reprinted in David G. Mandelbaum (Ed.), *Selected Writings of Edward Sapir in Language, Culture and Personality.* Berkeley and Los Angeles: University of California Press. 1949. Pp. 206–212.

———, 1933, La réalité psychologique des phonèmes. *Journal de Psychologie Normale et Pathologique* 30:247–265. Reprinted, as The psychological reality of phonemes, in Mandelbaum 1949:46–60.

SAPON, STANLEY M., 1957, *A Pictorial Linguistic Interview Manual.* Columbus: Ohio State University (American Library of Recorded Dialect Studies). 34 pp.

———, 1958, A note on the gathering and exchange of linguistic data. *Orbis* 7:183–185.

SAPORTA, SOL, 1963, Phoneme distribution and language universals. In Greenberg (Ed.) 1963:48–57.

————, and HELEN CONTRERAS, 1962, *A Phonological Grammar of Spanish*. Seattle: University of Washington Press. iv, 43 pp.

SCHÜTZ, ALBERT J., 1963, A phonemic typology of Fijian dialects. *Oceanic Linguistics* 2:62–79.

SHAFEEV, D. A., 1964, *A Short Grammatical Outline of Pashto*. Bloomington: Indiana University Research Center in Anthropolgy, Folklore, and Linguistics (*IJAL*, Vol. 30, Part III). 89 pp.

SHELTON, AUSTIN J., 1964, The "Miss Ophelia" syndrome in African field research. *Practical Anthropology* 11:259–265.

————, 1965, Anthropological 'values' and culture change: a note. *American Anthropologist* 67:103–106.

SHIPLEY, WILLIAM, 1956, The phonemes of Northeastern Maidu. *IJAL* 22:233–237.

SHUY, ROGER W. (Ed.), 1964, *Social Dialects and Language Learning* (Report of a conference sponsored by the Illinois Institute of Technology and the National Council of Teachers of English). Champaign, Ill.: National Council of Teachers of English. 157 pp.

SMALLEY, WILLIAM A., 1957, Finding out how close related dialects are. Part II: Conducting a dialect survey. *The Bible Translator* 8:114–126.

————, 1963, *Manual of Articulatory Phonetics*, rev. ed. Tarrytown, N. Y.: *Practical Anthropology*. 512 pp.

SPENCER, JOHN (Ed.), 1963, *Language in Africa* (Papers of the Leverhulme Conference on Universities and the Language Problems of Tropical Africa, University College, Ibadan, Nigeria). Cambridge, England: University Press. 167 pp.

STARK, DONALD S., 1962, Boundary markers in Dakota. *IJAL* 28:19–35.

STEVICK, EARL W., 1963, *A Workbook in Language Teaching (with Special Reference to English as a Foreign Language)*. Nashville, Tenn.: Abingdon Press. 127 pp.

STIMSON, HUGH M., 1963, Review of W. A. C. H. Dobson, *Early Archaic Chinese: A Descriptive Grammar*. *Language* 39:567–574.

STREET, JOHN C., 1963, Review of Samuel E. Martin, *Dagur Mongolian Grammar, Texts, and Lexicon*. *Language* 39:336–341.

STURTEVANT, WILLIAM C., and GEORGE W. GRACE, 1954, *Linguistic Questionnaire*. New Haven, Conn.: Tri-Institutional Pacific Program, Department of Anthropology, Yale University. 13 pp., duplicated.

SULLIVAN, HARRY STACK, 1954, *The Psychiatric Interview*. New York: W. W. Norton & Company, Inc. xxiii, 246 pp.

SUTTLES, W., 1965, Linguistic means for anthropological ends on the Northwest Coast. *Canadian Journal of Linguistics* 10(2, 3):156–166.

SWADESH, MORRIS, 1937, A method for phonetic accuracy and speed. *American Anthropologist* 39:728–732.

————, 1950, Salish internal relationships. *IJAL* 16:157–167.

————, 1951a, Diffusional cumulation and archaic residue as historical explanations. *Southwestern Journal of Anthropology* 7:1–21. Slightly revised version in Hymes (Ed.) 1964:624–635.

————, 1951b, Kleinschmidt Centennial III: Unaaliq and Proto-Eskimo. *IJAL* 17:66–70.

————, 1954, On the Penutian vocabulary survey. *IJAL* 20:123–133.

————, 1955, Towards greater accuracy in lexicostatistic dating. *IJAL* 21:121–137.

————, 1965, Language universals and research efficiency in descriptive linguistics. *Canadian Journal of Linguistics* 10(2, 3):147–155.

TABER, CHARLES R., 1965, *A Dictionary of Sango*. Hartford, Conn.: Hartford Seminary Foundation. xxi, 338 pp., duplicated.

TAYLOR, DOUGLAS, 1959, Concerning the validity of some translations. *IJAL* 25:70–71.

TEETER, KARL V., 1964a, *The Wiyot Language*. Berkeley and Los Angeles: University of California Press (University of California Publications in Linguistics, Vol. 37). xvii, 251 pp.

————, 1964b, "Anthropological linguistics" and linguistic anthropology. *American Anthropologist* 66:878–879.

————, 1966, The history of linguistics: New lamps for old. A paper read at the Seventeenth Annual Round Table Meeting on Linguistics and Language Studies, Georgetown University, Washington, D. C.

THOMAS, JACQUELINE M. C., 1963, *Le Parler Ngbaka de Bokanga. Phonologie, Morphologie, Syntaxe*. The Hague: Mouton and Co. 307 pp.

TRAGER, GEORGE L., 1948, Taos I: A language revisited. *IJAL* 14:155–160.

————, 1958, *Phonetics: Glossary and Tables*. Buffalo, N. Y.: University of Buffalo (*Studies in Linguistics*, Occasional Papers, No. 6). 27 pp.

TURNER, GLEN D., 1958, Alternative phonemicizing in Jivaro. *IJAL* 24:87–94.

TURNER, LORENZO DOW, 1949, *Africanisms in the Gullah Dialect*. Chicago: University of Chicago Press. xi, 317 pp.

TWADDELL, W. F., 1954, A linguistic archive as an indexed depot. *IJAL* 20:108–110.

UHLENBECK, E. M., 1960, The study of the so-called exotic languages and general linguistics. *Lingua* 9:417–434.

VOEGELIN, CARL F., 1942, Review of Eugene Buechal, *A Grammar of Lakota, the Language of the Teton Sioux Indians* and Hans Vogt, *The Kalispel Language. An Outline of the Grammar with Texts, Translations, and Dictionary. Language* 18:69–73.

————, 1949, Review of Kenneth L. Pike, *Phonemics. IJAL* 15:75–85.

————, 1950, Magnetic recording of American Indian languages and the relationship of this to other kinds of memory. *Proceedings of the American Philosophical Society* 94:295–300.

————, 1952, Training in anthropological linguistics. *American Anthropologist* 54:322–327.

————, 1953, From FL (Shawnee) to TL (English), autobiography of a woman. *IJAL* 19:1–25.

————, 1954a, A modern method for field work treatment of previously collected texts. *Journal of American Folklore* 67:15–20.

————, 1954b, Multiple stage translation. *IJAL* 20:271–280.

————, 1959a, Model-directed structuralization. *Anthropological Linguistics* 1(1):9–26.

————, 1959b, Review of Leonard Bloomfield, *Eastern Ojibwa: Grammatical Sketch, Texts and Word List. Language* 35:109–125.

————, 1960, Subsystem typology in linguistics. In Anthony F. C. Wallace (Ed.),

Man and Cultures: Selected Papers (Fifth International Congress of Anthropological and Ethnological Sciences). Philadelphia: University of Pennsylvania Press. Pp. 202–206.

———, 1961, Anthropological linguistics in the context of other fields of linguistics. In [Summer Institute of Linguistics], *À William Cameron Townsend en el XXV Aniversario del Instituto Lingüístico de Verano.* México, D. F. Pp. 673–685.

———, and ZELLIG S. HARRIS, 1945, Linguistics in ethnology. *Southwestern Journal of Anthropology* 1:455–465.

———, and FLORENCE M. ROBINETT, 1954, Obtaining a linguistic sample. *IJAL* 20:89–100.

———, and FLORENCE M. VOEGELIN, 1957, *Hopi Domains. A Lexical Approach to the Problem of Selection.* Bloomington: Indiana University Publications in Anthropology and Linguistics (*IJAL,* Memoir 14, Vol. 23). vi, 82 pp.

———, 1959, Guide for transcribing unwritten languages in field work. *Anthropological Linguistics* 1(6)1–28.

———, 1963, On the history of structuralizing in 20th century America. *Anthropological Linguistics* 5(1):12–37.

VOGT, HANS, 1940, *The Kalispel Language. An Outline of the Grammar with Texts, Translations, and Dictionary.* Oslo: Det Norske Videnskaps-Akademi. 178 pp.

VOORHOEVE, JAN, 1962, *Sranan Syntax.* Amsterdam: North-Holland Publishing Co. 91 pp.

WATERHOUSE, VIOLA, 1949, Learning a second language first. *IJAL* 15:106–109.

WAX, ROSALIE HANKEY, 1952, Reciprocity as a field technique. *Human Organization* 11(3):34–37. Reprinted, as Reciprocity in field work, in Adams and Preis 1960:90–98.

———, 1960, Twelve years later: an analysis of field experience. In Adams and Preis 1960:166–178.

WEINREICH, URIEL, 1962, Lexicographic definition in descriptive semantics. In Householder and Saporta (Eds.) 1962:25–43.

WERNER, OSWALD, 1965, Semantics of Navaho medical terms: I. *IJAL* 31:1–7.

WESTCOTT, ROGER W., 1962, *A Bini Grammar. Part 1: Phonology.* East Lansing: African Language Center, Michigan State University. 119 pp.

WESTERMANN, DIEDRICH, and IDA C. WARD, 1933, *Practical Phonetics for Students of African Languages.* London: Oxford University Press. xvi, 169 pp.

WHITE, LESLIE A., 1963, *The Ethnography and Ethnology of Franz Boas.* Austin: Texas Memorial Museum (Bulletin No. 6). 76 pp.

WHITELEY, W. H., 1964, Suggestions for recording a Bantu language in the field. *Tanganyika Notes and Records,* No 62, pp. 1–19.

WILSON, R., 1956, The implication of tape recording in the field of dialect geography. *Journal of the Canadian Linguistic Association* 2:17–21.

WOLFE, ALVIN W., 1959, *Field Guide to West and Central Africa.* Washington, D.C.: National Academy of Sciences—National Research Council (Field Guide Series Number 2, Committee on International Anthropology of the Division of Anthropology and Psychology). 40 pp.

WOLFF, HANS, 1951, Yuchi text with analysis. *IJAL* 17:48–53.

———, 1958, An Osage graphemic experiment. *IJAL* 24:30–35.

YAMPOLSKY, HELENE BOAS, 1958, Excerpts from the letter diary of Franz Boas on his first field trip to the Northwest Coast. *IJAL* 24:312–320.

YEGERLEHNER, JOHN, 1955, A note on eliciting techniques *IJAL* 21:286–288.

ZWIRNER, EBERHARD, 1963, A guide to linguistic tape recording. In Council for Cultural Co-operation of the Council of Europe, *New Trends in Linguistic Research*. Strasbourg. Pp. 9–47.

AUTHOR INDEX

241

SUBJECT INDEX